# TWO TRACTS ON CIVIL LIBERTY

A Da Capo Press Reprint Series

## THE ERA OF THE AMERICAN REVOLUTION

GENERAL EDITOR: LEONARD W. LEVY
*Claremont Graduate School*

# TWO TRACTS
## ON
# CIVIL LIBERTY
# THE WAR WITH AMERICA
# THE DEBTS AND FINANCES
# OF THE KINGDOM

By Richard Price

DA CAPO PRESS · NEW YORK · 1972

Library of Congress Cataloging in Publication Data

Price, Richard, 1723-1791.

Two tracts on civil liberty, the war with America, the debts and finances of the kingdom.

(The Era of the American Revolution)

Reprint of the 1778 ed.

CONTENTS: Observations on the nature of civil liberty, the principles of government, and the justice and policy of the war with America.—Additional observations on the nature and value of civil liberty, and the war with America.

1. U.S.—Politics and government—Revolution. 2. U.S.—History—Revolution—Causes. 3. Finance, Public—Gt. Brit.—1688-1815. 4. Finance, Public—France—To 1789. I. Price, Richard, 1723-1791. Additional observations on the nature and value of civil liberty, and the war with America. 1972. II. Title.

E211.P9692 320.9′42′073 74-169641

ISBN 0-306-70233-9

This Da Capo Press edition of *Two Tracts on Civil Liberty* is an unabridged republication of the first combined edition, published in London in 1778, of the following two works by Richard Price:

*Observations on the Nature of Civil Liberty, the Principles of Government, and the Justice and Policy of the War with America* (first edition, 1776; eighth edition, 1778)

*Additional Observations on the Nature and Value of Civil Liberty, and the War with America* (first edition, 1777; third edition, 1778)

This one-volume edition contains corrections and additions to the last previous edition (as indicated) of each work.

Published by Da Capo Press, Inc.
A Subsidiary of Plenum Publishing Corporation
227 West 17th Street, New York, New York 10011


Manufactured in the United States of America

# TWO TRACTS ON CIVIL LIBERTY

# TWO TRACTS

ON

# CIVIL LIBERTY,

THE

# WAR WITH AMERICA,

AND

# THE DEBTS AND FINANCES OF THE KINGDOM:

WITH

A GENERAL INTRODUCTION and SUPPLEMENT.

---

By RICHARD PRICE, D.D. F.R.S.

---

LONDON:

Printed for T. CADELL, in the STRAND.

MDCCLXXVIII.

# GENERAL INTRODUCTION.

THE first of the following tracts was published in the beginning of the year 1776; and the second in the beginning of last year. They are now offered to the public in one volume, with corrections and additions. All the calculations, in the *Appendix* to the first tract, have been transferred to the *second* and *fourth* sections, in the third part of the second tract.

The section on PUBLIC LOANS, in the second tract, has been revised with care; and a *supplement* to it, containing additional proposals and some necessary explanations, has been given at the end of the whole.——This is a subject to which I have applied (perhaps too unprofitably) much of my attention. I have now done with it; and the whole is referred to the candid examination of those who may be better informed, hoping for their indulgence should they find that, in any instance, I have been mistaken. I have not meant, in any thing I have said on this subject, to censure any persons. That accumulation of artificial debt which I have pointed out, and by which the danger of the kingdom from its growing burdens

 has

has been so needlessly increased, has, I doubt not, been the effect of inattention in our ministers; and the scheme, by which the loan of last year has been procured, gives reason to hope that better plans of borrowing will be adopted for the future.

The principal design of the first part of the second tract was (as I have observed in the introduction to it) to remove the misapprehensions of my sentiments on CIVIL LIBERTY AND GOVERNMENT into which some had fallen. It gives me concern to find that it has not answered that end in the degree I wished. I am still charged with maintaining opinions which tend to subvert all civil authority. I paid little regard to this charge, while it was confined to the advocates for the principles which have produced the present war; but as it seems lately to have been given the public from the authority of a writer of the first character, (*a*) it is impossible I should not be impressed by it; and I find myself under a necessity of taking farther notice of it.

There are two accounts, directly opposite to one another, which have been given of the origin of civil government. One of them is, that "civil government is an expedient contrived by

(*a*) See Mr. *Burke's* Letter to the Sheriffs of *Bristol*, page 53, 54.

4 "human

"human prudence for gaining security against
"oppression; and that, consequently, the power
"of civil governors is a delegation or trust from
"the people for accomplishing this end."

The other account is, that "civil government
"is an ordinance of the Deity, by which the
"body of mankind are given up to the will of a
"few; and, consequently, that it is a trust from
"the Deity, in the exercise of which civil go-
"vernors are accountable only to him."

The question "which of these accounts we ought
"to receive," is important in the highest degree.
There is no question which more deeply affects
the happiness and dignity of man as a citizen of this world.——If the former account is
right, the people (that is, the body of independent agents) in every community are their
own legislators. All civil authority is properly
*their* authority. Civil governors are only public
*servants*; and their power, being *delegated*, is by
its nature *limited*.——On the contrary, If the latter account is right, the people have nothing to
do with their own government. They are placed
by their maker in the situation of cattle on an
estate, which the owner has a right to dispose of
as he pleases. Civil Governors are a body of
*masters*; and their power is a commission from
Heaven held by divine right, and unbounded in
its extent.

 I have

I have espoused, with some zeal, the first of these accounts; and in the following tracts, endeavoured to explain and defend it. And this is *all* I have done to give countenance to the charge I have mentioned.——Even the masterly writer who, after a croud of writers infinitely his inferiors, seems to have taken up this accusation against me, often expresses himself as if he had adopted the same idea of government (*a*). Such indeed is my opinion of his good sense, and such has been the zeal which he has discovered for the rights of mankind, that I think it scarcely possible his ideas and mine on this subject should be very different. His language, however, sometimes puzzles me; and, particularly, when he intimates that government is an institution of divine authority; (*b*) when he scouts all discussions of the nature of civil liberty, the foundation of civil rights, and the principles of free government; and when he asserts the *competence* of our legislature to revive the *High-Commission Court* and *Star-Chamber*, and its BOUNDLESS AUTHO-

(*a*) "To follow, not to force the public inclination; to "give a direction, a form, a technical dress and a specific "sanction to the general sense of the community, is the "true end of legislature. When it goes beyond this, its "authority will be precarious, let its rights be what they "will." Letter to the Sheriffs of Bristol, p. 49.

(*b*) Ibid. p. 55. Thoughts on the causes of the present discontents, p. 67. "Government certainly, is an institution of

AUTHORITY not only over the people of *Britain*, but over distant communities who have no voice in it.

But

" of divine authority; though its *forms* and the *persons* who " administer it, all originate from the people." It is probable that Mr. *Burke* means only that government is a divine institution, in the same sense in which any other expedient of human prudence for gaining protection against injury, may be called a Divine institution. All that we owe *immediately* to our own foresight and industry, must *ultimately* be ascribed to God the giver of all our powers, and the cause of all causes. It is in this sense that St. Paul in Rom. xiii. 1, 2. calls civil magistracy the *ordinance of God*, and says that *there is no power but of God*. If any one wants to be convinced of this, he should read the excellent bishop HOADLY's Sermon entitled *The Measures of Submission to the civil Magistrate*, and the defences of it.

It is further probable, that when Mr. *Burke* asserts the *omnipotence* of Parliaments, or their *competence* to establish any oppressions (Letter, p. 46, 49) he means mere *power*, abstracted from *right*, or the same sort of *power* and *competence* that trustees have to betray their trust, or that armed ruffians have to rob and murder. Nor should I doubt whether this is his meaning, were it not for the passage I have quoted from him in the last page, the latter part of which seems to imply, that a legislature may contradict its *end*, and yet retain its *rights*.——Some of the justest remarks on this subject may be found in the Earl of ABINGDON's thoughts on Mr. *Burke*'s letter, a pamphlet which (on account of the excellent public principles it maintains, and the spirit of liberty it breathes, as well as the rank of the writer) must give to every friend to the true interests of this country particular pleasure.

A 3

In

But whatever may be Mr. BURKE's sentiments on this subject, he cannot possibly think of the

In p. 46, Mr. *Burke* says, that "if there is one man in "the world more zealous than another for the supremacy of "parliament and the rights of this imperial crown, it is "himself; though many may be more knowing in the ex-"tent and the foundation of these rights." He adds, that "he has constantly declined such disquisitions, not "being qualified for the chair of a professor in metaphysics, "and not chusing to put the solid interests of the kingdom "on speculative grounds."——*The less knowledge, the more zeal*, is a maxim which experience has dreadfully verified in *religion*. But he that, in the present case, should apply this maxim to Mr. *Burke*, would, whatever he may say of himself, greatly injure him. Though he chuses to decry enquiries into the nature of liberty, there are, I am persuaded, few in the world whose zeal for it is more united to extensive knowledge and an exalted understanding.——He calls it, p. 55. "the vital spring and energy of a state, and a blessing "of the first order." He cannot, therefore, think that too much pains may be taken to UNDERSTAND it. He must know, that nothing but usurpation and error can suffer by enquiry and discussion.

Mr. WILKES, in an excellent speech which he lately made in moving for the repeal of the declaratory law, observed, that this law was a *compromise* to which the great men, under whose administration it was passed, were forced in order to obtain the repeal of the *Stamp-act*. I think so highly of that administration and of the service it did the public, that I have little doubt of the truth of this observation. But, at the same time, I cannot help wishing Mr. *Burke* had given no reason for doubt by defending the *principle* of that act; a *principle* which, unquestionably, he and his friends would never have acted upon; but which others have since acted upon, with a violence which has brought us to the brink of ruin.

former

former account of government that "it is a "speculation which destroys all authority."—Both accounts establish an authority. The difference is, that one derives it from the *people*, and makes it a *limited* authority; and the other derives it from *Heaven*; and makes it *unlimited*.——I have repeatedly declared my admiration of such a constitution of government as our own would be, were the House of Commons a fair representation of the kingdom, and under no undue influence.——The sum of all I have meant to maintain is, "that LEGITIMATE GOVERNMENT, as "opposed to OPPRESSION and TYRANNY, con- "sists in the dominion of equal laws made with "common consent, or of men over *themselves*; "and not in the dominion of communities over "communities, or of any men over other men." Introduction to the second Tract, p. 9.——How then can it be pretended, that I have aimed at destroying all authority? Does our own constitution destroy all authority? Is the authority of equal laws made with common consent no authority? Must there be no government in a state that governs itself? Or, must an institution, contrived by the united counsels of the members of a community, for restraining licentiousness and gaining security against injury and violence, *encourage* licentiousness, and give to every one a power to commit what outrages he pleases?

The Archbishop of York, (in a sermon preached before the society for propagating the gospel in foreign parts, Feb. 21, 1777,) has taken notice of some loose opinions, as he calls them, which have been lately current on civil liberty; some who mean delinquency having given accounts of it "by "which every man's humour is made to be the "rule of his obedience, all the bad passions are "let loose, and those dear interests abandoned "to outrage for the protection of which we trust "in law," 4to edit. p. 15 and 16. It is not difficult to guess at one of the delinquents intended in these words. In opposition to the horrid sentiments of liberty which they describe, but which in reality no man in his senses ever entertained, the Archbishop defines it to be simply, the supremacy of law, or GOVERNMENT by LAW, without adding to *law*, as I had done, the words *equal* and *made with common consent*; (*a*) and without opposing a GOVERNMENT by LAW to a GOVERNMENT BY MEN, as others had done.——According

(*a*) In p. 19. he calls liberty "a freedom from all re- "straints except such as established law imposes for THE "GOOD OF THE COMMUNITY." But this addition can make no difference of any consequence, as long as it is not specified *where* the power is lodged of judging what laws are for the good of the community. In countries where the *laws* are the *edicts* of absolute princes, the end professed is always the good of the Community

cording

cording to him, therefore, the ſupremacy of law muſt be liberty, whatever the law is, or whoever makes it.——In deſpotic countries government by law is the ſame with government by the will of one man, which HOOKER has called *the miſery of all men*; but, according to this definition, it is liberty.——In ENGLAND *formerly*, the law conſigned to the flames all who denyed certain eſtabliſhed points of faith. Even *now*, it ſubjects to fines, impriſonment and baniſhment all teachers of religion who have not ſubſcribed the doctrinal articles of the church of England; and the good Archbiſhop, not thinking the law in this caſe ſufficiently rigorous, has propoſed putting Proteſtant Diſſenters under the ſame reſtraints with the Papiſts. (*a*) And ſhould this be done,

(*a*) "The laws againſt Papiſts have been extremely ſevere. "New dangers may ariſe; and if at any time ANOTHER "DENOMINATION of men ſhould be equally dangerous to "our civil intereſts, it would be juſtifiable to lay them "under ſimilar reſtraints." Page 17.——In another part of this ſermon the great men in oppoſition (ſome of the firſt in the kingdom in reſpect of rank, ability, and virtue) are deſcribed as a body of men void of principle, who, without regarding the relation in which they ſtand to the community, have entered into a league for advancing their private intereſt, and "who "are held together by the ſame bond that keeps together "the loweſt and wickedeſt combinations."——Was there ever ſuch a cenſure delivered from a pulpit? What wonder is

done, if done by *law*, it will be the establishment of *liberty*.

The truth is, that a government by law is or is not liberty, just as the laws are just or unjust; and as the body of the people do or do not participate in the power of making them. The learned Prelate seems to have thought otherwise, and therefore has given a definition of liberty, which might as well have been given of slavery.

At the conclusion of his sermon, the Archbishop adds words which he calls comfortable, addressed

is it that the Dissenters should come in for a share in his Grace's abuse?——Their political principles, he says, are growing dangerous.——On what does he ground this insinuation? He is mistaken if he imagines that they are all such delinquents as the author of the following tracts, or that they think universally as he does of the war with America. On this subject they are, like other bodies of men in the kingdom, of different opinions.——But I will tell him in what they agree.——They agree in detesting the doctrines of passive obedience and non-resistance. They are all WHIGS, enemies to arbitrary power, and firmly attached to those principles of civil and religious liberty which produced the GLORIOUS REVOLUTION and the HANOVERIAN SUCCESSION.——Such principles are the nation's best defence; and Protestant Dissenters have hitherto reckoned it their glory to be distinguished by zeal for them, and an adherence to them. ONCE these principles were *approved* by men in power. No good can be expected, if they are now reckoned dangerous.

addreſſed to thoſe who had been *patient in tribulation*,(*a*) and intimating that they might *rejoice in hope*, "a ray of brightneſs then appearing "after a proſpect which had been long dark." And in an account which follows the ſermon, from one of the miſſionaries in the province of New-York, it is ſaid, that "the rebellion would "undoubtedly be cruſhed, and that THEN will "be the time for taking ſteps for the increaſe of "the church in America, by granting it an epiſ-"copate." In conformity to the ſentiments of

(*a*) That is, the miſſionaries of the ſociety in America.—The charter of the ſociety declares the end of its incorporation to be "propagating the goſpel in foreign parts, "and making proviſion for the worſhip of God in thoſe "plantations which wanted the adminiſtration of God's "word and ſacraments, and were abandoned to atheiſm "and infidelity." The chief buſineſs, on the contrary, of the ſociety has been to provide for the ſupport of *epiſcopalianiſm* in the northern colonies, and particularly NEW-ENGLAND, where the ſacraments are more regularly adminiſtered, and the people leſs abandoned to infidelity, than perhaps in any country under heaven. The miſſionaries employed and paid by the ſociety for this purpoſe, have generally been clergymen of the higheſt principles in church and ſtate. *America*, having been for ſome time very hoſtile to men of ſuch principles, moſt of them have been obliged to take refuge in this country; and here they have, I am afraid, been too ſucceſsful in propagating their own reſentments, in miſleading our rulers, and widening the breach which has produced the preſent war.

this

this missionary, the Archbishop also expresses his hope, that the opportunity which such an event will give, for establishing episcopacy among the colonists, will not be lost; and advises, that measures should be thought of for that purpose, and for thereby rescuing the church from the persecution it has long suffered in *America*.

This is a subject so important, and it has been so much misrepresented, that I cannot help going out of my way to give a brief account of it.

It does not appear that the lay members themselves of the church in *America* have ever wished for Bishops. On the contrary, the assembly of *Virginia* (the first episcopal colony) some years ago returned thanks to two clergymen in that colony, who had protested against a resolution of the other clergy to petition for Bishops. The church *here* cannot have a right to *impose* Bishops on the church in another country; and therefore, while churchmen in *America* are averse to Bishops, it must be persecution to send Bishops among them. The *Presbyterians*, and other religious sects there, are willing, from a sense of the reasonableness of toleration, to admit Bishops whenever the body of episcopalian laity shall desire them, provided security is given that they shall be officers merely spiritual, possessed of no other powers than those which are necessary to the full exercise of that

mode

mode of religious worship. It is not Bishops, as *spiritual* officers, they have opposed; but Bishops on a state-establishment; Bishops with *civil* powers; Bishops at the head of ecclesiastical courts, maintained by taxing other sects, and possessed of a PRE-EMINENCE which would be incompatible with the equality which has long subsisted among all religious sects in *America*. In this last respect, the colonies have hitherto enjoyed a happiness which is unparalleled, but which the introduction of such Bishops as would be sent from hence would destroy. In *Pensilvania* (one of the happiest countries under heaven before we carried into it desolation and carnage) all sects of christians have been always perfectly on a level, the legislature taking no part with any one sect against others, but protecting all equally as far as they are peaceable. The state of the colonies north of *Pensilvania* is much the same; and, in the province of *Massachusett's-Bay* in particular, civil authority interposes no farther in religion than by imposing a tax for supporting public worship, leaving to all the power of applying the tax to the support of that mode of public worship which they like best. This tax the episcopalians were, at one time, obliged to pay in common with others; but so far did the province carry its indulgence to them, that an act was passed on purpose to excuse them.

them.—With this let the state of Protestant Dissenters in this country be compared. Not only are they obliged to pay tithes for the support of the established church, but their worship is not even tolerated, unless their ministers will subscribe the articles of the church. In consequence of having long scrupled this subscription, they have lost all legal right to protection, and are exposed to the cruellest penalties. Uneasy in such a situation, they not long ago applied twice to parliament for the repeal of the penal laws against them. Bills for that purpose were brought into the *House of Commons*, and passed that House. But, in the House of Lords, they were rejected in consequence of the opposition of the Bishops.—There are few I reverence so much as some on the sacred bench; but such conduct (and may I not add the alacrity with which most of them support the present measures?) must leave an indelible stain upon them, and w llprobably exclude them for ever from *America*.

On this occasion, I cannot help thinking with concern of the learned Prelate's feelings. After a prospect long dark, he had discovered a ray of brightness shewing him *America* reduced, and the church triumphant: But lately, that ray of brightness has vanished, and defeat has taken place of victory and conquest.—And what do we *now* see?—What a different prospect, mortifying

to

to the learned Prelate, presents itself?—A great people likely to be formed, in spite of all our efforts, into free communities, under governments which have (*a*) no religious tests and establishments!—A new æra in future annals, and a new

(*a*) I am sorry to mention one exception to the fact here intimated. The new constitution for *Pensilvania* (in other respects wise and liberal) is dishonoured by a religious test. It requires an acknowledgment of the divine inspiration of the Old and New Testament, as a condition of being admitted to a seat in the House of Representatives; directing however, at the same time, that no other religious test shall *for ever* hereafter be required of any civil officer.——This has been, probably, an accommodation to the prejudices of some of the narrower sects in the province, to which the more liberal part have for the present thought fit to yield; and, therefore, it may be expected that it will not be of long continuance.

Religious tests and subscriptions in general, and all establishments of particular systems of faith, with civil emoluments annexed, do inconceivable mischief, by turning religion into a trade, by engendering strife and persecution, by forming hypocrites, by obstructing the progress of truth, and fettering and perverting the human mind; nor will the world ever grow much *wiser*, or *better*, or *happier*, till, by the abolition of them, truth can gain fair play, and reason free scope for exertion. The Archbishop, page 11, speaks of christianity as "insufficient to rely on its own energies; and "of the assistances which it is the business of civil authority "to provide for gospel truths."——A worse slander was never thrown on gospel truths. Christianity disdains such assistances, as the corrupted governments of this world are capable of giving it. Politicians and statesmen know little of it. Their *enmity* has sometimes done it good; but their *friendship*, by supporting corruptions carrying its name, has been almost fatal to it.

opening

opening in human affairs beginning, among the descendants of *Englishmen*, in a new world;—A rising empire, extended over an immense continent, without BISHOPS,—without NOBLES,—and without KINGS.

*O the depth of the riches of the wisdom of God! How unsearchable are his judgments!*

But to proceed to another subject.

In the second of the following tracts, page 48. I have observed, that in former times it was the custom of parliament to pass bills for appointing commissioners to take, state, and examine the public accounts. I have lately had it in my power to inform myself more particularly on this subject; and I shall here beg leave to give a brief recital of some of the principal facts relating to it.

The first bill for the purpose I have mentioned was passed in the times of the commonwealth, and in the year 1653. It was called an "act for accounts, and for clearing of public "debts, and discovering frauds and conceal-"ments." Seven commissioners were named in it, and the necessary powers given them. In 1667, another act was passed for the same purpose; after which I find no account of any such acts till the beginning of the reign of King William.

William. At this time complaints of mismanagement and embezzlements in the disposition of public money were become so prevalent, that the *House of Commons* thought it necessary to enter into measures for effectually preventing them, by obliging all revenue officers to make up their accounts, and bringing defaulters to justice.

With these views, six of the acts I have mentioned were passed between the years 1690 and 1701. Another was passed in the first of Queen *Anne*; and *three* more in her four last years. In King *William*'s reign they were always passed by the *House of Commons* without a division. In *Queen Anne's reign*, not *one* passed without a division. In 1717, a motion for such an act was *rejected* without a division; and since 1717, only one motion (*a*) has been made for such a bill, and it was rejected by a majority of 136 to 66.

The preamble to these acts declares the reason of them to be, that "the kingdom may be "satisfied and truly informed, whether all the "monies granted by parliament have been faith-"fully issued and applied to the end for which "they had been given; and that all loyal subjects "may be thereby encouraged more chearfully to "bear the burthens laid upon them." The number of commissioners named in them was generally nine or seven, all members of the *House*

(*a*) In 1742, after the resignation of Sir *Robert Walpole*.

*of Commons.* It was particularly ordered, that they ſhould take an account of all the revenues brought into the receipt of the Exchequer, and all arrears thereof; of all monies in the hands of the receivers general of the land-tax, cuſtoms and exciſe; of all the public ſtores, proviſions, &c. as well for land as ſea ſervice; of all ſhips of war, and the ſums of money provided or paid for the uſe of the forces by ſea and land, and the number of them reſpectively; and of any briberies or corruptions in any perſons concerned in the receiving or diſpoſing of the national treaſure. And, for theſe purpoſes, they were impowered to call before them, and to examine upon oath the officers of the exchequer, the ſecretary at war, paymaſter of the forces, commiſſioners of the navy and ordnance, and all perſons whatever employed as commiſſioners, or otherwiſe, in or about the *Treaſury.*

The reports, which the commiſſioners thus appointed delivered from time to time to parliament, contain accounts of a waſte of public money, ariſing from the rapacity of contractors, and many ſcandalous abuſes and frauds in every part of the public ſervice, which muſt ſhock every perſon not grown callous to all the feelings of honeſty and honour. In conſequence of theſe reports, the *Houſe of Commons* addreſſed the throne, and remonſtrated; ſeveral great men were

were accuſed, and brought to ſhame; ſome were diſmiſſed from their places, and ordered to be proſecuted; ſome expelled, and ſome committed to the Tower. Thus did our repreſentatives in thoſe times diſcharge their duty as guardians of the public property; and it is, in my opinion, only by ſuch means that they are capable of doing this properly and effectually. It muſt, however, be acknowledged, that theſe commiſſions of enquiry did not produce all the good effects which might have been expected from them. The influence of the crown, and the intereſt in parliament of many great men entruſted with the diſpoſition of public money, rendered the proper execution of them extremely difficult. This led ſome even of the *Tories*, at the time of the great change of miniſtry in 1710, to propoſe, that the receiving and iſſuing of the public money ſhould be taken from the crown; and, in defence of this propoſal, it was urged, that the iſſuingof public money, being in ſome of the moſt deſpotic countries left in the hands of the people, it was by no means a neceſſary part of the royal prerogative. This would indeed have provided a complete remedy; and it might have perpetuated the conſtitution. But, even in theſe times, it was a reformation too great and too impracticable to engage much attention.

Ever ſince thoſe times the public accounts have been growing more complicated; and the temptations to profuſion and embezzlement have been increaſing with increaſing luxury and diſſipation. How aſtoniſhing then is it that every idea of ſuch *commiſſions* ſhould be now loſt; and that, at a time when the nation is labouring under expences almoſt too heavy to be borne, the paſſing of accounts by the *Houſe of Commons* is become little more than a matter of form; our repreſentatives ſcarcely thinking it worth their while to attend on ſuch occaſions, and MILLIONS of the public treaſure being ſometimes given away, in a few hours, juſt as propoſed by the *Treaſury*, without debate or enquiry.

I muſt not forget to mention particularly on this ſubject, that the commiſſioners named in the acts I have deſcribed, were always declared incapable of holding any place or office of profit under the crown; and directed to take an account "of all " penſions, ſalaries, and ſums of money paid " or payable to members of parliament out of " the revenue or otherwiſe."——Not long before this time, the *Houſe of Commons* would not ſuffer even the *Attorney-general* (*a*) to ſit and vote in the

(*a*) Sir FRANCIS BACON was the *ſecond* ATTORNEY-GENERAL who ſat in the *Houſe of Commons*; but, to prevent its being drawn into a precedent, the Houſe would not admit him, till they had made an order, that no Attorney-General

the houſe becauſe he was the king's ſervant; and in 1678, a member, as Mr. *Trenchard* ſays, was committed to the Tower, for only ſaying in the houſe that the king might keep guards for his defence, if he could pay them.——Such *once* was the Houſe of Commons——So jealous of the power of the crown, and ſo chaſte.——Since the reign of Queen *Ann* and the paſſing of the *Septennial Act*, a great change has taken place. (*a*) A change

General ſhould for the future be allowed to ſit and vote in that Houſe.——In conformity to this order, whenever afterwards a member was appointed Attorney-General, his place was vacated, and a new writ iſſued. This continued to be the practice till the year 1670, when Sir HENEAGE FINCH (afterwards EARL OF NOTTINGHAM) being appointed Attorney-General, he was allowed by connivance to preſerve his ſeat, which connivance has been continued ever ſince.—I give theſe facts not from any enquiry or knowledge of my own, but from the authority of a friend, who is perhaps better informed than any perſon in the kingdom on every ſubject of this kind.

(*a*) The following facts will ſhew, in ſome degree, how this change has been brought about.——For ten years ending Aug. 1, 1717 (a period comprehending in it a general war abroad; and the demiſe of the crown, the eſtabliſhment of a new family, and an open rebellion at home) the money expended in ſecret ſervices amounted only to 279,444 l.——For TEN YEARS ending Feb. 11, 1742, it amounted to no leſs a ſum than 1.384,600; of which 50,077 l. was paid to printers of News-papers and writers for government; and a greater ſum expended, in the laſt *ſix weeks* of theſe ten years, than had been ſpent in *three years* before Aug. 1710.——See the

A change which is little less than the total ruin of the constitution, and which may end in a tyranny the most oppressive and insupportable. It is, therefore, the greatest evil, which could have happened to us; and the men, by whose abominable

the Report of the COMMITTEE appointed March 23, 1742, to enquire into the conduct of ROBERT EARL OF ORFORD, printed in the Journals of the House of Commons, vol. 24, p. 295, 296, 300.—One passage, in this report, contains remarks, so much to my present purpose and so important, that I cannot help copying it.——"There are no laws particularly "adapted to the case of a minister who clandestinely em-"ploys the money of the public, and the whole power and "profitable employments that attend the collecting and dis-"posing of it, *against* the people: And, by this profusion "and criminal distribution of offices, in some measure jus-"tifies the expence that particular persons are obliged to be "at, by making it necessary to the preservation of all that "is valuable to a free nation. For in that case, the contest "is plain and visible. It is, whether the Commons shall "retain the *third* state in their own hands; while this "whole dispute is carried on at the expence of the people, "and, on the side of the minister, out of the money granted "to support and secure the constitutional independence of "the three branches of the legislature.——This method of "corruption is as sure, and, therefore, as criminal a way of "subverting the constitution as by an armed force. It is a "crime, productive of a total destruction of the very being "of this government; and is so *high* and *unnatural*, that no-"thing but the powers of parliament can reach it; and, as "it never can meet with parliamentary animadversion but "when it is unsuccessful, it must seek for its *security* in the "extent

able policy it has been accompliſhed, ought to be followed with the everlaſting execrations of every friend to public virtue and liberty.

I now withdraw to the ſituation of an anxious ſpectator of public events; but before I do this, I muſt leave with the public, at this threatening period, the following ſentiments.

Not long ago, the colonies might have been kept, without bloodſhed or trouble, by repealing the *acts* which have made us the aggreſſors in the preſent war; but *now* it would be great folly to expect this.—At the ſame time I think it certain, that they may be rendered more uſeful to us by a pacification on liberal terms, which ſhall bind them to us as FRIENDS, than by any victories or ſlaughters (were they poſſible) which can force them to ſubmit to us as SUBJECTS.—I think it alſo certain, that ſhould the offer of ſuch terms be delayed till they have formed an alliance with *France*, this country is UNDONE.——Such an alliance, we may hope, is not yet ſettled.——Our rulers, therefore, may *poſſibly*

" extent and efficacy of the miſchief it produces." P. 395. The obſtructions which this committee met with in their enquiry proved, that the crime they here deſcribe in ſuch emphatical language, had *even then* obtained that very ſecurity, in the extent of the miſchief it produced, which they obſerve it was under a neceſſity of ſeeking.

 have

have ſtill a moment for pauſing and retreating, and every dictate of prudence and feeling of humanity requires them to be ſpeedy and earneſt in improving it.—But what am I ſaying? I know this muſt not be expected. Too full of ideas of our own dignity; too proud to retract; and too tenacious of dominion, we ſeem determined to perſiſt: And the conſequence muſt be, that the colonies will become the allies of *France*; that a general war will be kindled; and, perhaps, this once happy country be made, in righteous judgment, the ſeat of that deſolation and miſery which it has produced in other countries.

January 19, 1778.

## Account of the Customs for the last Six Years.

IN the following tracts I have reckoned, among the deſtructive conſequences of the war with *America*, the loſs of a conſiderable part of our trade. In conſequence of ſeveral accidental cauſes, particularly the demand created by the war, this effect has not yet been ſo much felt as was generally expected. The truth, however, is, that the war has operated in this way to a degree that is remarkable and alarming, as will appear from the following account of the Customs for the laſt ſix years.

| | Groſs Receipt. | Debentures. | Net Receipt. | Payments into the Exchequer. |
|---|---|---|---|---|
| 1772 | 5.134,503 | 2.214,508 | 2.441,038 | 2.525,515 |
| 1773 | 5.159,800 | 2.463,767 | 2.221,460 | 2.431,071 |
| 1774 | 5.068,000 | 2.132,600 | 2.455,500 | 2.547,717 |
| 1775 | 5.146,900 | 1.904,900 | 2.709,340 | 2.476,302 |
| 1776 | 3.726,970 | 1.544,300 | 1.633,380 | 2.460,402 |

It ſhould be obſerved, that though, in 1776, there had been no importation of *tabacco*, yet the duties on *tobacco* brought into the *Exchequer* as much as ever, theſe duties having been paid for old ſtock taken out of the warehouſes for *home conſumption*, inſtead of *exportation*. This is one of the cauſes which contributed to keep up the payments into the *Exchequer* in 1776, notwithſtanding a ſudden fall of near a million and a half in the groſs receipt, and above a million in the net produce.——In the laſt year, or 1777, the payments into the *Exchequer*, for the three quarters ended at *Michaelmas* laſt, had ſunk near a quarter of a million. But what may be of more importance is, that the

the debentures (or duties returned at exportation) which had fallen in 1775 and 1776 above a *fourth*, continued to fall in 1777; and, in the port of LONDON (where commonly about three-fourths of the cuſtoms are paid) they did not amount laſt year to *half* the uſual ſum.

I have examined the cuſtoms from the Revolution to the preſent time; but I cannot find that any thing like ſuch a fall in them has ever happened before. A diſmal prelude, probably, to greater falls.

---

# ADVERTISEMENT.

THE preſent ſtate of the public funds makes it neceſſary for me to acquaint the reader, that when the *Supplement* to the following Tracts was written, the 3 *per cent.* annuities were at the price which the calculations in it ſuppoſe, or nearly at 78. They have ſince fallen to 72, and once even below 69, which is a lower price than they were ever at during the whole laſt war, except juſt at the pinch of the loan of twelve millions in 1762.—The difference of price alſo between them and the new 4 *per cents.* is fallen, (for no reaſon that I can diſcover) from 14 to about 10½.—I find, likewiſe, that in conſequence of a diſtreſſing ſcarcity of money, the ſubſcribers to the laſt loan of *five millions* have not yet been able to complete their payments.—Theſe facts afford a dark proſpect; and make it doubtful whether, if things don't mend, it will be poſſible, by any ſchemes, to procure the money neceſſary to bear the expence of another campaign.——Should it happen, for theſe reaſons, that what I have written on loans can be of no uſe; or, though capable of being of uſe, ſhould it be neglected; I ſhall ſtill reflect with ſatisfaction, that I have now given what I wiſhed to offer on this ſubject with more correctneſs; and proved, beyond a doubt, that a great part of the National Debt is an *artificial* debt, for which no money has been received, and which might have been eaſily avoided.

# OBSERVATIONS

ON THE NATURE OF

# CIVIL LIBERTY,

THE PRINCIPLES OF

# GOVERNMENT,

AND THE

# JUSTICE AND POLICY

OF THE

# WAR WITH AMERICA.

*Quis furor iste novus? quo nunc, quo tenditis ——*
*Heu! miseri cives? non Hostem, inimicaque castra,*
*—— Vestras Spes uritis.* VIRG.

By RICHARD PRICE, D. D. F. R. S.

THE EIGHTH EDITION,
With CORRECTIONS and ADDITIONS.

LONDON:
Printed for T. CADELL, in the STRAND.
M.DCC.LXXVIII.

# PREFACE

## TO

## The FIRST EDITION.

*IN the following Observations, I have taken that liberty of examining public measures, which, happily for this kingdom, every person in it enjoys. They contain the sentiments of a private and unconnected man; for which, should there be any thing wrong in them, he alone is answerable.*

*After all that has been written on the dispute with* America, *no reader can expect to be informed, in this publication, of much that he has not before known. Perhaps, however, he may find in it some new matter; and if he should, it will be chiefly in the Observations on the Nature of Civil Liberty, and the Policy of the War with America.*

February 8th, 1776.

PRE-

# PREFACE

TO

## The FIFTH EDITION.

THE favourable reception which the following Tract has met with, makes me abundant amends for the abuse it has brought upon me. I should be ill employed were I to take much notice of this abuse: But there is one circumstance attending it, which I cannot help just mentioning.—The principles on which I have argued form the foundation of every state as far as it is free; and are the same with those taught by Mr. Locke, and all the writers on Civil Liberty who have been hitherto most admired in this country. But I find with concern, that our Governors chuse to decline trying by them their present measures: For, in a Pamphlet which has been circulated by government with great industry, these principles are pronounced to be " unnatural and wild, in" compatible with practice, and the off-

" spring

" ſpring of the diſtempered imagination of
" a man who is biaſſed by party, and who
" writes to deceive."

I muſt take this opportunity to add, that I love quiet too well to think of entering into a controverſy with any writers; particularly, NAMELESS ones. Conſcious of good intentions, and unconnected with any party, I have endeavoured to plead the cauſe of general liberty and juſtice: And happy in knowing this, I ſhall, in ſilence, commit myſelf to that candour of the public of which I have had ſo much experience.

March 12th, 1776.

CON-

# OBSERVATIONS,

## &c.

OUR Colonies in NORTH AMERICA appear to be now determined to risk and suffer every thing, under the persuasion, that GREAT BRITAIN is attempting to rob them of that Liberty to which every member of society, and all civil communities, have a natural and unalienable title. The question, therefore, whether this is a right persuasion, is highly interesting, and deserves the careful attention of every *Englishman* who values Liberty, and wishes to avoid staining himself with the guilt of invading it. But it is impossible to judge properly of this question without just ideas of Liberty *in general*; and of the nature, limits, and principles of Civil Liberty *in particular*.—The following observations on this subject appear to me of some importance; and I cannot make myself easy without offering them to the public at the present period, big with events of the last consequence to this kingdom. I do this, with reluctance and pain, urged by strong feelings, but at the same time checked by the consciousness that I am likely to deliver sentiments not favourable to the present measures of that government, under which I live, and to which I am a constant and zealous well-wisher. Such, however, are my present sentiments and views, that this is a consideration of inferior moment with me; and, as I hope never to go beyond the bounds of decent discussion and expostulation, I flatter myself, that I shall be able to avoid giving any person reason for offence.

The observations with which I shall begin, are of a more general and abstracted nature; but being necessary to introduce what I have principally in view, I hope they will be patiently read and considered.

## SECT. I.

### *Of the Nature of Liberty in General.*

IN order to obtain a more distinct view of the nature of Liberty as such, it will be useful to consider it under the four following general divisions.

First, *Physical* Liberty.——Secondly, *Moral* Liberty. —— Thirdly, *Religious* Liberty. —— And Fourthly, *Civil* Liberty.——These heads comprehend all the different kinds of Liberty. And I have placed *Civil* Liberty last, because caufe I mean to apply to it all I fhall fay of the other kinds of Liberty.

By PHYSICAL LIBERTY I mean that principle of *Spontaneity*, or *Self-determination*, which conftitutes us *Agents*; or which gives us a command over our actions, rendering them properly *ours*, and not effects of the operation of any foreign caufe.——MORAL LIBERTY is the power of following, in all circumftances, our fenfe of right and wrong; or of acting in conformity to our reflecting and moral principles, without being controuled by any contrary principles.——RELIGIOUS LIBERTY fignifies the power of exercifing, without moleftation, that mode of religion which we think beft; or of making the decifions of our own confciences refpecting religious truth, the rule of our conduct, and not any of the decifions of our fellow-men.—In like manner; CIVIL LIBERTY is the power of a *Civil Society* or *State* to govern itfelf by its own difcretion, or by laws of its own making, without being fubject to the impofitions of *any* power, in appointing and directing which the collective body of the people have no concern, and over which they have no controul.

It fhould be obferved, that, according to thefe definitions of the different kinds of liberty, there is one general idea, that runs through them all; I mean, the idea of *Self-direction*, or *Self-government*.—Did our volitions originate not with *ourfelves*, *ſelves*, but with ſome cauſe over which we have no power; or were we under a neceſſity of always following ſome will different from our own, we ſhould want PHYSICAL LIBERTY.

In like manner; he whoſe perceptions of moral obligation are controuled by his paſſions has loſt his *Moral Liberty*; and the moſt common language applied to him is, that he wants *Self-government.*

He likewiſe who, in religion, cannot govern himſelf by his convictions of religious duty, but is obliged to receive formularies of faith, and to practiſe modes of worſhip impoſed upon him by others, wants *Religious Liberty.*——And the Community alſo that is governed, not by itſelf, but by ſome will independent of it, wants *Civil Liberty.*

In all theſe caſes there is a force which ſtands oppoſed to the agent's *own* will; and which, as far as it operates, produces *Servitude.*——In the *firſt* caſe, this force is incompatible with the very idea of voluntary motion; and the ſubject of it is a mere paſſive inſtrument which never *acts*, but is always *acted upon.*——In the *ſecond* caſe; this force is the influence of paſſion getting the better of reaſon; or the *brute* overpowering and conquering the will of the *man.*——In the *third* caſe; it is *Human Authority* in religion requiring conformity to particular modes of faith and worſhip, and ſuperſeding *private judgment.*——And in the laſt

caſe,

case, it is any will distinct from that of the Majority of a Community, which claims a power of making laws for it, and disposing of its property.

This it is, I think, that marks the limit between *Liberty* and *Slavery*. As far as, in any instance, the operation of any cause comes in to restrain the power of Self-government, so far Slavery is introduced: Nor do I think that a preciser idea than this of Liberty and Slavery can be formed.

I cannot help wishing I could here fix my reader's attention, and engage him to consider carefully the dignity of that blessing to which we give the name of LIBERTY, according to the representation now made of it. There is not a word in the whole compass of language which expresses so much of what is important and excellent. It is, in every view of it, a blessing truly sacred and invaluable.——Without *Physical Liberty*, man would be a machine acted upon by mechanical springs, having no principle of motion in himself, or command over events; and, therefore, incapable of all merit and demerit.——Without *Moral Liberty*, he is a wicked and detestable being, subject to the tyranny of base lusts, and the sport of every vile appetite.——And without *Religious* and *Civil Liberty* he is a poor and abject animal, without rights, without property, and without a conscience, bending his neck to the yoke, and crouching to the will of every ſilly creature who has the inſolence to pretend to authority over him.——Nothing, therefore, can be of ſo much conſequence to us as *Liberty*. It is the foundation of all honour, and the chief privilege and glory of our natures.

In fixing our ideas on the ſubject of Liberty, it is of particular uſe to take ſuch an enlarged view of it as I have now given. But the immediate object of the preſent enquiry being *Civil Liberty*, I will confine to it all the ſubſequent obſervations.

## SECT. II.

### *Of Civil Liberty and the Principles of Government.*

FROM what has been ſaid it is obvious, that all civil government, as far as it can be denominated *free*, is the creature of the people. It originates with them. It is conducted under their direction; and has in view nothing but their happineſs. All its different forms are no more than ſo many different modes in which they chuſe to direct their affairs, and to ſecure the quiet enjoyment of their rights.——In every free ſtate every man is his own Legiſlator. (*a*)——All *taxes* are free-gifts for public ſervices.——All *laws* are particular proviſions or regulations eſtabliſhed by COMMON

(*a*) See a particular explanation of this aſſertion in the Second Tract, Page 9.

CONSENT

CONSENT for gaining protection and safety.—— And all *Magistrates* are Trustees or Deputies for carrying these regulations into execution.

Liberty, therefore, is too imperfectly defined when it is said to be "a Government by LAWS, and not by MEN." If the laws are made by one man, or a junto of men in a state, and not by COMMON CONSENT, a government by them does not differ from Slavery. In this case it would be a contradiction in terms to say that the state governs itself.

From hence it is obvious that *Civil Liberty*, in its most perfect degree, can be enjoyed only in small states, where every independent agent is capable of giving his suffrage in person, and of being chosen into public offices. When a state becomes so numerous, or when the different parts of it are removed to such distances from one another, as to render this impracticable, a diminution of Liberty necessarily arises. There are, however, in these circumstances, methods by which such near approaches may be made to perfect Liberty as shall answer all the purposes of government, and at the same time secure every right of human nature.

Tho' all the members of a state should not be capable of giving their suffrages on public measures, *individually* and *personally*, they may do this by the appointment of *Substitutes* or *Representatives*. They may entrust the powers of legislation, ſubject to ſuch reſtrictions as they ſhall think neceſſary, with any number of *Delegates*; and whatever can be done by ſuch delegates within the limits of their truſt, may be conſidered as done by the united voice and counſel of the Community. ——In this method a free government may be eſtabliſhed in the largeſt ſtate; and it is conceivable that by regulations of this kind, any number of ſtates might be ſubjected to a ſcheme of government, that would exclude the deſolations of war, and produce univerſal peace and order.

Let us think here of what may be practicable in this way with reſpect to *Europe* in particular. ——While it continues divided, as it is at preſent, into a great number of independent kingdoms whoſe intereſts are continually claſhing, it is impoſſible but that diſputes will often ariſe which muſt end in war and carnage. It would be no remedy to this evil to make one of theſe ſtates ſupreme over the reſt; and to give it an abſolute plenitude of power to ſuperintend and controul them. This would be to ſubject all the ſtates to the arbitrary diſcretion of one, and to eſtabliſh an ignominious ſlavery not poſſible to be long endured. It would, therefore, be a remedy worſe than the diſeaſe; nor is it poſſible it ſhould be approved by any mind that has not loſt every idea of Civil Liberty. On the contrary.—Let every ſtate, with reſpect to all its internal concerns, be con-

tinued

tinued independent of all the reſt; and let a general confederacy be formed by the appointment of a SENATE conſiſting of Repreſentatives from all the different ſtates. Let this SENATE poſſeſs the power of managing all the *common* concerns of the united ſtates, and of judging and deciding between them, as a common *Arbiter* or *Umpire*, in all diſputes; having, at the ſame time, under its direction, the common force of the ſtates to ſupport its deciſions.——In theſe circumſtances, each ſeparate ſtate would be ſecure againſt the interference of foreign power in its private concerns, and, therefore, would poſſeſs *Liberty*; and at the ſame time it would be ſecure againſt all oppreſſion and inſult from every neighbouring ſtate.——Thus might the ſcattered force and abilities of a whole continent be gathered into one point; all litigations ſettled as they roſe; univerſal peace preſerved; and nation prevented *from any more lifting up a ſword againſt nation.*

I have obſerved, that tho', in a great ſtate, all the individuals that compoſe it cannot be admitted to an immediate participation in the powers of legiſlation and government, yet they may participate in theſe powers by a delegation of them to a body of repreſentatives.——In this caſe it is evident that the ſtate will be ſtill *free* or *ſelf-governed*; and that it will be more or leſs ſo in proportion

as

as it is more or leſs fairly and adequately repreſented. If the perſons to whom the truſt of government is committed hold their places for ſhort terms; if they are choſen by the unbiaſſed voices of a majority of the ſtate, and ſubject to their inſtructions; Liberty will be enjoyed in its higheſt degree. But if they are choſen for long terms by a part only of the ſtate; and if during that term they are ſubject to no controul from their conſtituents; the very idea of Liberty will be loſt, and the power of chuſing repreſentatives becomes nothing but a power, lodged in a *few*, to chuſe at certain periods, a body of *Maſters* for themſelves and for the reſt of the Community. And if a ſtate is ſo ſunk that the majority of its repreſentatives are elected by a handful of the meaneſt *(a)* perſons in it, whoſe votes are always paid for; and if alſo, there is a higher will on which even theſe mock repreſentatives themſelves depend, and that directs their voices: In theſe circumſtances, it will be an abuſe of language to ſay that the ſtate poſſeſſes Liberty. Private men, indeed, might be allowed the exerciſe of Liberty; as they might alſo under the moſt deſpotic government; but it would be an *indul-*

(*a*) In *Great Britain,* conſiſting of near ſix *millions* of inhabitants, 5723 perſons, moſt of them the loweſt of the people, elect one half of the *Houſe of Commons*; and 364 votes chuſe a ninth part. This may be ſeen diſtinctly made out in the *Political Diſquiſitions*, Vol. 1. Book 2. C. 4. a work full of important and uſeful inſtruction.

*gence,*

*gence* or *connivance* derived from the ſpirit of the times, or from an accidental mildneſs in the adminiſtration. And, rather than be governed in ſuch a manner, it would perhaps be better to be governed by the will of one man without any repreſentation: For a repreſentation ſo degenerated could anſwer no other end than to miſlead and deceive, by diſguiſing ſlavery, and keeping up a *form* of Liberty when the *reality* was loſt.

Within the limits now mentioned, Liberty may be enjoyed in every poſſible degree; from that which is complete and perfect, to that which is merely nominal; according as the people have more or leſs of a ſhare in government, and of a controuling power over the perſons by whom it is adminiſtered.

In general, to be *free* is to be guided by one's own will; and to be guided by the will of another is the characteriſtic of *Servitude.* This is particularly applicable to Political Liberty. That ſtate, I have obſerved, is *free*, which is guided by its own will; or, (which comes to the ſame) by the will of an aſſembly of repreſentatives appointed by itſelf and accountable to itſelf. And every ſtate that is not ſo governed; or in which a body of men repreſenting the people make not an eſſential part of the Legiſlature, is in *ſlavery.*——In order to form the moſt perfect conſtitution of government,

ment, there may be the beſt reaſons for joining to ſuch a body of repreſentatives, an *Hereditary Council* conſiſting of men of the firſt rank in the ſtate, with a *Supreme executive Magiſtrate* at the head of all. This will form uſeful checks in a legiſlature; and contribute to give it vigour, union, and diſpatch, without infringing liberty: for, as long aa that part of a government which repreſents the people is a *fair repreſentation*; and alſo has a negative on all public meaſures, together with the ſole power of impoſing taxes and originating ſupplies; the eſſentials of liberty will be preſerved. ——We make it our boaſt in this country, that this is our own conſtitution. I will not ſay with how much reaſon.

Of ſuch Liberty as I have now deſcribed, it is impoſſible there ſhould be an exceſs. Government is an inſtitution for the benefit of the people governed, which they have power to model as they pleaſe; and to ſay, that they can have too much of this power, is to ſay, that there ought to be a power in the ſtate ſuperior to that which gives it being, and from which all juriſdiction in it is derived.——Licentiouſneſs, which has been commonly mentioned, as an extreme of liberty, is indeed its oppoſite. It is government by the will of rapacious individuals, in oppoſition to the will

of

of the community, made known and declared in the laws. A free ſtate, at the ſame time that it is free itſelf, makes all its members free, by excluding licentiouſneſs, and guarding their perſons and property and good name againſt inſult. It is the end of all juſt government, at the ſame time that it ſecures the liberty of the public againſt *foreign* injury, to ſecure the liberty of the individual againſt *private* injury. I do not, therefore, think it ſtrictly juſt to ſay, that it belongs to the nature of government to entrench on private liberty. It ought never to do this, except as far as the exerciſe of private liberty encroaches on the liberties of others. That is; it is licentiouſneſs it reſtrains, and liberty itſelf only when uſed to deſtroy liberty.

It appears from hence, that licentiouſneſs and deſpotiſm are more nearly allied than is commonly imagined. They are both alike inconſiſtent with liberty, and the true end of government; nor is there any other difference between them, than that the one is the licentiouſneſs of *great* men, and the other the licentiouſneſs of *little* men; or that, by the one, the perſons and property of a people are ſubject to outrage and invaſion from a King, or a lawleſs body of *Grandees*; and that, by the other, they are ſubject to the like outrage from a *lawleſs mob*.——In avoiding one of theſe evils, mankind have often run into the other. But all well conſtituted governments guard equally againſt both.

Indeed of the two, the laſt is, on ſeveral accounts, the leaſt to be dreaded, and has done the leaſt miſchief. It may be truly ſaid, that if licentiouſneſs has deſtroyed its thouſands, deſpotiſm has deſtroyed its millions. The former, having little power, and no ſyſtem to ſupport it, neceſſarily finds its own remedy; and a people ſoon get out of the tumult and anarchy attending it. But a deſpotiſm, wearing the form of government, and being armed with its force, is an evil not to be conquered without dreadful ſtruggles. It goes on from age to age, debaſing the human faculties, levelling all diſtinctions, and preying on the rights and bleſſings of ſociety.——It deſerves to be added, that in a ſtate diſturbed by licentiouſneſs, there is an animation which is favourable to the human mind, and which puts it upon exerting its powers. But in a ſtate habituated to a deſpotiſm, all is ſtill and torpid. A dark and ſavage tyranny ſtifles every effort of genius; and the mind loſes all its ſpirit and dignity.

Before I proceed to what I have farther in view, I will obſerve, that the account now given of the principles of public Liberty, and the nature of an equal and free government, ſhews what judgment we ſhould form of that OMNIPOTENCE, which, it has been ſaid, muſt belong to every government as ſuch. Great ſtreſs has been laid on this, but moſt

moſt unreaſonably.——Government, as has been before obſerved, is, in the very nature of it, a TRUST; and all its powers a DELEGATION for gaining particular ends. This *truſt* may be miſapplied and abuſed. It may be employed to defeat the very ends for which it was inſtituted; and to ſubvert the very rights which it ought to protect.——A PARLIAMENT, for inſtance, conſiſting of a body of repreſentatives, choſen for a limited period, to make laws, and to grant money for public ſervices, would forfeit its authority by making itſelf perpetual, or even prolonging its own duration; by nominating its own members; by accepting bribes; or ſubjecting itſelf to any kind of foreign influence. This would convert a *Parliament* into a *conclave* or *junto* of ſelf-created tools; and a ſtate that has loſt its regard to its own rights, ſo far as to ſubmit to ſuch a breach of truſt in its rulers, is enſlaved.——Nothing, therefore, can be more abſurd than the doctrine which ſome have taught, with reſpect to the omnipotence of parliaments. They poſſeſs no power beyond the limits of the truſt for the execution of which they were formed. If they contradict this truſt, they betray their conſtituents, and diſſolve themſelves. All delegated power muſt be ſubordinate and limited.—If omnipotence can, with any ſenſe, be aſcribed to a legiſlature, it muſt be lodged where all legiſlative authority originates; that is, in the PEOPLE. For

*their*

*their* ſakes government is inſtituted; and their's is the only real omnipotence.

I am ſenſible, that all I have been ſaying would be very abſurd, were the opinions juſt which ſome have maintained concerning the origin of government. According to theſe opinions, government is not the creature of the people, or the reſult of a convention between them and their rulers: But there are certain men who poſſeſs in themſelves, independently of the will of the people, a right of governing them, which they derive from the Deity. This doctrine has been abundantly refuted by many (*a*) excellent writers. It is a doctrine which avowedly ſubverts Civil Liberty; and which repreſents mankind as a body of vaſſals, formed to deſcend like cattle from one ſet of owners to another, who have an abſolute dominion over them. It is a wonder, that thoſe who view their ſpecies in a light ſo humiliating, ſhould ever be able to think of themſelves without regret and ſhame. The intention of theſe obſervations is not to oppoſe ſuch ſentiments; but, taking for granted the reaſonableneſs of Civil Liberty, to ſhew wherein it conſiſts, and what diſtinguiſhes it from its con-

(*a*) See among others Mr. Locke on Government, and Dr. Prieſtley's Eſſay on the firſt Principles of Government.

trary.

trary.——And, in considering this subject, as it has been now treated, it is unavoidable to reflect on the excellency of a free government, and its tendency to exalt the nature of man.——Every member of a free state, having his property secure, and knowing himself his own governor, possesses a consciousness of dignity in himself, and feels incitements to emulation and improvement, to which the miserable slaves of arbitrary power must be utter strangers. In such a state all the springs of action have room to operate, and the mind is stimulated to the noblest exertions (*a*).—But to be obliged, from our birth, to look up to a creature no better than ourselves as the master of our fortunes; and to receive his will as our law—What can be more humiliating? What elevated ideas can enter a mind in such a situation?——Agreeably to this remark; the subjects of free states have, in all ages, been most distinguished for genius and knowledge. Liberty is the soil where the arts and sciences have flourished; and the more free a state has been, the more have the powers of the human mind been drawn forth into action, and the greater number of brave men has it produced. With what lustre do the antient free states of *Greece* shine in the annals of the world? How different is that country now, under the Great *Turk*? The differ-

(*a*) See Dr. Priestley on Government, page 68, 69, &c.

ence between a country inhabited by men and by brutes is not greater.

These are reflexions which ſhould be conſtantly preſent to every mind in this country.——As *Moral* Liberty is the prime bleſſing of man in his *private* capacity, ſo is *Civil* liberty in his *public* capacity. There is nothing that requires more to be *watched* than power. There is nothing that ought to be oppoſed with a more determined reſolution than its encroachments. Sleep in a ſtate, as *Monteſquieu* ſays, is always followed by ſlavery.

The people of this kingdom were once warmed by ſuch ſentiments as theſe. Many a ſycophant of power have they ſacrificed. Often have they fought and bled in the cauſe of Liberty. But that time ſeems to be going. The fair inheritance of Liberty left us by our anceſtors many of us are willing to reſign. An abandoned venality, the inſeparable companion of diſſipation and extravagance, has poiſoned the ſprings of public virtue among us: And ſhould any events ever ariſe that ſhould render the ſame oppoſition neceſſary that took place in the times of King *Charles* the Firſt, and *James* the Second, I am afraid all that is valuable to us would be loſt. The terror of the ſtanding army, the danger of the public funds, and the all-corrupting influence of the treaſury, would deaden all zeal, and produce general acquieſcence and ſervility.

## SECT. III.

### *Of the Authority of one Country over another.*

FROM the nature and principles of Civil Liberty, as they have been now explained, it is an immediate and neceſſary inference that no one community can have any power over the property or legiſlation of another community, which is not incorporated with it by a juſt and adequate repreſentation.——Then only, it has been ſhewn, is a ſtate *free*, when it is governed by its own will. But a country that is ſubject to the legiſlature of another country, in which it has no voice, and over which it has no controul, cannot be ſaid to be governed by its own will. Such a country, therefore, is in a ſtate of ſlavery. And it deſerves to be particularly conſidered, that ſuch a ſlavery is worſe, on ſeveral accounts, than any ſlavery of private men to one another, or of kingdoms to deſpots within themſelves.—Between one ſtate and another, there is none of that fellow-feeeling that takes place between perſons in private life. Being detached bodies that never ſee one another, and reſiding perhaps in different quarters of the globe, the ſtate that governs cannot be a witneſs to the ſufferings occaſioned by its oppreſſions; or a competent judge of the circumſtances and abilities of the people who are governed. They muſt alſo have in a great degree ſeparate intereſts; and the more the one is loaded, the more the other may be eaſed. The infamy likewiſe of oppreſſion, being in ſuch circumſtances ſhared among a multitude, is not likely to be much felt or regarded.——On all theſe accounts there is, in the caſe of one country ſubjugated to another, little or nothing to check rapacity; and the moſt flagrant injuſtice and cruelty may be practiſed without remorſe or pity.——I will add, that it is particularly difficult to ſhake off a tyranny of this kind. A ſingle deſpot, if a people are unanimous and reſolute, may be ſoon ſubdued. But a deſpotic ſtate is not eaſily ſubdued; and a people ſubject to it cannot emancipate themſelves without entering into a dreadful, and, perhaps, very unequal conteſt.

I cannot help obſerving farther, that the ſlavery of a people to internal deſpots may be qualified and limited; but I don't ſee what can limit the authority of one ſtate over another. The exerciſe of power in this caſe can have no other meaſure than diſcretion; and, therefore, muſt be indefinite and abſolute.

Once more. It ſhould be conſidered that the government of one country by another, can only be ſupported by a military force; and, without

ſuch

ſuch a ſupport, muſt be deſtitute of all weight and efficiency.

This will be beſt explained by putting the following caſe.——There is, let us ſuppoſe, in a province ſubject to the ſovereignty of a diſtant ſtate, a ſubordinate legiſlature conſiſting of an Aſſembly choſen by the people; a Council choſen by that Aſſembly; and a Governor *appointed* by the Sovereign ſtate, and paid by the Province. There are, likewiſe, judges and other officers, appointed and paid in the ſame manner, for adminiſtering *juſtice* agreeably to the laws, by the verdicts of juries fairly choſen.——This forms a conſtitution ſeemingly free, by giving the people a ſhare in their own government, and ſome check on their rulers. But, while there is a higher legiſlative power, to the controul of which ſuch a conſtitution is ſubject, it does not itſelf poſſeſs Liberty, and therefore cannot be of any uſe as a ſecurity to Liberty; nor is it poſſible that it ſhould be of long duration. Laws offenſive to the Province will be enacted by the Sovereign State. The legiſlature of the Province will remonſtrate againſt them. The magiſtrates will not execute them. Juries will not convict upon them; and conſequently, like the Pope's Bulls which once governed *Europe*, they will become nothing but forms and empty ſounds, to which no regard will be ſhewn.——In order to remedy this evil, and to give efficiency to its government, the supreme state will naturally be led to withdraw the *Governor*, the *Council*, and the *Judges* (*a*) from the controul

(*a*) The independency of the Judges we esteem in this country one of our greatest privileges.——Before the revolution they generally, I believe, held their places *during pleasure*. King William gave them their places *during good behaviour*. At the accession of the present Royal Family their places were given them *during good behaviour*, in consequence of the Act of Settlement, 12 and 13 W. III. C. 2. But an opinion having been entertained by some, that though their commissions were made under the Act of Settlement to continue, during good behaviour, yet that they determined on the demise of the Crown; it was enacted by a statute made in the first year of his present Majesty, Chap. 23. "That the commissions of Judges for "the time being shall be, continue, and remain in full force, "during their good behaviour, notwithstanding the demise "of his Majesty, or of any of his Heirs and Successors;" with a proviso, "that it may be lawful for his Majesty, his "Heirs and Successors, to remove any Judge upon the address "of both Houses of Parliament." And by the same Statute their salaries are secured to them during the continuance of their commissions: His Majesty, according to the preamble of the Statute, having been pleased to declare from the Throne to both Houses of Parliament, "That he looked upon the "independency and uprightness of Judges as essential to the "impartial administration of Justice, as one of the best securities to the Rights and Liberties of his loving Subjects, and "as most conducive to the honour of his Crown."

A worthy friend and able Lawyer has supplied me with this note. It affords, when contrasted with that *dependence* of the Judges which has been thought reasonable in *America*, a sad specimen of the different manner in which a kingdom may think proper to govern itself, and the provinces subject to it.

of the Province, by making them entirely dependant on itſelf for their *pay* and *continuance in office*, as well as for their appointment. It will alſo alter the mode of chuſing Juries on purpoſe to bring them more under its influence: And in ſome caſes, under the pretence of the impoſſibility of gaining an impartial trial where government is reſiſted, it will perhaps ordain, that offenders ſhall be removed from the Province to be tried within its own territories: And it may even go ſo far in this kind of policy, as to endeavour to prevent the effects of diſcontents, by forbidding all meetings and aſſociations of the people, except at ſuch times, and for ſuch particular purpoſes, as ſhall be permitted them.

Thus will ſuch a Province be exactly in the ſame ſtate that *Britain* would be in, were our firſt executive magiſtrate, our Houſe of Lords, and our Judges, nothing but the inſtruments of a foreign democratical power; were our Juries nominated by that power; or were we liable to be tranſported to a diſtant country to be tried for offences committed here, and reſtrained from calling any meetings, conſulting about any grievances, or aſſociating for any purpoſes, except when leave ſhould be given us by a *Lord Lieutenant* or *Viceroy*.

It is certain that this is a ſtate of oppreſſion which no country could endure, and to which it would be vain to expect, that any people should submit an hour without an armed force to compel them.

The late transactions in *Massachuset's Bay* are a perfect exemplification of what I have now said. The government of *Great Britain* in that Province has gone on exactly in the train I have described; till at last it became necessary to station troops there, not amenable to the civil power; and all terminated in a government by the SWORD. And such, if a people are not sunk below the character of men, will be the issue of all government in similar circumstances.

It may be asked——"Are there not causes by "which one state may acquire a *rightful* authority "over another, though not consolidated by an adequate Representation?"——I answer, that there are no such causes.——All the causes to which such an effect *can* be ascribed are CONQUEST, COMPACT, or OBLIGATIONS CONFERRED.

Much has been said of the right of *conquest*; and history contains little more than accounts of kingdoms reduced by it under the dominion of other kingdoms, and of the havock it has made among mankind. But the authority derived from hence, being founded on violence, is never *rightful*. The *Roman Republic* was nothing but a faction against the general liberties of the world; and

had

had no more right to give law to the Provinces ſubject to it, than thieves have to the property they ſeize, or to the houſes into which they break. ——Even in the caſe of a juſt war undertaken by one people to defend itſelf againſt the oppreſſions of another people, conqueſt gives only a right to an indemnification for the injury which occaſioned the war, and a reaſonable ſecurity againſt future injury.

Neither can any ſtate acquire ſuch an authority over other ſtates in virtue of any *compacts* or *ceſſions*. This is a caſe in which compacts are not binding. *Civil* Liberty is, in this reſpect, on the ſame footing with *Religious* Liberty. As no people can lawfully ſurrender their *Religious* Liberty, by giving up their right of judging for themſelves in religion, or by allowing any human beings to preſcribe to them what faith they ſhall embrace, or what mode of worſhip they ſhall practiſe; ſo neither can any civil ſocieties lawfully ſurrender their *Civil* Liberty, by giving up to any extraneous juriſdiction their power of legiſlating for themſelves and diſpoſing their property. Such a ceſſion, being inconſiſtent with the unalienable rights of human nature, would either not bind at all; or bind only the individuals who made it. This is a bleſſing which no one generation of men can give up for another; and which, when loſt, a people have always a right to reſume.——Had our anceſtors

anceſtors in this country been ſo mad as to have ſubjected themſelves to any foreign Community, we could not have been under any obligation to continue in ſuch a ſtate. And all the nations now in the world who, in conſequence of the tameneſs and folly of their predeceſſors, are ſubject to arbitrary power, have a right to emancipate themſelves as ſoon as they can.

If neither *conqueſt* nor *compact* can give ſuch an authority, much leſs can any favours received, or any ſervices performed by one ſtate for another. ——Let the favour received be what it will, Liberty is too dear a price for it. A ſtate that has been *obliged* is not, therefore, bound to be *enſlaved*. It ought, if poſſible, to make an adequate return for the ſervices done to it; but to ſuppoſe that it ought to give up the power of governing itſelf, and the diſpoſal of its property, would be to ſuppoſe, that, in order to ſhew its gratitude, it ought to part with the power of ever afterwards exerciſing gratitude.——How much has been done by this kingdom for *Hanover?* But no one will ſay that on this account, we have a right to make the laws of *Hanover*; or even to draw a ſingle penny from it without its own conſent.

After what has been ſaid it will, I am afraid, be trifling to apply the preceding arguments to the caſe of different communities, which are conſidered

ſidered as different parts of the ſame *Empire*. But there are reaſons which render it neceſſary for me to be explicit in making this application.

What I mean here is juſt to point out the difference of ſituation between communities forming an *Empire*; and particular bodies or claſſes of men forming different parts of a *Kingdom*. Different communities forming an *Empire* have no connexions, which produce a neceſſary reciprocation of intereſts between them. They inhabit different diſtricts, and are governed by different legiſlatures. ——On the contrary. The different claſſes of men *within* a *kingdom* are all placed on the ſame ground. Their concerns and intereſts are the ſame; and what is done to one part muſt affect all. ——Theſe are ſituations totally different; and a conſtitution of government that may be conſiſtent with Liberty in one of them, may be entirely inconſiſtent with it in the other. It is, however, certain that, even in the laſt of theſe ſituations, no one part ought to govern the reſt. In order to a fair and equal government, there ought to be a fair and equal repreſentation of all that are governed; and as far as this is wanting in any government, it deviates from the principles of Liberty, and becomes unjuſt and oppreſſive.——But in the circumſtances of different communities, all this holds with unſpeakably more force. The government of a part in this caſe becomes compleate tyranny;

ranny; and subjection to it becomes complete slavery.

But ought there not, it is asked, to exist somewhere in an *Empire* a supreme legislative authority over the whole; or a power to controul and bind all the different states of which it consists? — This enquiry has been already answered. The truth is, that such a supreme controuling power ought to exist no-where except in such a SENATE or body of delegates as that described in page 8; and that the authority or supremacy of even this senate ought to be limited to the common concerns of the *Empire*.——I think I have proved that the fundamental principles of Liberty necessarily require this.

In a word. An *Empire* is a collection of states or communities united by some common bond or tye. If these states have each of them free constitutions of government, and, with respect to taxation and internal legislation, are independent of the other states, but united by compacts, or alliances, or subjection to a Great *Council*, representing the whole, or to one monarch entrusted with the supreme executive power: In these circumstances, the Empire will be an Empire of Freemen.—If, on the contrary, like the different provinces subject to the *Grand Seignior*, none of the states possess any independent legislative authority; but are all ſubject to an abſolute monarch, whoſe will is their law; then is the Empire an Empire of Slaves.—— If one of the ſtates is free, but governs by its will all the other ſtates; then is the Empire, like that of the Romans in the times of the republic, an Empire conſiſting of one ſtate free, and the reſt in ſlavery: Nor does it make any more difference in this caſe, that the governing ſtate is itſelf free, than it does, in the caſe of a kingdom ſubject to a *deſpot*, that this deſpot is himſelf free. I have before obſerved, that this only makes the ſlavery worſe. There is, in the one caſe, a chance, that, in the quick ſucceſſion of deſpots, a good one will ſometimes ariſe. But bodies of men continue the ſame; and have generally proved the moſt unrelenting of all tyrants.

A great writer before (*a*) quoted, obſerves of the *Roman Empire*, that while Liberty was at the center, tyranny prevailed in the diſtant provinces; that ſuch as were free under it were extremely ſo, while thoſe who were ſlaves groaned under the extremity of ſlavery; and that the ſame events that *deſtroyed* the liberty of the former, *gave* liberty to the latter.

The Liberty of the *Romans*, therefore, was only an additional calamity to the provinces governed by them; and though it might have been ſaid of the *citizens* of *Rome*, that they were the "freeſt

(*a*) Monteſquieu's Spirit of Laws, Vol. I. Book 11. C. xix.

"members

" members of any civil ſociety in the known " world ;" yet of the *ſubjects* of *Rome*, it muſt have been ſaid, that they were the completeſt ſlaves in the known world.——How remarkable is it, that this very people, once the freeſt of mankind, but at the ſame time the moſt proud and tyrannical, ſhould become at laſt the moſt contemptible and abject ſlaves that ever exiſted ?

# PART II.

IN the foregoing disquisitions, I have, from one leading principle, deduced a number of consequences, that seem to me incapable of being disputed. I have meant that they should be applied to the great question between this kingdom and the Colonies which has occasioned the present war with them.

It is impossible, but my readers must have been all along making this application; and if they still think, that the claims of this kingdom are reconcileable to the principles of true liberty and legitimate government, I am afraid, that nothing I shall farther say will have any effect on their judgments. I wish, however, they would have the patience and candour to go with me, and grant me a hearing some time longer.

Though clearly decided in my own judgment on this subject, I am inclined to make great allowances for the different judgments of others. We have been so used to speak of the Colonies as *our* Colonies

Colonies, and to think of them as in a ſtate of ſubordination to us, and as holding their exiſtence in *America* only for our uſe, that it is no wonder the prejudices of many are alarmed, when they find a different doctrine maintained. The meaneſt perſon among us is diſpoſed to look upon himſelf as having a body of ſubjects in *America*; and to be offended at the denial of his right to make laws for them, though perhaps he does not know what colour they are of, or what language they talk. ——Such are the natural prejudices of this country.——But the time is coming, I hope, when the unreaſonableneſs of them will be ſeen; and more juſt ſentiments prevail.

Before I proceed, I beg it may be attended to, that I have choſen to try this queſtion by the general principles of Civil Liberty; and not by the practice of former times; or by the *Charters* granted the colonies.——The arguments *for* them, drawn from theſe laſt topics, appear to me greatly to outweigh the arguments *againſt* them. But I wiſh to have this queſtion brought to a higher teſt, and ſurer iſſue. The queſtion with all liberal enquirers ought to be, not what juriſdiction over them *Precedents*, *Statutes*, and *Charters* give, but what reaſon and equity, and the rights of humanity give.——This is, in truth, a queſtion which no kingdom has ever before had occaſion to agitate.

The

The caſe of a free country branching itſelf out in the manner *Britain* has done, and ſending to a diſtant world colonies which have there, from ſmall beginnings, and under free legiſlatures of their own, increaſed, and formed a body of powerful ſtates, likely ſoon to become ſuperior to the parent ſtate—This is a caſe which is new in the hiſtory of mankind; and it is extremely improper to judge of it by the rules of any narrow and partial policy; or to conſider it on any other ground than the general one of reaſon and juſtice.——Thoſe who will be candid enough to judge on this ground, and who can diveſt themſelves of national prejudices, will not, I fancy, remain long unſatisfied.——But alas! Matters are gone too far. The diſpute probably muſt be ſettled another way; and the ſword alone, I am afraid, is now to determine what the rights of *Britain* and *America* are.——Shocking ſituation!—Deteſted be the meaſures which have brought us into it: And, if we are endeavouring to enforce injuſtice, curſed will be the war.——A retreat, however, is not yet impracticable. The duty we owe our gracious ſovereign obliges us to rely on his diſpoſition to ſtay the ſword, and to promote the happineſs of all the different parts of the Empire at the head of which he is placed. With ſome hopes, therefore, that it may not be too late to reaſon on this ſubject, I will, in the following Sections, enquire what the war with *America* is in the following respects.

1. In respect of Justice.
2. The Principles of the Constitution.
3. In respect of Policy and Humanity.
4. The Honour of the Kingdom.

And lastly, The Probability of succeeding in it.

## SECT. I.

### *Of the Justice of the War with America.*

THE enquiry, whether the war with the Colonies is a *just* war, will be best determined by stating the power over them, which it is the end of the war to maintain: And this cannot be better done, than in the words of an act of parliament, made on purpose to define it. That act, it is well known, declares, "That this kingdom has "power, and of right ought to have power to "make laws and statutes to bind the Colonies, "and people of *America*, in all cases whatever." ——Dreadful power indeed! I defy any one to express slavery in stronger language. It is the same with declaring "that we have a right to do with them what we please."——I will not waste my time by applying to such a claim any of the preceding arguments. If my reader does not feel more

more in this caſe, than words can expreſs, all reaſoning muſt be vain.

But, probably, moſt perſons will be for uſing milder language; and for ſaying no more than, that the united legiſlatures of *England* and *Scotland* have of right power to tax the Colonies, and a *ſupremacy* of legiſlation over *America.*——But this comes to the ſame. If it means any thing, it means, that the property and the legiſlations of the Colonies, are ſubject to the abſolute diſcretion of *Great Britain*, and ought of right to be ſo. The nature of the thing admits of no limitation. The Colonies can never be admitted to be judges, how far the authority over them in theſe caſes ſhall extend. This would be to deſtroy it entirely.—— If *any* part of their property is ſubject to our diſcretion, the *whole* muſt be ſo. If we have a right to interfere at all in their internal legiſlations, we have a right to interfere as far as we think proper. ——It is ſelf-evident, that this leaves them nothing they can call *their own.*——And what is it that can give to any people ſuch a ſupremacy over another people?———I have already examined the principal anſwers which have been given to this enquiry. But it will not be amiſs in this place to go over ſome of them again.

It has been urged, that ſuch a right muſt be lodged ſomewhere, "in order to preſerve the "UNITY of the Britiſh Empire."

D 2 Pleas

Pleas of this ſort have, in all ages, been uſed to juſtify tyranny.———They have in RELIGION given riſe to numberleſs oppreſſive claims, and ſlaviſh Hierarchies. And in the *Romiſh Communion* particularly, it is well known, that the POPE claims the title and powers of the ſupreme head on earth of the Chriſtian church, in order to preſerve its UNITY.———With reſpect to the *Britiſh Empire*, nothing can be more prepoſterous than to endeavour to maintain its unity, by ſetting up ſuch a claim. This is a method of eſtabliſhing unity, which, like the ſimilar method in religion, can produce nothing but diſcord and miſchief.——— The truth is, that a common relation to one ſupreme executive head; an exchange of kind offices; tyes of intereſt and affection, and *compacts*, are ſufficient to give the Britiſh Empire all the unity that is neceſſary. But if not———If, in order to preſerve its *Unity*, one half of it muſt be enſlaved to the other half, let it, in the name of God, want Unity.

Much has been ſaid of "the *Superiority* of the "Britiſh State." But what gives us our ſuperiority?—Is it our *Wealth?*—This never confers real dignity. On the contrary: Its effect is always to debaſe, intoxicate, and corrupt.———Is it the *number of our people?* The colonies will ſoon be equal to us in number.—Is it our *Knowledge* and *Virtue?* They are probably *equally* knowing, and *more*

virtuous.

virtuous. There are names among them that will not ſtoop to any names among the philoſophers and politicians of this iſland.

But we are the PARENT STATE."—These are the magic words which have faſcinated and miſled us.———The Engliſh came from *Germany*. Does that give the *German* ſtates a right to tax us?—Children, having no property, and being incapable of guiding themſelves, the author of nature has committed the care of them to their parents, and ſubjected them to their abſolute authority. But there is a period when, having acquired property, and a capacity of judging for themſelves, they become independent agents; and when, for this reaſon, the authority of their parents ceaſes, and becomes nothing but the reſpect and influence due to benefactors. Suppoſing, therefore, that the order of nature in eſtabliſhing the relation between parents and children, ought to have been the rule of our conduct to the Colonies, we ſhould have been gradually relaxing our authority as they grew up. But, like mad parents, we have done the contrary; and, at the very time when our authority ſhould have been moſt relaxed, we have carried it to the greateſt extent, and exerciſed it with the greateſt rigour. No wonder then, that they have turned upon us; and obliged us to remember, that they are not Children.

" But we have, it is said, protected them, and " run deeply in debt on their account."—The full answer to this has been already given, (page 26.) Will any one say, that all we have done for them has not been more on our *own* account, (*a*) than on *theirs?*——But suppose the contrary. Have they done nothing for us? Have they made no compensation for the protection they have received? Have they not helped us to pay our *taxes*, to support our poor, and to bear the burthen of our debts, by taking from us, at our own price, all the commodities with which we can supply them?—Have they not, for our advantage, submitted to

(*a*) This is particularly true of the *bounties* granted on some American commodities (as pitch, tar, indigo, &c.) when imported into *Britain*; for it is well known, that the end of granting them was, to get those commodities cheaper from the Colonies, and in return for our manufactures, which we used to get from *Russia* and other foreign countries. And this is expressed in the preambles of the laws which grant these bounties. See the Appeal to the Justice, &c. page 21, third edition. It is, therefore, strange that Doctor TUCKER and others, should have insisted so much upon these bounties as favours and indulgencies to the Colonies.—But it is still more strange, that the same representation should have been made of the compensations granted them for doing more during the last war in assisting us than could have been reasonably expected; and also of the sums we have spent in maintaining troops among them *without* their consent; and in opposition to their wishes.——See a pamphlet, entitled " The rights of Great Britain asserted against the claims of America."

many

many reſtraints in acquiring property? Muſt they likewiſe reſign to us the diſpoſal of that property? —Has not their excluſive trade with us been for many years one of the chief ſources of our wealth and power?—In all our wars have they not fought by our ſide, and contributed much to our ſucceſs? In the laſt war, particularly, it is well known, that they ran themſelves deeply in debt; and that the parliament thought it neceſſary to grant them conſiderable ſums annually as compenſations for going beyond their abilities in aſſiſting us. And in this courſe would they have continued for many future years; perhaps, for ever.—In ſhort; were an accurate account ſtated, it is by no means certain which ſide would appear to be moſt indebted. When aſked as *freemen*, they have hitherto ſeldom diſcovered any reluctance in giving. But, in obedience to a demand, and with the bayonet at their breaſts, they will give us nothing but blood.

It is farther ſaid, "that the land on which they "ſettled was ours."—But how came it to be ours? If ſailing along a coaſt can give a right to a country, then might the people of *Japan* become, as ſoon as they pleaſe, the proprietors of *Britain*. Nothing can be more chimerical than property founded on ſuch a reaſon. If the land on which the Colonies firſt ſettled had any proprietors, they were the natives. The greateſt part of it they bought of the natives. They have ſince cleared and cultivated it; and, without any help from us, converted a wilderneſs into fruitful and pleaſant fields. It is, therefore, now on a double account their property; and no power on earth can have any right to diſturb them in the poſſeſſion of it, or to take from them, without their conſent, any part of its produce.

But let it be granted, that the land was ours. Did they not ſettle upon it under the faith of charters, which promiſed them the enjoyment of all the rights of *Engliſhmen*; and allowed them to tax themſelves, and to be governed by legiſlatures of their own, ſimilar to ours? Theſe charters were given them by an authority, which at the time was thought competent; and they have been rendered ſacred by an acquieſcence on our part for near a century. Can it then be wondered at, that the Colonies ſhould revolt, when they found their charters violated; and an attempt made to force INNOVATIONS upon them by famine and the ſword; ——But I lay no ſtreſs on charters. They derive their rights from a higher ſource. It is inconſiſtent with common ſenſe to imagine, that any people would ever think of ſettling in a diſtant country, on any ſuch condition, as that the people from whom they withdrew, ſhould for ever be maſters of their property, and have power to ſubject them to any modes of government they pleaſed. And had there

there been exprefs ftipulations to this purpofe in all the charters of the colonies, they would, in my opinion, be no more bound by them, than if it had been ftipulated with them, that they fhould go naked, or expofe themfelves to the incurfions of wolves and tigers.

The defective ftate of the reprefentation of this kingdom has been farther pleaded to prove our right to tax *America*. We fubmit to a parliament that does not reprefent us, and therefore they ought.——How ftrange an argument is this? It is faying we want liberty; and therefore, they ought to want it.——Suppofe it true, that they are indeed contending for a better conftitution of government, and more liberty than we enjoy: Ought this to make us angry?——Who is there that does not fee the danger to which this country is expofed?——Is it generous, becaufe we are in a fink, to endeavour to draw them into it? Ought we not rather to wifh earneftly, that there may at leaft be ONE FREE COUNTRY left upon earth, to which we may fly, when venality, luxury, and vice have completed the ruin of liberty here?

It is, however, by no means true, that *America* has no more right to be exempted from taxation by the *Britifh* parliament, than *Britain* itfelf.—— *Here*, all freeholders, and burgeffes in boroughs, are reprefented. *There*, not one *Freeholder*, or any other perfon, is reprefented.——*Here*, the *aids* granted

granted by the represented part of the kingdom must be proportionably *paid* by themselves; and the laws they make for *others*, they at the same time make for *themselves*. *There*, the aids they would grant would not be *paid*, but *received*, by themselves; and the laws they made would be made for *others only*.—In short. The relation of one country to another country, whose representatives have the power of taxing it (and of appropriating the money raised by the taxes) is much the same with the relation of a country to a single despot, or a body of despots, within itself, invested with the like power. In both cases, the people taxed and those who tax have separate interests; nor can there be any thing to check oppression, besides either the abilities of the people taxed, or the humanity of the *taxers*.—But indeed I can never hope to convince that person of any thing, who does not see an essential difference (*a*) between the two cases now

(*a*) It is remarkable that even the author of the *Remarks on the Principal Acts of the 13th Parliament of Great Britain*, &c. finds himself obliged to acknowledge this difference.——There cannot be more detestable principles of government, than those which are maintained by this writer. According to him, the *properties* and *rights* of a people are only a kind of *alms* given them by their civil governors. Taxes, therefore, he asserts, are not the *gifts* of the people. See page 58, and 191.

mentioned;

mentioned; or between the circumſtances of individuals, and claſſes of men, making parts of a community imperfectly repreſented in the legiſlature that governs it; and the circumſtances of a whole community, in a diſtant world, not at all repreſented.

But enough has been ſaid by others on this point; nor is it poſſible for me to throw any new light upon it. To finiſh, therefore, what I meant to offer under this head, I muſt beg that the following conſiderations may be particularly attended to.

The queſtion now between us and the Colonies is, Whether, in reſpect of taxation and internal legiſlation, they are bound to be ſubject to the juriſdiction of this kingdom: Or, in other words, Whether the *Britiſh* parliament has or has not of right, a power to diſpoſe of their property, and to model as it pleaſes their governments?——To this ſupremacy over them, we ſay, we are entitled; and in order to maintain it, we have begun the preſent war.——Let me here enquire,

1*ſt*. Whether, if we have now this ſupremacy, we ſhall not be equally entitled to it in any future time?——They are now but little ſhort of half our number. To this number they have grown, from a ſmall body of original ſettlers, by a very rapid increaſe. The probability is, that they will

go

go on to increase; and that, in 50 or 60 years, they will be *double* our number; (*a*) and form a mighty Empire, consisting of a variety of states, all equal or superior to ourselves in all the arts and accomplishments, which give dignity and happiness to human life. In that period, will they be still bound to acknowledge that supremacy over them which we now claim? Can there be any person who will assert this; or whose mind does not revolt at the idea of a vast continent, holding all that is valuable to it, at the discretion of a handful of people on the other side the *Atlantic*?—— But if, at *that* period, this would be unreasonable; what makes it otherwise *now*?—Draw the line, if you can.—But there is a still greater difficulty.

*Britain* is now, I will suppose, the seat of Liberty and Virtue; and its legislature consists of a body of able and independent men, who govern with wisdom and justice. The time may come when all will be reversed: When its excellent constitution of government will be subverted: When, pressed by debts and taxes, it will be greedy to draw to itself an increase of revenue from every distant Province, in order to ease its own burdens: When the influence of the crown, strengthened by luxury and an universal profligacy of manners, will have tainted every heart, broken down every fence

(*a*) See Observations on Reversionary Payments, page 207, &c.

of Liberty, and rendered us a nation of tame and contented vaſſals: When a General *Election* will be nothing but a general *Auction* of *Boroughs*: And when the PARLIAMENT, the Grand Council of the nation, and once the faithful guardian of the ſtate, and a terror to evil miniſters, will be degenerated into a body of *Sycophants*, dependent and venal, always ready to confirm *any* meaſures; and little more than a public court for regiſtering royal edicts.——Such, it is poſſible, may, ſome time or other, be the ſtate of *Great Britain.*——What will, at that period, be the duty of the Colonies? Will they be ſtill bound to unconditional ſubmiſſion? Muſt they always continue an appendage to our government; and follow it implicitly through every change that can happen to it?——Wretched condition, indeed, of millions of freemen as good as ourſelves.——Will you ſay that we now govern equitably; and that there is no danger of any ſuch revolution?—Would to God this were true.——But will you not always ſay the ſame? Who ſhall judge whether we govern equitably or not? Can you give the Colonies any *ſecurity* that ſuch a period will never come? Once more.

If we have indeed that power which we claim over the legiſlations, and internal rights of the Colonies, may we not, whenever we pleaſe, ſubject them to the arbitrary power of the crown? —— I do not mean, that this would be a diſadvantageous

vantageous change: For I have before obſerved, that if a people are to be ſubject to an external power over which they have no command, it is better that power ſhould be lodged in the hands of one man than of a multitude. But many perſons think otherwiſe; and ſuch ought to conſider that, if this would be a calamity, the condition of the Colonies muſt be deplorable.——" A government by King, Lords, and Commons, (it has been ſaid) is the perfection of government;" and ſo it is, when the Commons are a juſt repreſentation of the people; and when alſo, it is not extended to any diſtant people, or communities, not repreſented. But if this is the *beſt*, a government by a king only muſt be the *worſt*; and every claim implying a right to eſtabliſh ſuch a government among any people muſt be unjuſt and cruel.——It is ſelf-evident, that by claiming a right to alter the conſtitutions of the Colonies, according to our diſcretion, we claim this power: And it is a power that we have thought fit to exerciſe in *one* of our Colonies; and that we have attempted to exerciſe in *another*.——*Canada*, according to the late extenſion of its limits, is a country almoſt as large as half *Europe*; and it may poſſibly come in time to be filled with Britiſh ſubjects. The *Quebec* act makes the king of *Great Britain* a deſpot over all that country.——In the Province of *Maſſachuſet's Bay* the ſame thing has been attempted and begun.

 The

The act for BETTER *regulating their government*, passed at the same time with the *Quebec* act, gives the king the right of appointing, and removing at his pleasure, the members of one part of the legislature; alters the mode of chusing juries, on purpose to bring it more under the influence of the king; and takes away from the province the power of calling any meetings of the people without the king's consent. (*a*)——The judges, likewise, have been made dependent on the king, for their nomination and pay, and continuance in office.—If all this is no more than we have a right to do; may we not go on to abolish the house of representatives, to destroy all trials by juries, and to give up the province absolutely and totally to the will of the king?——May we not even establish popery in the province, as has been lately done in *Canada*, leaving the support of protestantism to the king's discretion?—Can there be any Englishman who, were it his own case, would not sooner lose his heart's blood than yield to claims so pregnant with evils, and destructive to every thing that can distinguish a *Freeman* from a *Slave*?

I will take this opportunity to add, that what I have now said, suggests a consideration that demonstrates, on how different a footing the Colonies are with respect to our government, from particular bodies of men *within* the kingdom, who hap-

(*a*) See page 22.

pen

pen not to be reprefented. Here, it is impoffible that the reprefented part fhould fubject the unrepresented part to arbitrary power, without including themfelves. But in the Colonies it is *not* impoffible. We know that it *has* been done.

## SECT. II.

### *Whether the War with* America *is juftified by the Principles of the Conftitution.*

I Have propofed, in the next place, to examine the war with the Colonies by the principles of the conftitution.—I know, that it is common to fay that we are now maintaining the conftitution in *America*. If this means that we are endeavouring to eftablifh our own conftitution of government there; it is by no means true; nor, were it true, would it be right. They have chartered governments of their own, with which they are pleafed; and which, if any power on earth may change without their confent, that power may likewife, if it thinks proper, deliver them over to the *Grand Seignior*.——Suppofe the Colonies of *France* had, by compacts, enjoyed for many years, free governments open to all the world, under which they had grown and flourifhed; what fhould we think of that kingdom, were it to attempt to deftroy their governments, and to force upon them its own mode of government? Should we not applaud

any

any zeal they discovered in repelling such an injury?——But the truth is, in the present instance, that we are not maintaining but violating our own constitution in *America*. The essence of our constitution consists in its independency. There is in this case no difference between *subjection* and *annihilation*. Did, therefore, the Colonies possess governments perfectly the same with ours, the attempt to subject them to ours would be an attempt to ruin them. A free government loses its nature from the moment it becomes liable to be commanded or altered by any superior power.

But I intended here principally to make the following observation.

The fundamental principle of our government is, "The right of a people to give and grant their own money."——It is of no consequence, in this case, whether we enjoy this right in a proper manner or not. Most certainly we do not. It is, however, the *principle* on which our government, as a *free* government, is founded. The *spirit* of the constitution gives it us; and, however imperfectly enjoyed, we glory in it as our first and greatest blessing. It was an attempt to encroach upon this right, in a trifling instance, that produced the civil war in the reign of *Charles* the First.—Ought not our brethren in *America* to enjoy this right as well as ourselves? Do the principles of the constitution give it *us*, but deny it to *them*?

Or can we, with any decency, pretend that when we give to the king *their* money, we give him *our own?* (a)——What difference does it make, that in the time of *Charles the First* the attempt to take away this right was made by *one man:* but that, in the case of *America*, it is made by a body of men?

In a word. This is a war undertaken not only against the principles of our own constitution; but on purpose to destroy other similar constitutions in *America*; and to substitute in their room a military force. See page 23, 24.——It is, therefore, a gross and flagrant violation of the constitution.

## SECT. III.

### *Of the Policy of the War with* America.

IN writing the present Section, I enter upon a subject of the last importance, on which much has been said by other writers with great force, and in the ablest manner (b). But I am not

(a) The author of *Taxation no Tyranny* will undoubtedly assert this without hesitation, for in page 69 he compares our present situation with respect to the Colonies to that of the antient *Scythians*, who, upon returning from a war, *found themselves shut out of their* OWN HOUSES *by their* SLAVES.

(b) See particularly, a speech intended to have been spoken on the bill for altering the Charter of the Colony of Massachuset's Bay; the *Considerations on the Measures carrying on with respect to the British Colonies*; the *Two Appeals to the Justice and Interests of the People*; and the *further Examination*, just published, *of our present American Measures*, by the Author of the Considerations, &c.

willing

willing to omit any topic which I think of great consequence, merely because it has already been discussed: And, with respect to this in particular, it will, I believe, be found that some of the observations on which I shall insist, have not been sufficiently attended to.

The object of this war has been often enough declared to be "maintaining the supremacy of this "country over the colonies." I have already enquired how far reason and justice, the principles of Liberty, and the rights of humanity, entitle us to this supremacy. Setting aside, therefore, now all considerations of this kind, I would observe, that this supremacy is to be maintained, either merely *for its own sake*, or for the sake of some public interest connected with it and dependent upon it.——If *for its own sake*; the only object of the war is the extension of dominion; and its only motive is the lust of power.——All government, even *within* a state, becomes tyrannical, as far as it is a needless and wanton exercise of power; or is carried farther than is absolutely necessary to preserve the peace and to secure the safety of the state. This is what an excellent writer calls GOVERNING TOO MUCH; and its effect must always be, weakening government by rendering it contemptible and odious.—Nothing can be of more importance, in go-

 verning

verning diſtant provinces and adjuſting the claſhing intereſts of different ſocieties, than attention to this remark. In theſe circumſtances it is *particularly* neceſſary to make a ſparing uſe of power, in order to preſerve power.——Happy would it have been for *Great Britain*, had this been remembered by thoſe who have lately conducted its affairs. But our policy has been of another kind. At the period when our authority ſhould have been moſt concealed, it has been brought moſt in view; and by a progreſſion of violent meaſures, every one of which has increaſed diſtreſs, we have given the world reaſon to conclude, that we are acquainted with no other method of governing than *by force*—What a ſhocking miſtake!—If our object is power, we ſhould have known better how to uſe it; and our rulers ſhould have conſidered, that freemen will always revolt at the ſight of a naked ſword; and that the complicated affairs of a great kingdom, holding in ſubordination to it a multitude of diſtant communities, all jealous of their rights, and warmed with ſpirits as high as our own, require not only the moſt ſkilful, but the moſt cautious and tender management. The conſequences of a different management we are now feeling. We ſee ourſelves driven among rocks, and in danger of being loſt.

The following reaſons make it too probable, that the preſent conteſt with *America* is a conteſt for

for power only (*a*), abstracted from all the advantages connected with it.

*1st.* There is a love of power inherent in human nature; and it cannot be uncharitable to suppose that the nation in general, and the cabinet in particular, are too likely to be influenced by it. What can be more flattering than to look across the *Atlantic*, and to see in the boundless continent of *America*, increasing MILLIONS whom we have a right to order as we please, who hold their property at our disposal, and who have no other law than our will. With what complacency have we been used to talk of them as OUR subjects?——Is it not the interruption they now give to this pleasure; is it not the opposition they make to our pride; and not any injury they have done us, that is the secret spring of our present animosity against them?———I wish all in this kingdom would examine themselves carefully on this point. Perhaps, they might find, that they have not known what spirit they are of.—Perhaps, they would become sensible, that it was a spirit of domination, more than a regard to the true interest of

(*a*) I have heard it said by a person in one of the first departments of the state, that the present contest is for DOMINION on the side of the Colonies, as well as on ours: And so it is indeed; but with this essential difference. *We* are struggling for dominion over OTHERS. *They* are struggling for SELF-dominion: The noblest of all blessings.

this country, that lately led ſo many of them, with ſuch ſavage folly, to addreſs the throne for the ſlaughter of their brethren in *America*, if they will not ſubmit to them; and to make offers of their lives and fortunes for that purpoſe.——Indeed, I am perſuaded, that, were pride and the luſt of dominion exterminated from every heart among us, and the humility of Chriſtians infuſed in their room, this quarrel would be ſoon ended.

2*dly*. Another reaſon for believing that this is a conteſt for power only is, that our miniſters have frequently declared, that their object is not to draw a revenue from *America*; and that many of thoſe who are warmeſt for continuing it, repreſent the *American trade* as of no great conſequence.

But what deſerves particular conſideration here is, that this is a conteſt from which no advantages can poſſibly be derived.——Not a revenue: For the provinces of America, when deſolated, will afford no revenue; or if they ſhould, the expence of ſubduing them and keeping them in ſubjection will much exceed that revenue.——Not any of the advantages of trade: For it is a folly, next to inſanity, to think trade can be promoted by impoveriſhing our cuſtomers, and fixing in their minds an everlaſting abhorrence of us.—It remains, therefore, that this war can have no other object than the extenſion of power.——Miſerable lerable reflection !——To ſheath our ſwords in the bowels of our brethren, and ſpread miſery and ruin among a happy people, for no other end than to oblige them to acknowledge our ſupremacy. How horrid !—This is the curſed ambition that led a *Cæſar* and an *Alexander*, and many other mad conquerors, to attack peaceful communities, and to lay waſte the earth.

But a worſe principle than even this, influences ſome among us. Pride and the love of dominion are principles hateful enough ; but blind reſentment and the deſire of revenge are infernal principles : And theſe, I am afraid, have no ſmall ſhare at preſent in guiding our public conduct.——One cannot help indeed being aſtoniſhed at the virulence, with which ſome ſpeak on the preſent occaſion againſt the Colonies.——For, what have they done?—Have they croſſed the ocean and invaded us ? Have they attempted to take from us the fruits of our labour, and to overturn that form of government which we hold ſo ſacred ?—This cannot be pretended.—On the contrary. This is what we have done to them.——We have tranſported ourſelves to their peaceful retreats, and employed our fleets and armies to ſtop up their ports, to deſtroy their commerce, to ſeize their effects, and to burn their towns. Would we but let them alone, and ſuffer them to enjoy in ſecurity their property and governments, inſtead of disturbing us, they would thank and bless us. And yet it is WE who imagine ourselves ill-used. ——The truth is, we expected to find them a cowardly rabble who would lie quietly at our feet; and they have disappointed us. They have risen in their own defence, and repelled force by force. They deny the plenitude of our power over them; and insist upon being treated as free communities.——It is THIS that has provoked us; and kindled our governors into rage.

I hope I shall not here be understood to intimate, that *all* who promote this war are actuated by these principles. Some, I doubt not, are influenced by no other principle, than a regard to what they think the just authority of this country over its colonies, and to the unity and indivisibility of the British Empire. I wish such could be engaged to enter thoroughly into the enquiry, which has been the subject of the first part of this pamphlet; and to consider, particularly, how different a thing maintaining the authority of government *within* a state is from maintaining the authority of one people over another, already happy in the enjoyment of a government of their own. I wish farther they would consider, that the desire of maintaining authority is warrantable, only as far as it is the means of promoting some end, and doing some good; and that, before we resolve to spread famine and fire through a country in order to make

it

it acknowledge our authority, we ought to be aſſured that great advantages will ariſe not only to ourſelves, but to the country we wiſh to conquer. ——That from the preſent conteſt no advantage to *ourſelves* can ariſe, has been already ſhewn, and will preſently be ſhewn more at large.——That no advantage to the Colonies can ariſe from it, need not, I hope, be ſhewn. It has however been aſſerted, that even *their* good is intended by this war. Many of us are perſuaded, that they will be much happier under our government, than under any government of their own; and that their liberties will be ſafer when held for them by us, than when truſted in their own hands.——How kind is it thus to take upon us the trouble of judging for them what is moſt for their happineſs? Nothing can be kinder except the reſolution we have formed to exterminate them, if they will not ſubmit to our judgment.——What ſtrange language have I ſometimes heard? By an armed force we are now endeavouring to deſtroy the laws and governments of America; and yet I have heard it ſaid, that we are endeavouring to ſupport law and government there. We are inſiſting upon our right to levy contributions upon them; and to maintain this right, we are bringing upon them all the miſeries a people can endure; and yet it is aſſerted, that we mean nothing but their ſecurity and happineſs.

But I have wandered a little from the point I attended principally to insist upon in this section, which is, "the folly, in respect of policy, of the "measures which have brought on this contest; "and its pernicious and fatal tendency."

The following observations will, I believe, abundantly prove this.

*1st*, There are points which are likely always to suffer by discussion. Of this kind are most points of authority and prerogative; and the best policy is to avoid, as much as possible, giving any occasion for calling them into question.

The colonies were at the beginning of this reign in the habit of acknowledging our authority, and of allowing us as much power over them as our interest required; and more, in some instances, than we could reasonably claim. This habit they would have retained: and had we, instead of imposing new burdens upon them, and increasing their restraints, studied to promote their commerce, and to grant them new indulgences, they would have been always growing more attached to us. Luxury, and, together with it, their dependence upon us, and our influence (*a*) in their assemblies, would have increased, till in time perhaps they would have become as corrupt as our-

(*a*) This has been our policy with respect to the people of *Ireland*; and the consequence is, that we now see their parliament as obedient as we can wish.

selves;

ſelves; and we might have ſucceeded to our wiſhes in eſtabliſhing our authority over them.——But, happily for *them*, we have choſen a different courſe. By exertions of authority which have alarmed them, they have been put upon examining into the grounds of all our claims, and forced to give up their luxuries, and to ſeek all their reſources within themſelves: And the iſſue is likely to prove the loſs of *all* our authority over them, and of all the advantages connected with it. So little do men in power ſometimes know how to preſerve power; and ſo remarkably does the deſire of extending dominion ſometimes deſtroy it.——Mankind are naturally diſpoſed to continue in ſubjection to that mode of government, be it what it will, under which they have been born and educated. Nothing rouſes them into reſiſtance but groſs abuſes, or ſome particular oppreſſions out of the road to which they have been uſed. And he who will examine the hiſtory of the world will find, there has generally been more reaſon for complaining that they have been too patient, than that they have been turbulent and rebellious.

Our governors, ever ſince I can remember, have been jealous that the Colonies, ſome time or other, would throw off their dependence. This jealouſy was not founded on any of their acts or declarations. They have always, while at *peace* with us, diſclaimed any ſuch deſign; and they have continued to diſclaim it ſince they have been at *war* with us. I have reaſon, indeed, to believe, that independency is, even at this moment, (*a*) generally dreaded among them as a calamity to which they are in danger of being driven, in order to avoid a greater.——The jealouſy I have mentioned, was, however, natural; and betrayed a ſecret opinion, that the ſubjection in which they were held was more than we could expect them always to endure. In ſuch circumſtances, all poſſible care ſhould have been taken to give them no reaſon for diſcontent, and to preſerve them in ſubjection, by keeping in that line of conduct to which cuſtom had reconciled them, or at leaſt never deviating from it, except with great caution; and particularly, by avoiding all direct attacks on their property and legiſlations. Had we done this, the different intereſts of ſo many ſtates ſcattered over a vaſt continent, joined to our own prudence and moderation, would have enabled us to maintain them in dependence for ages to come.——But inſtead of this, how have we acted?——It is in truth too evident, that our whole conduct, inſtead of being directed by that ſound policy and foreſight which in ſuch circumſtances were abſolutely neceſſary, has been nothing (to ſay the beſt of it) but a ſeries of the blindeſt rigour followed by re-

(*a*) It ſhould be remembered, that this was written ſome time before the Declaration of Independence in July 1776. See page 85 of the next Tract.

tractation;

tractation; of violence followed by concession; of mistake, weakness and inconsistency.——A recital of a few facts, within every body's recollection, will fully prove this.

In the 6th of *George the Second*, an act was passed for imposing certain duties on all foreign spirits, molasses and sugars imported into the plantations. In this act, the duties imposed are said to be GIVEN and GRANTED by the Parliament to the King; and this is the first *American* act in which these words have been used. But notwithstanding this, as the act had the appearance of being only a regulation of trade, the colonies submitted to it; and a small direct revenue was drawn by it from them.——In the 4th of the present reign, many alterations were made in this act, with the declared purpose of making provision for raising a revenue in America. This alarmed the Colonies; and produced discontents and remonstrances, which might have convinced our rulers this was tender ground, on which it became them to tread very gently.——There is, however, no reason to doubt but in time they would have sunk into a quiet submission to this revenue act, as being at worst only the exercise of a power which then they seem not to have thought much of contesting; I mean, the power of taxing them EXTERNALLY.——But before they had time to cool, a worse provocation was given them; and the STAMP-ACT was passed. This being an attempt

tempt to tax them INTERNALLY; and a direct attack on their property, by a power which would not suffer itself to be questioned; which eased *itself* by loading *them*; and to which it was impossible to fix any bounds; they were thrown at once, from one end of the continent to the other, into resistance and rage.——Government, dreading the consequences, gave way; and the Parliament (upon a change of ministry) repealed the *Stamp-Act*, without requiring from them any recognition of its authority, or doing any more to preserve its dignity, than asserting, by the declaratory law, that it was possessed of full power and authority to make laws to bind them in all cases whatever.——Upon this, peace was restored; and, had no farther attempts of the same kind been made, they would undoubtedly have suffered us (as the people of *Ireland* have done) to enjoy quietly our declaratory law. They would have recovered their former habits of subjection; and our connexion with them might have continued an increasing source of our wealth and glory.——But the spirit of despotism and avarice, always blind and restless, soon broke forth again. The scheme for drawing a revenue from *America*, by parliamentary taxation, was resumed; and in a little more than a year after the repeal of the *Stamp-Act*, when all was peace, a third act was passed, imposing duties payable in *America* on tea, paper, glass, painters colours, &c.

——This,

——This, as might have been expected, revived all the former heats; and the Empire was a ſecond time threatened with the moſt dangerous commotions.———Government receded again; and the Parliament (under another change of miniſtry) repealed all the obnoxious duties, EXCEPT that upon tea. This exception was made in order to maintain a ſhew of dignity. But it was, in reality, ſacrificing ſafety to pride; and leaving a ſplinter in the wound to produce a gangrene. ——For ſome time, however, this relaxation anſwered its intended purpoſes. Our commercial intercourſe with the Colonies was again recovered; and they avoided nothing but that tea which we had excepted in our repeal. In this ſtate would things have remained, and even tea would perhaps in time have been gradually admitted, had not the evil genius of *Britain* ſtepped forth once more to embroil the Empire.

The *Eaſt India* company having fallen under difficulties, partly in conſequence of the loſs of the *American* market for tea, a ſcheme was formed for aſſiſting them by an attempt to recover that market. With this view an act was paſſed to enable them to export their tea to *America* free of all duties here, and ſubject only to 3d. per pound duty, payable in *America*. It was to be offered at a low price; and it was expected the conſequence would prove that the

Colonies

Colonies would be tempted to buy it; a precedent gained for taxing them; and at the ſame time the company relieved. Ships were, therefore, fitted out; and large cargoes ſent. The ſnare was too groſs to eſcape the notice of the Colonies. They ſaw it, and ſpurned at it. They refuſed to admit the tea; and at BOSTON ſome perſons in diſguiſe threw it into the ſea.—Had our governors in this caſe ſatisfied themſelves with requiring a compenſation from the province for the damage done, there is no doubt but it would have been granted. Or had they proceeded no farther in the infliction of puniſhment, than ſtopping up the port and deſtroying the trade of Boſton, till compenſation was made, the province might poſſibly have ſubmitted, and a ſufficient ſaving would have been gained for the honour of the nation. But having hitherto proceeded without wiſdom, they obſerved now no bounds in their reſentment. To the Boſton port bill was added a bill which deſtroyed the chartered government of the province; a bill which withdrew from the juriſdiction of the province, perſons who in particular caſes ſhould commit murder; and the *Quebec* bill. At the ſame time a ſtrong body of troops was ſtationed at *Boſton* to enforce obedience to theſe bills.

All who knew any thing of the temper of the Colonies ſaw that the effect of this ſudden accumulation

mulation of vengeance, would probably be not intimidating but exasperating them, and driving them into a general revolt. But our ministers had different apprehensions. They believed that the malecontents in the Colony of *Massachusett's* were a small party, headed by a few factious men; that the majority of the people would take the side of government, as soon as they saw a force among them capable of supporting them; that, at worst, the Colonies in general would never make a common cause with this province; and that, the issue would prove, in a few months, order, tranquility and submission.—Every one of these apprehensions was falsified by the events that followed.

When the bills I have mentioned came to be carried into execution, the whole province was thrown into confusion. The courts of justice were shut up, and all government was dissolved. The commander in chief found it necessary to fortify himself in Boston; and the other Colonies immediately resolved to make a common cause with this Colony.

Disappointed by these consequences, our ministers took fright. Once more they made an effort to retreat; but indeed the most ungracious one that can well be imagined. A proposal was sent to the Colonies, called Conciliatory; and the substance of which was, that if any of them would raise such sums as should be demanded of them by taxing themselves, the Parliament would forbear to tax them.——It will be ſcarcely believed, hereafter, that ſuch a propoſal could be thought conciliatory. It was only telling them; "If "you will tax yourſelves BY OUR ORDER, we will "ſave ourſelves the trouble of taxing you."—— They received the propoſal as an inſult; and rejected it with diſdain.

At the time this conceſſion was tranſmitted to *America*, open hoſtilities were not begun. In the ſword our miniſters thought they had ſtill a reſource which would immediately ſettle all diſputes. They conſidered the people of *New-England* as nothing but a mob, who would be ſoon routed and forced into obedience. It was even believed, that a few thouſands of our army might march through all *America*, and make all quiet whereever they went. Under this conviction our miniſters did not dread urging the Province of *Maſſachuſett's Bay* into rebellion, by ordering the army to ſeize their ſtores, and to take up ſome of their leading men.——The attempt was made.—— The people fled immediately to arms, and repelled the attack.——A conſiderable part of the flower of the Britiſh army has been deſtroyed. ——Some of our beſt Generals, and the braveſt of our troops, are now (*a*) diſgracefully and miſ-

(*a*) In February 1776.—In a few weeks after this, they were driven from *Boſton*; and took refuge at *Hallifax* in *Nova Scotia*; from whence, after a ſtrong reinforcement, they invaded the Province of *New-York*.

erably

erably imprisoned at *Boston*.——A horrid civil war is commenced;——And the Empire is distracted and convulsed.

Can it be possible to think with patience of the policy that has brought us into these circumstances? Did ever Heaven punish the vices of a people more severely by darkening their counsels? How great would be our happiness could we now recal former times, and return to the policy of the last reigns?—But those times are gone. ——I will, however, beg leave for a few moments to look back to them; and to compare the ground we have left with that on which we find ourselves. This must be done with deep regret; but it forms a necessary part of my present design.

In those times our Colonies, foregoing every advantage which they might derive from trading with foreign nations, consented to send only to us whatever it was for our interest to receive from them; and to receive only from us whatever it was for our interest to send to them. They gave up the power of making sumptuary laws, and exposed themselves to all the evils of an increasing and wasteful luxury, because we were benefited by vending among them the materials of it. The iron with which providence had blessed their country, they were required by laws, in which they acquiesced, to transport hither, that our people might be maintained by working it for them into nails, ploughs, axes, &c. And, in ſeveral inſtances, even one Colony was not allowed to ſupply any neighbouring Colonies with commodities, which could be conveyed to them from hence.——But they yielded much farther. They conſented that we ſhould have the appointment of one branch of their legiſlature. By recognizing as their King, a King reſident among us and under our influence, they gave us a negative on all their laws. By allowing an appeal to us in their civil diſputes, they gave us likewiſe the ultimate determination of all civil cauſes among them. ——In ſhort. They allowed us every power we could deſire, except that of taxing them, and interfering in their internal legiſlations: And they had admitted precedents which, even in theſe inſtances, gave us no inconſiderable authority over them. By purchaſing our goods they paid our taxes; and, by allowing us to regulate their trade in any manner we thought moſt for our advantage, they enriched our merchants, and helped us to bear our growing burdens. They fought our battles with us. They gloried in their relation to us. All their gains centered among us; and they always ſpoke of this country and looked to it as their home.

Such WAS the ſtate of things.——What is it now?

Not

Not contented with a degree of power, ſufficient to ſatisfy any reaſonable ambition, we have attempted to extend it.——Not contented with drawing from them a large revenue *indirectly*, we have endeavoured to procure one *directly* by an authoritative ſeizure; and, in order to gain a pepper-corn in this way, have choſen to hazard millions, acquired by the peaceable intercourſe of trade.——Vile policy! What a ſcourge is government ſo conducted? ——Had we never deſerted our old ground: Had we nouriſhed and favoured *America*, with a view to commerce, inſtead of conſidering it as a country to be governed: Had we, like a liberal and wiſe people, rejoiced to ſee a multitude of free ſtates branched forth from ourſelves, all enjoying independent legiſlatures ſimilar to our own: Had we aimed at binding them to us only by the tyes of affection and intereſt; and contented ourſelves with a moderate power rendered durable by being lenient and friendly, an umpire in their differences, an aid to them in improving their own free governments, and their common bulwark againſt the aſſaults of foreign enemies: Had this, I ſay, been our policy and temper; there is nothing ſo great or happy that we might not have expected. With their increaſe our ſtrength would have increaſed. A growing ſurplus in the revenue might have been gained, which, invariably applied to the gradual diſcharge of the national debt, would have delivered us from the ruin with which it threatens us.

 The

The Liberty of *America* might have preſerved our Liberty; and, under the direction of a patriot king or wiſe miniſter, proved the means of reſtoring to us our almoſt loſt conſtitution. Perhaps, in time, we might alſo have been brought to ſee the neceſſity of carefully watching and reſtricting our paper-credit: And thus we might have regained ſafety; and, in union with our Colonies, have been more than a match for every enemy, and riſen to a ſituation of honour and dignity never before known amongſt mankind.——But I am forgetting myſelf.——Our Colonies are likely to be loſt for ever. Their love is turned into hatred; and their reſpect for our government into reſentment and abhorrence.——We ſhall ſee more diſtinctly what a calamity this is, and the obſervations I have now made will be confirmed, by attending to the following facts.

Our American Colonies, particularly the Northern ones, have been for ſome time in the happieſt ſtate of ſociety; or, in that middle ſtate of civilization, between its firſt rude and its laſt refined and corrupt ſtate. Old countries conſiſt, generally, of three claſſes of people; a GENTRY; a YEOMANRY; and a PEASANTRY. The Colonies conſiſt only of a body of YEOMANRY (a) ſupported by

(a) Except the *Negroes* in the Southern Colonies, who probably will now either ſoon become extinct, or have their condition

by agriculture, and all independent, and nearly upon a level; in consequence of which, joined to a boundless extent of country, the means of subsistence are procured without difficulty, and the temptations to wickedness are so inconsiderable, that executions (*b*) are seldom known among them. From hence arises an encouragement to population so great, that in some of the Colonies they double their own number in fifteen years; in others, in eighteen years; and in all, taken one with another, in twenty-five years.——Such an increase was, I believe, never before known. It demonstrates that they must live at their ease; and be free from those cares, oppressions, and diseases which depopulate and ravage luxurious states.

With the population of the Colonies has increased their trade; but much faster, on account of the gradual introduction of luxury among them.——In 1723 the exports to *Pensylvania* were 16,000 l.—In 1742 they were 75,295 l.——In 1757 they

condition changed into that of *Freemen*.——It is not the fault of the Colonies that they have among them so many of these unhappy people. They have made laws to prohibit the importation of them; but these laws have always had a negative put upon them here, because of their tendency to hurt our Negro trade.

(*b*) In the county of Suffolk, where Boston is, there has not been, I am informed, more than one execution these 18 years.

were increaſed to 268,426l. and in 1773 to half a million.

The exports to all the Colonies in 1744 were 640,114l.——In 1758, they were increaſed to 1,832,948l. and in 1773, to three millions. (a) And the probability is, that, had it not been for the diſcontents among the Colonies ſince the year 1764, our trade with them would have been this year double to what it was in 1773; and that in a few years more, it would not have been poſſible for the whole kingdom, though conſiſting only of manufacturers, to ſupply the American demand.

This trade, it ſhould be conſidered, was not only thus an increaſing trade; but it was a trade in which we had no rivals; a trade certain, conſtant, and uninterrupted; and which, by the ſhipping employed in it, and the naval ſtores ſupplied by it, contributed greatly to the ſupport of that navy which is our chief national ſtrength.——Viewed in theſe lights it was an object unſpeakably important. But it will appear ſtill more ſo if we view it in its connexions and dependencies. It is well known, that our trade with *Africa* and the *Weſt-Indies* cannot eaſily ſubſiſt without it. And, upon the whole, it is undeniable, that it has been one of the

(a) Mr. Burke (in his excellent and admirable Speech on moving his reſolutions for conciliation with the Colonies, P. 9. &c.) has ſhewn, that our trade to the Colonies, including that to *Africa* and the *Weſt-Indies*, was in 1772 nearly equal to the trade which we carried on with the whole world at the beginning of this Century.

main ſprings of our opulence and ſplendour; and that we have, in a great meaſure, been indebted to it for our ability to bear a debt ſo much heavier, than that which, fifty years ago, the wiſeſt men thought would neceſſarily ſink us.

This ineſtimable prize, and all the advantages connected with *America*, we are now throwing away. Experience alone can ſhew what calamities muſt follow. It will indeed be aſtoniſhing if this kingdom can bear ſuch a loſs without dreadful conſequences.——Theſe conſequences have been amply repreſented by others; and it is needleſs to enter into any account of them——At the time we ſhall be feeling them——The Empire diſmembered; the blood of thouſands ſhed in an unrighteous quarrel; our ſtrength exhauſted; our merchants breaking; our manufacturers ſtarving; our debts increaſing; the revenue ſinking; the funds tottering; and all the miſeries of a public bankruptcy impending——At ſuch a *criſis* ſhould our natural enemies, eager for our ruin, ſeize the opportunity——The apprehenſion is too diſtreſſing. ——Let us view this ſubject in another light.

On this occaſion, particular attention ſhould be given to the preſent SINGULAR ſituation of this kingdom. This is a circumſtance of the utmoſt importance; and as I am afraid it is not much conſidered, I will beg leave to give a diſtinct account of it.

At the REVOLUTION, the *ſpecie* of the kingdom amounted, according to (*a*) *Davenant*'s account, to eighteen millions and a half.——From the ACCESSION to the year 1772, there were coined at the mint, near 29 millions of gold; and in ten years only of this time, or from January 1759 to January 1769, there were coined eight millions and a half. (*b*) But it has appeared lately, that the gold ſpecie now left in the kingdom is no more than about twelve millions and a half. (*c*)—Not ſo much as half a million of *Silver ſpecie* has been coined theſe ſixty years; and it cannot be ſuppoſed, that the quantity of it now in circulation exceeds two or three millions. The whole ſpecie of the kingdom, therefore, is probably at this time about fifteen millions. Of this ſome millions muſt be hoarded at the *Bank*.——Our circulating *ſpecie*, therefore, appears to be decreaſed. But our wealth, or the quantity of money in the

(*a*) See Dr. Davenant's works, collected and reviſed by Sir Charles Whitworth, Vol. I. Page 363, &c. 443, &c.

(*b*) See Conſiderations on Money, Bullion, &c. Page 2 and 11.

(*c*) The coin deficient between one grain and three grains was not called in at the time this was written. This call was made in the Summer of 1776; and it brought in above three millions more than was expected. The quantity of gold coin ſhould therefore have been ſtated at about SIXTEEN MILLIONS, and the whole coin of the kingdom at 18 or 19 millions.——The evidence from which I have drawn this eſtimate may be found in the firſt Section of the Second Part of the next Tract.

the kingdom, is greatly increaſed. This is paper to a vaſt amount, iſſued in almoſt every corner of the kingdom; and, particularly, by the BANK OF ENGLAND. While this paper maintains its credit it anſwers all the purpoſes of ſpecie, and is in all reſpects the ſame with money.

Specie repreſents ſome real value in goods or commodities. On the contrary; paper repreſents immediately nothing but ſpecie. It is a promiſe or obligation which the emitter brings himſelf under to pay a given ſum in coin; and it owes its currency to the credit of the emitter; or to an opinion that he is able to make good his engagement; and that the ſum ſpecified may be received upon being demanded.—Paper, therefore, repreſents coin; and coin repreſents real value. That is, the one is a *ſign* of wealth. The other is the *ſign* of that *ſign*.——But farther. Coin is an *univerſal* ſign of wealth, and will procure it every where. It will bear any alarm, and ſtand any ſhock. ——On the contrary. Paper, owing its currency to opinion, has only a local and imaginary value. It can ſtand no ſhock. It is deſtroyed by the approach of danger; or even the *ſuſpicion* of danger.

In ſhort. Coin is the baſis of our paper-credit; and were it either all deſtroyed, or were only the quantity of it reduced beyond a certain limit, the paper circulation of the kingdom would ſink at once. But, were our paper deſtroyed, the coin would

would not only remain, but riſe in value, in proportion to the quantity of paper deſtroyed.

From this account it follows, that as far as, in any circumſtances, ſpecie is not to be procured in exchange for paper, it repreſents *nothing*, and is, worth *nothing*.——The ſpecie of this kingdom is inconſiderable, compared with the amount of the paper circulating in it. This is generally believed; and, therefore, it is natural to enquire how its currency is ſupported.——The anſwer is eaſy. It is ſupported in the ſame manner with all other bubbles. Were all to demand ſpecie in exchange for their notes, payment could not be made; but, at the ſame time that this is known, every one truſts, that no alarm producing ſuch a demand will happen, while he holds the paper he is poſſeſſed of; and that if it ſhould happen, he will ſtand a chance for being firſt paid; and this makes him eaſy. And it alſo makes all with whom he traffics eaſy. —But let any events happen which threaten danger; and every one will become diffident. A run will take place; and a bankruptcy follow.

This is an account of what has often happened in *private* credit. And it is alſo an account of what *will* (if no change of meaſures takes place) happen ſome time or other in *public* credit. The deſcription I have given of our paper-circulation implies, that nothing can be more delicate or hazardous. It is an immenſe fabrick, with its head in the clouds, that is continually trembling with every

every adverſe blaſt and every fluctuation of trade; and which, like the baſeleſs fabrick of a viſion, may in a moment vaniſh, and leave no wreck behind.——The deſtruction of a few books at the *Bank*; an improvement in the art of forgery; the landing of a body of *French* troops on our coaſts; inſurrections threatening a revolution in government; or any events that ſhould produce a general panic, however groundleſs, would at once annihilate it, and leave us without any other medium of traffic, than a quantity of *ſpecie* not much more than the money now drawn from the public by the taxes. It would, therefore, become impoſſible to pay the taxes. The revenue would fail. Near a hundred and forty millions of property would be deſtroyed. The whole frame of government would fall to pieces; and a ſtate of nature would take place.——What a dreadful ſituation? It has never had a parallel among mankind; except at one time in *France* after the eſtabliſhment there of the Royal *Miſſiſipi* Bank. In 1720 this bank broke; (*a*) and, after involving for ſome time the whole kingdom in a golden dream, ſpread through it in one day, deſolation and ruin.——The diſtreſs attending ſuch an event, in this free country, would be greater than it was in *France*. Happily for that kingdom, they have ſhot this gulph. Paper-credit has never ſince recovered it

(*a*) See Sir James Steuart's Enquiry into the Principles of political Œconomy, Vol. II. Book 4, Chap. 32.

ſelf

self there; and their circulating cash consists now all of solid coin, amounting, according to the lowest account, to no less a sum than 1500 millions of *Livres*; (*a*) or near 67 millions of pounds sterling. This gives them unspeakable advantages; and, joined to that quick reduction of their debts which is inseparable (*b*) from their nature, places them on a ground of safety which we have reason to admire and envy.

These are subjects on which I should have chosen to be silent, did I not think it necessary, that this country should be apprized and warned of the danger which threatens it. This danger is created chiefly by the national debt. High taxes are necessary to support a great public debt; and a large supply of cash is necessary to support high taxes. This cash we owe to our paper; and, in proportion to our paper, must be the productiveness of our taxes.——King William's wars drained the

(*a*) See the Second Tract, P. 65.

(*b*) Their debts consist chiefly of money raised by annuities on lives, short annuities, anticipations of taxes for short terms, &c. During the whole last war they added to their *perpetual* annuities only 12 millions sterling, according to Sir James Steuart's account; whereas we added to these annuities near 60 millions. In consequence therefore of the nature of their debts, as well as of the management they are now using for hastening the reduction of them, they must in a few years, if peace continues, be freed from most of their incumbrances; while we probably (if no event comes soon that will unburthen us at once) shall continue with them all upon us.

kingdom

kingdom of its specie. This sunk the revenue, and distressed government. In 1694 the BANK was established; and the kingdom was provided with a substitute for specie. The taxes became again productive. The revenue rose; and government was relieved.——Ever since that period our paper and taxes have been increasing together, and supporting one another; and one reason, undoubtedly, of the late increase in the productiveness of our taxes has been the increase of our paper.

Was there no public debt, there would be no occasion for half the present taxes. Our paper-circulation might be reduced. The balance of trade would turn in our favour. Specie would flow in upon us. The quantity of property destroyed by a failure of paper-credit (should it in such circumstances happen) would be 140 millions less; and, therefore, the shock attending it would be *tolerable*. But, in the present state of things, whenever any calamity or panic shall produce such a failure, the shock attending it will be *intolerable*.——May heaven soon raise up for us some great statesman who shall see these things; and enter into effectual measures, if not now too late, for extricating and preserving us.

Public banks are, undoubtedly, attended with great conveniencies. But they also do great harm; and, if their emissions are not restrained, and conducted with great wisdom, they may prove the most pernicious of all institutions; not only, by substituting *fictitious* for *real* wealth; by increasing luxury; by raising the prices of provisions; by concealing an unfavourable balance of trade; and by rendering a kingdom incapable of bearing any *internal* tumults or *external* attacks, without the danger of a dreadful convulsion: But, particularly, by becoming instruments in the hands of ministers of state to increase their influence, to lessen their dependence on the people, and to keep up a delusive shew of public prosperity, when perhaps ruin may be near. There is, in truth, nothing that a government may not do with such a mine at its command as a public Bank, while it can maintain its credit; nor, therefore, is there any thing more likely to be IMPROPERLY and DANGEROUSLY used.——But to return to what may be more applicable to our own state at present.

Among the causes that may produce a failure of paper-credit, there are two which the present quarrel with *America* calls upon us particularly to consider.——The first is, "An unfavourable balance of trade." This, in proportion to the degree in which it takes place, must turn the course of foreign exchange against us; raise the price of bullion; and carry off our specie. The danger to which this would expose us is obvious; and it has been

been much increased by the new coinage of the gold specie which begun in 1773. Before this coinage, the greatest part of our gold coin being light, but the same in currency as if it had been heavy, always remained in the kingdom. But, being now nearly of full weight, whenever a wrong balance of foreign trade alters the course of exchange, and gold in *coin* becomes of less value than in *bullion*, there is reason to fear, that it will be melted down in such great quantities, and exported so fast, as in a little time to leave none behind; (*a*) the consequence of which must prove, that the whole super-

(*a*) Mr. *Lowndes* in the dispute between him and Mr. *Locke*, contended for a reduction of the standard of silver. One of his reasons was, that it would render the silver-coin more commensurate to the wants of the nation; and CHECK HAZARDOUS PAPER-CREDIT.—Mr. CONDUIT, Sir ISAAC NEWTON's successor in the mint, has proposed, in direct contradiction to the laws now in being, that all the bullion imported into the kingdom should be carried into the mint to be coined; and only coin allowed to be exported. "The height, he says, of "paper-credit is the strongest argument for trying this and *every* "*other* method that is likely to increase the coinage. For "whilst paper-credit does in a great measure the business of mo-"ney at home, Merchants and Bankers are not under a necessi-"ty, as they were formerly, of coining a quantity of specie for "their home trade; and as Paper-credit brings money to the "Merchants to be exported, the money may go away insensi-"bly, and NOT BE MISSED TILL IT BE TOO LATE: And "where Paper-credit is large and increasing, if the money "be exported and the coinage decrease, THAT CREDIT "MAY SINK AT ONCE, for want of a proportionable quan-

 "tity

ſuperſtructure of paper-credit, now ſupported by it, will break down.——The only remedy, in ſuch circumſtances, is an increaſe of coinage at the mint. But this will operate too ſlowly; and, by raiſing the price of bullion, will only increaſe the evil.—It is the *Bank* that at ſuch a time muſt be the immediate ſufferer: For it is from thence that thoſe who want coin for any purpoſe will always draw it.

For many years before 1773, the price of gold in *bullion* had been, from 2 to 3 or 4 *per cent.* higher than in *coin*. This was a temptation to melt down and export the coin, which could not be reſiſted. Hence aroſe a demand for it on the BANK; and, conſequently, the neceſſity of purchaſing bullion at a loſs for a new coinage. But the more coin the Bank procured in this way, the lower its price became in compariſon with that of bullion, and the faſter it vaniſhed; and, conſequently, the more neceſſary it became to coin again, and the greater loſs fell upon the Bank.——Had things continued much longer in this train, the conſequences might have proved very ſerious. I am by no means ſufficiently informed to be able to aſſign the cauſes which have produced the change that happened in 1772. But, without doubt, the ſtate of things which took place before that year muſt be

" tity of *Specie*, which alone can ſupport it in a time of diſ-" treſs."——See Mr. *Conduit*'s Obſervations on the ſtate of our Gold and Silver Coins in 1730, Page 36, to 46.

expected

expected to return. The fluctuations of trade, in its best state, render this unavoidable. But the contest with our Colonies has a tendency to bring it on soon; and to increase unspeakably the distress attending it. All know that the balance of trade with them is greatly in our favour; (*a*) and that this balance is paid partly by direct remittances of bullion; and partly by circuitous remittances through *Spain*, *Portugal*, *Italy*, &c. which diminish the balance against us with these countries.—During the last year they have been employed in paying their debts, without adding to them; and their exportations and remittances for that purpose have contributed to render the general balance of trade more favourable to us, and, also, (in conjunction with the late operations of the Bank) to keep up our funds. These remittances are now ceased; and a few years will determine, if this contest goes on, how far we can sustain such a loss without suffering the consequences I have described.

The second event, ruinous to our paper circulation, which may arise from our rupture with *America*, is a deficiency in the revenue. As a failure of our paper would destroy the revenue, so a

(*a*) According to the accounts of the exports to, and imports from the North-American Colonies, laid before Parliament, the balance in our favour appears to have been, for 11 years before 1774, near a *million and a half* annually.

failure of the revenue, or any considerable diminution of it, would destroy our paper. The BANK is the support of our paper; and the support of the BANK is the credit of government. Its principal securities, are a capital of eleven millions lent to government; and money continually advanced to a vast amount on the Land-tax and Malt-tax, Sinking Fund, Exchequer Bills, Navy Bills, &c. Should, therefore, deficiencies in the revenue bring government under any difficulties, all these securities would lose their value, and the *Bank* and Government, and all private and public credit, would fall together.—Let any one here imagine, what would probably follow, were it but suspected by the public in general, that the taxes were so fallen, as not to produce enough to pay the interest of the public debts, besides bearing the *ordinary* expences of the nation; and that, in order to supply the deficiency and to hide the calamity, it had been necessary in any one year to anticipate the taxes, and to borrow of the Bank.——In such circumstances I can scarcely doubt, but an alarm would spread of the most dangerous tendency.——The next foreign war, should it prove *half* as expensive as the last, will probably occasion such a deficiency; and bring our affairs to that crisis towards which they have been long tending.——But the war with *America* has a greater tendency to do this; and the reason is, that it affects our resources more; and is

 attended

attended more with the danger of internal diſturbances.

Some have made the proportion of our trade depending on *North America* to be near ONE HALF. A moderate computation makes it a THIRD. (*a*) Let it, however, be ſuppoſed to be only a FOURTH. I will venture to ſay, this is a proportion of our foreign trade, the loſs of which, when it comes to be felt, will be found inſupportable.——In the article of *Tobacco* alone it will cauſe a deduction from the *Cuſtoms* of at leaſt 300,000*l. per ann.* (*b*) including the duties paid on foreign commodities purchaſed by the exportation of tobacco. Let the whole deduction from the revenue be ſuppoſed to be only half a million. This alone is more than the kingdom can at preſent bear, without having recourſe

(*a*) See the ſubſtance of the evidence on the petition preſented by the *Weſt-India* Planters and Merchants to the Houſe of Commons as it was introduced at the BAR, and ſummed up by Mr. GLOVER.

(*b*) The annual average of the payments into the Exchequer, on account of the duties on tobacco, was for five years, from 1770 to 1774, 219,117 l. excluſive of the payments from *Scotland*.——Near one half of the *tobacco* trade is carried on from *Scotland*; and above *four fifths* of the tobacco imported is afterwards exported to *France*, *Germany* and other countries. From *France* alone it brings annually into the Kingdom, I am informed, about 150,000 l. in money.

In 1775, being, alas! the *parting* year, the duties on tobacco in ENGLAND brought into the *Exchequer* no leſs a ſum than 298,202 l.

to lotteries, and the land-tax at 4s. in order to defray the common and neceſſary expences of peace. But to this muſt be added a deduction from the produce of the *Exciſes*, in conſequence of the increaſe of the poor, of the difficulties of our merchants and manufacturers, of leſs national wealth, and a retrenchment of luxury. There is no poſſibility of knowing to what theſe deductions may amount. When the evils producing them begin, they will proceed rapidly; and they may end in a general wreck before we are aware of any danger.

In order to give a clearer view of this ſubject, I will in an Appendix*, ſtate particularly the national expenditure and income for eleven years, from 1764 to 1774. From that account it will appear, that the money drawn every year from the public by the taxes, does not fall greatly ſhort of a ſum equal to the whole *ſpecie* of the kingdom; and that, notwithſtanding the late increaſe in the productiveneſs of the taxes, the whole ſurplus of the national income has not exceeded 338,759l. *per ann.* See the Second Tract, p. 160. This is a ſurplus ſo inconſiderable as to be ſcarcely ſufficient to guard againſt the deficiencies ariſing from the common fluctuations of foreign trade, and of home conſumption. It is NOTHING when conſidered as the

* All the accounts and calculations in the *Appendix* here referred to, have been transferred to the 2d and 4th Sections of the 3d Part of the Second Tract.

only

only fund we have for paying off a debt of near 140 millions.—Had we continued in a state of profound peace, it could not have admitted of any diminution. What then must follow, when one of the most profitable branches of our trade is destroyed; when a THIRD of the Empire is lost; when an addition of many millions is made to the public debt; and when, at the same time, perhaps some millions are taken away from the revenue?——I shudder at this prospect.——A KINGDOM ON AN EDGE SO PERILOUS, SHOULD THINK OF NOTHING BUT A RETREAT.

## SECT. IV.

### *Of the Honour of the Nation as affected by the War with* America.

ONE of the pleas for continuing the contest with *America* is, "That our honour is engaged; and that we cannot now recede without "the most humiliating concessions."

With respect to this, it is proper to observe, that a distinction should be made between the nation, and its rulers. It is melancholy that there should be ever any reason for making such a distinction. A government is, or ought to be, nothing but an institution for collecting and for carrying into execution the will of the people. But so far is this from being in general the fact, that the measures of government, and the sense of the people, are sometimes in direct opposition to one another; nor does it *often* happen that any certain conclusion can be drawn from the one to the other.——I will not pretend to determine, whether, in the present instance, the dishonour attending a retreat would belong to the nation at large, or only to the persons in power who guide its affairs. Be this as it will, no good argument can be drawn from it against receding. The disgrace which may be implied in making concessions, is nothing to that of being the aggressors in an unrighteous quarrel; and dignity, in such circumstances, consists in retracting freely and speedily.———For, (to adopt on this occasion, words which I have heard applied to this very purpose, in a great assembly, by a peer to whom this kingdom has often looked as its deliverer, and whose ill state of health at this awful moment of public danger every friend to *Britain* must deplore) to adopt, I say, the words of this great man——"RECTITUDE IS DIGNITY. OPPRESSION ONLY IS MEANNESS; AND JUSTICE, HONOUR."

I will add, that PRUDENCE, no less than true HONOUR, requires us to retract. For the time may come when, if it is not done voluntarily, we may be *obliged* to do it; and find ourselves under a necessity of granting that to our distresses, which we we now deny to equity and humanity, and the prayers of *America*. The possibility of this appears plainly from the preceding pages; and should it happen, it will bring upon us disgrace indeed, disgrace greater than the worst rancour can wish to see accumulated on a kingdom already too much dishonoured.——Let the reader think here what we are doing.——A nation, once the protector of Liberty in distant countries, and the scourge of tyranny, changed into an enemy to Liberty, and engaged in endeavouring to reduce to servitude its own brethren.——A great and enlightened nation, not content with a controuling power over millions of people which gave it every reasonable advantage, insisting upon such a supremacy over them as would leave them nothing they could call their own, and carrying desolation and death among them for disputing it. ——What can be more ignominious?——How have we felt for the brave *Corsicans*, in their struggle with the *Genoese*, and afterwards with the *French* government? Did GENOA or FRANCE want more than an absolute command over their property and legislations; or the power of binding them in all cases whatsoever?——The *Genoese*, finding it difficult to keep them in subjection, CEDED them to the *French*.——All such cessions of one people by another are disgraceful to human

man nature. But if our claims are just, may not we also, if we please, CEDE the Colonies to *France?* ——There is, in truth, no other difference between these two cases than that the *Corsicans* were not descended from the people who governed them, but that the *Americans* are.

There are some who seem to be sensible, that the authority of one country over another, cannot be distinguished from the servitude of one country to another; and that unless different communities, as well as different parts of the same community, are united by an equal representation, all such authority is inconsistent with the principles of Civil Liberty.——But they except the case of the Colonies and *Great Britain*; because the Colonies are communities which have branched forth from, and which, therefore, as they think, belong to *Britain.* Had the colonies been communities of *foreigners*, over whom we wanted to acquire dominion, or even to extend a dominion before acquired, they are ready to admit that their resistance would have been just.——In my opinion, this is the same with saying, that the Colonies ought to be worse off than the rest of mankind, because they are our own *Brethren.*

Again. The United Provinces of *Holland* were once subject to the *Spanish* monarchy; but, provoked by the violation of their charters; by levies of money, without their consent; by the introduction

tion of Spanish troops among them; by innovations in their antient modes of government; and the rejection of their petitions; they were driven to that resistance which we and all the world have ever since admired; and which has given birth to one of the greatest and happiest Republics that ever existed. ——— Let any one read also, the history of the war which the *Athenians*, from a thirst of Empire, made on the *Syracusans* in *Sicily*, a people derived from the same origin with them; and let him, if he can, avoid rejoicing in the defeat of the *Athenians*.

Let him, likewise, read the account of the social war among the Romans. The allied states of *Italy* had fought the battles of *Rome*, and contributed by their valour and treasure to its conquests and grandeur. They claimed, therefore, the rights of Roman citizens, and a share with them in legislation. The Romans, disdaining to make those their *fellow-citizens*, whom they had always looked upon as their *subjects*, would not comply; and a war followed, the most horrible in the annals of mankind, which ended in the ruin of the Roman Republic. The feelings of every *Briton* in this case must force him to approve the conduct of the Allies, and to condemn the proud and ungrateful Romans.

But not only is the present contest with *America* thus disgraceful to us, because inconsistent with

with our own feelings in similar cases; but also because condemned by our own practice in former times. The Colonies are persuaded that they are fighting for Liberty. We see them sacrificing to this persuasion every private advantage. If mistaken, and though guilty of irregularities, they should be pardoned by a people whose ancestors have given them so many examples of similar conduct. ENGLAND should venerate the attachment to Liberty amidst all its excesses; and, instead of indignation or scorn, it would be most becoming them, in the present instance, to declare their applause, and to say to the Colonies——"We excuse your mistakes. We admire your spirit. "It is the spirit that has more than once saved "*ourselves*. We aspire to no dominion over you. "We understand the rights of men too well to "think of taking from you the inestimable privilege of governing yourselves; and, instead of "employing our power for any such purpose, "we offer it to you as a friendly and guardian "power, to be a mediator in your quarrels; a "protection against your enemies; and an aid "to you in establishing a plan of Liberty that shall "make you great and happy. In return, we "ask nothing but your gratitude and your commerce."

This would be a language worthy of a brave and enlightened nation. But alas! it often happens

pens in the *Political World* as it does in *Religion*, that the people who cry out moſt vehemently for Liberty to themſelves are the moſt unwilling to grant it to others.

But farther. This war is diſgraceful on account of the perſuaſion which led to it, and under which it has been undertaken. The general cry was laſt winter, that the people of NEW-ENGLAND were a body of cowards, who would at once be reduced to ſubmiſſion by a hoſtile look from our troops. In this light were they held up to public deriſion in both Houſes of Parliament; and it was this perſuaſion that, probably, induced a Nobleman of the firſt weight in the ſtate to recommend, at the paſſing of the *Boſton Port Bill*, coercive meaſures; hinting at the ſame time, that the *appearance* of hoſtilities would be ſufficient, and that all would be ſoon over, SINE CLADE.——Indeed no one can doubt, but that had it been believed ſome time ago, that the people of *America* were brave, more care would have been taken not to provoke them.

Again. The manner in which this war has been hitherto conducted, renders it ſtill more diſgraceful.——Engliſh valour being thought inſufficient to ſubdue the Colonies, the laws and religion of *France* were eſtabliſhed in *Canada*, on purpoſe to obtain the power of bringing upon them from thence an army of *French Papiſts*. The wild *Indi-*

*ans*

*ans* and their own Slaves have been inſtigated to attack them; and attempts have been made to gain the aſſiſtance of a large body of *Ruſſians.*—— With like views, *German* troops have been hired; and the defence of our Forts and Garriſons truſted in their hands.

Theſe are meaſures which need no comment. The laſt of them, in particular, having been carried into execution without the conſent of parliament, threatens us with imminent danger; and ſhews that we are in the way to loſe even the *Forms* of the conſtitution.——If, indeed, our miniſters can at any time, without leave, not only ſend away the national troops, but introduce *foreign* troops in their room, we lie entirely at mercy; and we have every thing to dread.

## SECT. V.

### *Of the Probability of Succeeding in the War with* America.

LET us next conſider how far there is a poſſibility of ſucceeding in the preſent war.

Our own people, being unwilling to enliſt, and the attempts to procure armies of *Ruſſians*, *Indians*, and *Canadians* having miſcarried; the utmoſt force we can employ, including foreigners, does not exceed, if I am rightly informed, 40,000 effective men. This is the force that is to conquer half a million *at leaſt* (*a*) of determined men fighting on their own ground, within ſight of their houſes and families, and for that ſacred bleſſing of Liberty, without which man is a beaſt, and government a curſe. All hiſtory proves, that in ſuch a ſituation, a handful is a match for millions.

In the *Netherlands*, a few ſtates thus circumſtanced, withſtood, for a long courſe of years, the whole force of the Spaniſh monarchy, when at its zenith; and at laſt humbled its pride, and emancipated themſelves from its tyranny.—The citizens of SYRACUSE alſo, thus circumſtanced, withſtood the whole power of the *Athenians*, and almoſt ruined them.—The ſame happened in the conteſt between the houſe of *Auſtria*, and the cantons (*b*) of *Switzerland*.——There is in this caſe an infinite difference between attacking and being attacked; between fighting to *deſtroy*, and fighting to *preſerve* or *acquire* Liberty.——Were we, therefore, capable of employing a *land* force againſt *America* equal to its own, there would be little probability of ſucceſs. But to think of conquering that whole continent with 30,000 or 40,000 men to be tranſported

(*a*) A quarter of the inhabitants of every country are fighting men.——If, therefore, the Colonies conſiſt only of two millions of inhabitants, the number of fighting men in them will be half a million.

(*b*) See the Appendix to Dr. Zubly's Sermon, preached at the opening of the Provincial Congreſs of *Georgia*.

ported acroſs the *Atlantic*, and fed from hence, and incapable of being recruited after any defeat ——This is indeed a folly ſo great, that language does not afford a name for it.

With reſpect to our naval force, could it ſail at land as it does at ſea, much might be done with it; but as that is impoſſible, *little* or *nothing* can be done with it, which will not hurt *ourſelves* more than the *Coloniſts*.——Such of their maritime towns as they cannot guard againſt our fleets, and have not been already deſtroyed, they are determined either to give up to our reſentment, or (*a*) deſtroy themſelves: The conſequence of which will be, that theſe towns will be rebuilt in ſafer ſituations; and that we ſhall loſe ſome of the principal pledges by which we have hitherto held them in ſubjection.—As to their trade; having all the neceſſaries and the chief conveniencies of life within themſelves, they have no dependence upon it; and the loſs of it will do them unſpeakable good, by preſerving them from the evils of luxury and the temptations of wealth; and keeping them in that ſtate of virtuous ſimplicity which is the greateſt happineſs. I know that I am now ſpeaking the ſenſe of ſome of the wiſeſt men in America. It has been long their wiſh that *Britain* would ſhut up all their ports. They will rejoice, particularly, in the laſt reſtraining act. It might have happened, that the people would have grown weary of

their

their agreements not to export or import. But this act will oblige them to keep these agreements; and confirm their unanimity and zeal. It will also furnish them with a reason for confiscating the estates of all the friends of our government among them, and for employing their sailors, who would have been otherwise idle, in making reprisals on British property. Their ships, before useless, and consisting of many hundreds, will be turned into ships of war; and that attention, which they have hitherto confined to trade, will be employed in fitting out a naval force for their own defence; and thus the way will be prepared for their becoming, much sooner than they would otherwise have been, a great maritime power. This act of parliament, therefore, crowns the folly of all our late measures.(*a*)—None who know me, can believe me to be disposed to superstition. Perhaps, however, I am not in the present instance, free from this weakness.——I fancy I see in these measures something that cannot be accounted for merely by human ignorance. I am inclined to think, that the hand of Providence is in them working to bring about some great ends.—But this leads me to one consideration more, which I

(*a*) The apprehensions here expressed have been verified by the events which have happened since this was written. American privateers have spread themselves over the Atlantick. They have frightened us even on our own coasts, and seized millions of British property.

 cannot

cannot help offering to the public, and which appears to me in the higheſt degree important.

In this hour of tremendous danger, it would become us to turn our thoughts to Heaven. This is what our brethren in the Colonies are doing. From one end of *North America* to the other, they are FASTING and PRAYING. But what are we doing?—We are ridiculing them as *Fanatics*, and ſcoffing at religion.——We are running wild after pleaſure, and forgetting every thing ſerious and decent at *Maſquerades*.——We are trafficking for Boroughs; perjuring ourſelves at Elections; and ſelling ourſelves for places.—Which ſide then is Providence likely to favour?

In *America* we ſee a number of riſing ſtates in the vigour of youth, inſpired by the nobleſt of all paſſions, the paſſion for being free; and animated by piety.——*Here* we ſee an old ſtate, great indeed, but inflated and irreligious; enervated by luxury; encumbred with debts; and hanging by a thread.——Can any one look without pain to the iſſue? May we not expect calamities that ſhall recover to *reflection* (perhaps to *devotion*) our *Libertines* and *Atheiſts*?

Is our cauſe ſuch as gives us reaſon to aſk God to bleſs it?——Can we in the face of Heaven declare, "that we are not the aggreſſors in this war; "and that we mean by it, not to acquire or even "preſerve dominion for its own ſake; not con-

"queſt

" queſt, or Empire, or the gratification of reſent-
" ment; but ſolely to deliver ourſelves from op-
" preſſion; to gain reparation for injury; and
" to defend ourſelves againſt men who would plun-
" der or kill us?"—Remember, reader, whoever
thou art, that there are no other juſt cauſes of war;
and that blood ſpilled, with any other views, muſt
ſome time or other be accounted for.——But not
to expoſe myſelf by ſaying more in this way, I will
now beg leave to recapitulate ſome of the arguments I have uſed; and to deliver the feelings
of my heart in a brief, but earneſt addreſs to my
countrymen.

I am hearing it continually urged——" Are
" they not our ſubjects?"——The plain anſwer is,
they are not your ſubjects. The people of *America* are no more the ſubjects of the people of *Britain*, than the people of *Yorkſhire* are the ſubjects
of the people of *Middleſex*. They are your *fellow-ſubjects*.

" But *we* are taxed; and why ſhould not *they*
be taxed?"——*You* are taxed by yourſelves. *They*
inſiſt on the ſame privilege.——They are taxed
to ſupport their own governments; and they help
alſo to pay your taxes by purchaſing your manufactures, and giving you a monopoly of their
trade. Muſt they maintain *two* governments?
Muſt they ſubmit to be *triple* taxed?—Has your
moderation in taxing yourſelves been ſuch as en-

 courages

courages them to truſt you with the power of taxing them?

"But they will not obey the *Parliament* and the *Laws*."——Say rather, they will not obey *your* parliament and *your* laws. Their reaſon is: They have no voice in your parliament. They have no ſhare in making (*a*) your laws.——"Neither have *moſt* of us."——Then you ſo far want Liberty; and your language is, "*We* are not free, Why will *they* be free?"——But *many* of you have a voice in parliament: *None* of them have. *All* your freehold land is repreſented: But not a foot of *their* land is repreſented. At worſt, therefore, you are only enſlaved *partially*.——Were they to ſubmit, they would be enſlaved *totally*.—— They are governed by parliaments choſen by themſelves, and by legiſlatures ſimilar to yours. Why will you diſturb them in the enjoyment of a bleſſing ſo valuable? Is it reaſonable to inſiſt, that your diſcretion alone ſhall be their law; that they

(*a*) "I have no other notion of ſlavery, but being bound "by a law to which I do not conſent." See the caſe of *Ireland*'s being bound by acts of Parliament in *England*, ſtated by William Molyneux, Eſq; Dublin.——In arguing againſt the authority of Communities, and all people not incorporated, over one another; I have confined my views to taxation and internal legiſlation. Mr. Molyneux carried his views much farther; and denied the right of *England* to make any laws even to regulate the trade of *Ireland*. He was the intimate friend of Mr. Locke; and writ his book in 1698, ſoon after the publication of Mr. Locke's Treatiſe on Government.

ſhall

ſhall have no conſtitutions of government, except ſuch as you ſhall be pleaſed to give them; and no property except ſuch as your parliament ſhall be pleaſed to leave them?—What is your parliament? —Is there not a growing intercourſe between it and the court? Does it awe miniſters of ſtate as it once did?—Inſtead of contending for a controuling power over the governments of *America*, ſhould you not think more of watching and reforming your own?—Suppoſe the worſt. Suppoſe, in oppoſition to all their own declarations, that the Coloniſts are now aiming at independence. (*a*)—" If they can ſubſiſt without you;" is it to be wondered at? Did there ever exiſt a *community*, or even an *individual*, that would not do the ſame?—" If they *cannot* ſubſiſt without you;" let them alone. They will ſoon come back.——" If you cannot ſubſiſt without them," reclaim them by (*b*) kindneſs; engage them by moderation and equity. It is madneſs to reſolve to butcher them. This will make

(*a*) See on this ſubject the ſecond Section of the ſecond Part of the next Tract, Page 77.

(*b*) Some perſons, convinced of the *folly* as well as *barbarity* of attempting to keep the Colonies by ſlaughtering them, have very humanely propoſed giving them up. But the higheſt authority has informed us, with great reaſon, " That " they are too important to be given up."—Dr. TUCKER has inſiſted on the depopulation, produced by migrations from this country to the Colonies, as a reaſon for this meaſure. But, unleſs

make them deteſt and avoid you for ever. Freemen are not to be governed by force; or dragooned into compliance. If capable of bearing to be ſo treated, it is a diſgrace to be connected with them.

"If *they* can ſubſiſt without *you*; and alſo *you* without *them*," the attempt to ſubjugate them by confiſcating their effects, burning their towns, and ravaging their territories, is a wanton exertion of cruel ambition, which, however common it has been among mankind, deſerves to be called by harder names than I chuſe to apply to it.—Suppoſe ſuch an attempt was to be ſucceeded: Would it not be a fatal preparation for ſubduing yourſelves? Would not the diſpoſal of *American* places, and the diſtribution of an *American* revenue, render that influence of the crown irreſiſtible, which has already ſtabbed your liberties?

Turn your eyes to *India*: There more has been done than is now attempted in *America*. There ENGLISHMEN, actuated by the love of plunder and

unleſs the kingdom is made a priſon to its inhabitants, theſe migrations cannot be prevented; nor do I think that they have any great tendency to produce depopulation. When a number of people quit a country, there is more employment and greater plenty of the means of ſubſiſtence left for thoſe who remain; and the vacancy is ſoon filled up. The grand cauſes of depopulation are, not migrations, or even famines and plagues, or any other *temporary* evils; but the permanent and ſlowly working evils of debauchery, luxury, high taxes, and oppreſſion.

the

the ſpirit of conqueſt, have depopulated whole kingdoms, and ruined millions of innocent people by the moſt infamous oppreſſion and rapacity.—The juſtice of the nation has ſlept over theſe enormities. Will the juſtice of heaven ſleep?——Are we not now execrated on both ſides of the globe?

With reſpect to the Coloniſts; it would be folly to pretend they are faultleſs. They were running faſt into our vices. But this quarrel gives them a ſalutary check: And it may be permitted on purpoſe to favour them, and in *them* the reſt of mankind; by making way for eſtabliſhing, in an extenſive country poſſeſſed of every advantage, a plan of government, and a growing power that will aſtoniſh the world, and under which every ſubject of human enquiry ſhall be open to free diſcuſſion, and the friends of Liberty, in every quarter of the globe, find a ſafe retreat from civil and ſpiritual tyranny.——I hope, therefore, our brethren in *America* will forgive their oppreſſors. It is certain *they know not what they are doing*.

# CONCLUSION.

HAVING ſaid ſo much of the war with America, and particularly of the danger with which it threatens us, it may be expected that I ſhould propoſe ſome method of eſcaping from this danger, and of reſtoring this once happy Empire to a ſtate of peace and ſecurity.—Various plans of pacification have been propoſed; and ſome of them, by perſons ſo diſtinguiſhed by their rank and merit, as to be above my applauſe. But till there is more of a diſpoſition to attend to ſuch plans; they cannot, I am afraid, be of any great ſervice. And there is too much reaſon to apprehend, that nothing but calamity will bring us to repentance and wiſdom.——In order, however, to complete my deſign in theſe obſervations, I will take the liberty to lay before the public the following ſketch of one of the plans juſt referred to, as it was opened before the holidays to the houſe of Lords by the *Earl of Shelburne*; who, while he held the ſeals of the Southern Department, with the buſineſs of the Colonies annexed, poſſeſſed their confidence, without ever compromiſing the authority of this country; a confidence which diſcovered itſelf by peace among themſelves, and duty and ſubmiſſion

to

to the Mother-country. I hope I ſhall not take an unwarrantable liberty, if, on this occation, I uſe his Lordſhip's own words, as nearly as I have been able to collect them.

" Meet the Colonies on their own ground, in
" the laſt petition from the Congreſs to the king.
" The ſureſt, as well as the moſt dignified
" mode of proceeding for this country.—Suſpend
" all hoſtilities——Repeal the acts which imme-
" diately diſtreſs America, namely, the laſt re-
" ſtraining act,—the charter act,—the act for the
" more impartial adminiſtration of juſtice;—and
" the Quebec act.—All the other acts (the cuſtom
" houſe act, the poſt office act, &c.) leave to a tem-
" perate reviſal.——There will be found much
" matter which both countries may wiſh repealed.
" *Some* which can never be given up, the prin-
" ciple being that regulation of trade for the
" common good of the Empire, which forms our
" *Palladium. Other* matter which is fair ſubject of
" mutual accommodation.——Preſcribe the moſt
" explicit acknowledgment of your right of regu-
" lating commerce in its moſt extenſive ſenſe; if
" the petition and other public acts of the Colonies
" have not already, by their declarations and ac-
" knowledgments, left it upon a ſufficiently ſecure
" foundation.—Beſides the power of regulating the
" general commerce of the Empire, ſomething
" further might be expected; provided a due and
" tender

" tender regard were had to the means and abili-
" ties of the ſeveral provinces, as well as to thoſe
" fundamental, unalienable rights of *Engliſhmen*,
" which no father can ſurrender on the part of his
" ſon, no repreſentative on the part of his elector,
" no generation on the part of the ſucceeding one;
" the right of judging not only of the *mode* of
" raiſing, but the *quantum*, and the appropriation
" of ſuch aids as they ſhall grant.——To be more
" explicit; the debt of *England*, without entering
" into invidious diſtinctions how it came to be
" contracted, might be acknowledged the debt of
" every individual part of the whole Empire,
" Aſia, as well as America, included.——Pro-
" vided, that full ſecurity were held forth to them,
" that ſuch free aids, together with the Sinking
" Fund (Great Britain contributing her ſuperior
" ſhare) ſhould not be left as the privy purſe of
" the miniſter, but be unalienably appropriated to
" the original intention of that fund, the diſcharge
" of the debt;—and that by an honeſt application
" of the *whole* fund, the taxes might in time be leſ-
" ſened, and the price of our manufactures conſe-
" quently reduced, ſo that every contributory part
" might feel the returning benefit—always ſuppo-
" ſing the laws of trade duly obſerved and enforced.

" The time *was*, I am confident—and per-
" haps *is*, when theſe points might be obtain-
" ed upon the eaſy, the conſtitutional, and,
" therefore, the indiſpenſible terms of an exemp-
" tion

"tion from parliamentary taxation, and an ad-
"mission of the sacredness of their charters; instead
"of sacrificing their good humour, their affec-
"tion, their effectual aids, and the act of NAVI-
"GATION itself, (which you are now in the direct
"road to do) for a commercial quit-rent, (a) or a
"barren metaphysical chimæra.——How long
"these ends may continue attainable, no man can
"tell.——But if no words are to be relied on ex-
"cept such as make against the Colonies—If
"nothing is acceptable, except what is attainable
"by force; it only remains to apply, what has
"been so often remarked of unhappy periods,
"——*Quos deus vult, &c.*"

These are sentiments and proposals of the last importance; and I am very happy in being able to give them to the public from so respectable an authority as that of the distinguished Peer I have mentioned; to whom, I know, this kingdom, as

(a) See the Resolutions on the *Nova-Scotia* petition reported to the House of Commons, November 29, 1775, by Lord North, Lord George Germaine, &c. and a bill ordered to be brought in upon the said Resolutions.——There is indeed, as Lord Shelburne has hinted, something very astonishing in these Resolutions. They offer a relaxation of the authority of this country, in points to which the Colonies have always consented, and by which we are great gainers; at the same time, that, with a rigour which hazards the Empire, we are maintaining its authority in points to which they will never consent; and by which nothing can be gained.

well

4

well as America, is much indebted for his zeal to promote thoſe grand public points on which the preſervation of Liberty among us depends; and for the firm oppoſition which, jointly with many others (Noblemen and Commoners of the firſt character and abilities,) he has made to the preſent meaſures.

Had ſuch a plan as that now propoſed been adopted a few months ago, I have little doubt but that a pacification would have taken place, on terms highly advantageous to this kingdom.—— In particular. It is probable, that the Colonies would have conſented to grant an annual ſupply, which, increaſed by a ſaving of the money now ſpent in maintaining troops among them, and by contributions which might have been gained from other parts of the Empire, would have formed a fund conſiderable enough, if unalienably applied, to redeem the public debt; in conſequence of which, agreeably to Lord Shelburne's ideas, ſome of our worſt taxes might be taken off, and the Colonies would receive our manufactures cheaper; our paper-currency might be reſtrained; our whole force would be free to meet at any time foreign danger; the influence of the Crown would be reduced; our Parliament would become leſs dependent; and the kingdom might, perhaps, be reſtored to a ſituation of permanent ſafety and proſperity.

To

To conclude.——An important revolution in the affairs of this kingdom ſeems to be approaching. If ruin is not to be our lot, all that has been lately done muſt be undone, and new meaſures adopted. At that period, an opportunity (never perhaps to be recovered, if loſt) will offer itſelf for ſerving eſſentially *this country*, as well as *America*; by putting the national debt into *a fixed* courſe of payment; by ſubjecting to new regulations, the adminiſtration of the finances; and by eſtabliſhing meaſures for exterminating corruption and reſtoring the conſtitution.——For my own part; if this is not to be the conſequence of any future changes in the miniſtry, and the ſyſtem of corruption, lately ſo much improved, is to go on; I think it totally indifferent to the kingdom who are *in*, or who are *out* of power.

THE following fact is of so much importance, that I cannot satisfy myself without laying it before the public.——In a Committee of the American CONGRESS in *June* 1775, a declaration was drawn up containing an offer to GREAT BRITAIN, "that the Colonies would not "only continue to grant extraordinary aids in "time of war, but also, if allowed a free commerce, pay into the SINKING-FUND such a sum "annually for ONE HUNDRED YEARS, as should "be *more* than sufficient in that time, if faithfully "applied, to extinguish all the present debts of "BRITAIN. Or, provided this was not accepted, "that, to remove the groundless jealousy of *Britain* that the Colonies aimed at Independence "and an abolition of the Navigation Act, which "in truth, they had never intended; and also, to "avoid all future disputes about the right of making that and other Acts for regulating their "commerce for the general benefit, they would "enter into a covenant with *Britain*, that she "should fully possess and exercise that right for "*one hundred years* to come."

At the end of the preceding Tract I have had the honor of laying before the public the Earl of *Shelburne*'s plan of Pacification with the Colonies. In that plan, it is particularly proposed, that the Colonies should grant an annual

supply

ſupply to be carried to the Sinking Fund, and unalienably appropriated to the diſcharge of the public debt.—It muſt give this excellent Peer great pleaſure to learn, from this reſolution, that even this part of his plan, as well as all the other parts, would, moſt probably, have been accepted by the Colonies. For though the reſolution only offers the alternative of either a *free* trade, with extraordinary aids and an annual ſupply, or an *excluſive* trade confirmed and extended; yet there can be little reaſon to doubt, but that to avoid the calamities of the preſent conteſt, BOTH would have been conſented to; particularly, if, on our part, ſuch a reviſal of the laws of trade had been offered as was propoſed in Lord Shelburne's plan.

The preceding reſolution was, I have ſaid, drawn up in a Committee of the Congreſs. But it was not entered in their minutes; a ſevere Act of Parliament happening to arrive at that time, which determined them not to give the ſum propoſed in it.

F I N I S.

# ADDITIONAL OBSERVATIONS

On the NATURE and VALUE of

# CIVIL LIBERTY,

AND THE

# WAR WITH AMERICA:

ALSO

OBSERVATIONS on Schemes for raiſing Money by PUBLIC LOANS;

An Hiſtorical Deduction and Analyſis of the NATIONAL DEBT;

And a brief Account of the DEBTS and RESOURCES of FRANCE.

---

Should the morals of the Engliſh be perverted by luxury;—ſhould they loſe their Colonies by reſtraining them, &c.—they will be enſlaved; they will become inſignificant and contemptible; and *Europe* will not be able to ſhew the world one nation in which ſhe can pride herſelf.

ABBE' RAYNAL.

TO

THE RIGHT HONOURABLE

THE LORD MAYOR,

THE ALDERMEN, AND THE COMMONS

OF THE

CITY OF LONDON,

THIS TRACT,

Containing ADDITIONS to thoſe OBSERVATIONS on CIVIL LIBERTY,

which they have honoured with their Approbation,

Is, with the greateſt Reſpect and Gratitude,

INSCRIBED,

BY

Their moſt obedient

and humble Servant,

RICHARD PRICE.

# CONTENTS.

*Published by the same Author,*

And printed for T. CADELL, in the Strand.

I. OBSERVATIONS on REVERSIONARY PAYMENTS; on Schemes for providing Annuities for Widows, and Persons in Old Age; on the Method of calculating the Values of Assurances on Lives; and on the National Debt. To which are added, Four Essays on different Subjects in the Doctrine of Life-Annuities and Political Arithmetic. Also, an Appendix, containing a complete Set of Tables; particularly four New Tables, shewing the Probabilities of Life in LONDON, NORWICH, and NORTHAMPTON, and the Values of two joint Lives.

The 3d Edition, with a Supplement, containing (besides several New Tables) additional Observations on the Probabilities of Human Life in different Situations; on the LONDON Societies for the Benefit of Widows and of Old Age; and on the present State of Population in this Kingdom. Price 6s.

II. A Review of the principal Questions and Difficulties in MORALS. Particularly, those relating to the Original of our Ideas of Virtue, its Nature, Foundation, Reference to the Deity, Obligation, Subject-matter, and Sanctions. The Second Edition corrected. Price 6s.

III. FOUR DISSERTATIONS.——I. On Providence.—II. On Prayer.—III. On the Reasons for expecting that virtuous Men shall meet after Death in a State of Happiness.—IV. On the Importance of Christianity, the Nature of Historical Evidence, and Miracles. The 4th Edition. Price 6s.

IV. An APPEAL to the PUBLIC, on the Subject of the NATIONAL DEBT. The 2d Edition; with an Appendix, containing Explanatory Observations and Tables; and an Account of the present State of Population in Norfolk. Price 2s.

V. OBSERVATIONS on the Nature of CIVIL LIBERTY, the Principles of GOVERNMENT, and the Justice and Policy of the WAR with AMERICA. To which is added an Appendix, containing a State of the National Debt, an Estimate of the Money drawn from the Public by the Taxes, and an Account of the National Income and Expenditure since the last War. The 7th Edition. Price 2s.

# INTRODUCTION.

BEFORE the reader enters on the following tract, I ſhall beg leave to detain him while I give a general account of the contents of it, and make a few introductory obſervations.

In the firſt part of the *Obſervations on Civil Liberty*, publiſhed laſt winter, I gave a brief account of the nature of Liberty in general, and of *Civil Liberty* in particular. That account appears to me, after carefully reconſidering it, to be juſt; nor do I think it in my power to improve it. In order, however, to be as explicit as poſſible on this ſubject, and to remove thoſe miſapprehenſions of my ſentiments into which ſome have fallen, I have thought proper to add the *ſupplemental* and *explanatory* obſervations, which will be found in the FIRST part of this pamphlet.——In writing with this view, I have been led to refer often to my former pamphlet, and to repeat ſome of the obſervations in it. But as this could not have been avoided, it will, I hope, be excuſed.

The remarks in the SECOND part, I offer to the public with all the deference due to the high ſtation and abilities of the noble Lord, whoſe ſpeech at opening the Budget in *April* laſt, has occaſioned them.——Theſe remarks, having been

 promiſed

promiſed long ago, ſhould have been publiſhed ſooner. The reaſons which have produced this delay are of little conſequence to the public; and, therefore, need not be mentioned.

In the firſt ſection of this *ſecond* part, it will, I think, appear, that I went upon as good grounds as the nature of the caſe admitted, when I ſtated the gold coin (*a*) of the kingdom at ABOUT TWELVE MILLIONS AND A HALF. It appears now, indeed, to be ſome millions more. But this is a diſcovery made by the call of laſt ſummer; which, I find, has brought in near double the ſum that the beſt judges expected. Nothing, however, very encouraging can be inferred from hence. It only ſhews that a great deal of gold has been hoarded; and will, probably, be again hoarded. This is the natural conſequence of public diffidence; and it is a circumſtance which may, hereafter, greatly increaſe diſtreſs. Before the REVOLUTION, according to Dr. *Davenant*, near half the coin was hoarded; and the ſame, undoubtedly, will be done again, whenever the nation comes to be thoroughly alarmed.

In the next ſection of this part, I have made ſome further obſervations on the conteſt with *America*.——I cannot expect any other than a tragical and deplorable iſſue to this conteſt. But let events turn out as they will, I ſhall always

(*a*) See Obſervatious on Civil Liberty, page 74.

reflect

reflect with satisfaction, that I have, though a private person of little consequence, bore my testimony, from deep-felt conviction, against a war which must shock the feelings and the reason of every considerate person; a war in which rivers of blood must be shed, not to repel the attacks of enemies, or to maintain the authority of government *within* the realm, but to maintain sovereignty and dominion in another world (*a*).—I wish the advocates for the measures against *America* would attend to the distinction now intimated.—The support of just government *within* the realm is always necessary, and therefore right. But to maintain, by fire and sword, dominion over the persons and the property of a people *out* of the realm, who have no share in its legislature, contradicts every principle of liberty and humanity.—Legitimate government, let it be remembered, as opposed to oppression and tyranny, consists "only in the dominion of "EQUAL LAWS made with COMMON CONSENT, or of "men over THEMSELVES; and not in the dominion "of communities over communities, or of ANY "MEN OVER OTHER MEN."—This is the great truth I have endeavoured to explain and defend; and

(*a*) Of all the writers against this war, the learned Dr. TUCKER is the severest. For if, as he maintains, contrary to repeated declarations from the throne, a separation from the Colonies would be an advantage to us, the attempt to keep them, by invasion and bloodshed, deserves a harsher censure than words can convey.

happy

happy would the world be, were a due conviction of it impressed on every human heart.

The representation I have given in this section and elsewhere, of the state of this kingdom, is, without doubt, gloomy. But it is not the effect, as some have intimated, of either a natural disposition to gloominess, or of sinister views. Few, who know me, will entertain such a suspicion. Valuing *most* what politicians and statesmen generally value *least*, I feel myself perfectly easy with respect to my interest as a citizen of this world; nor is there any change of situation that can make me happier, except a return to privacy and obscurity. The opinion I have entertained of the present danger of the kingdom is, therefore, the effect of evidence which appears to me irresistible. This evidence I have stated to the public; and every one may judge of it as he pleases. I am sensible of my own liableness to error. The measures which I condemn as the worst that ever disgraced and hazarded a great kingdom, others, whose integrity I cannot question, approve; and that very situation of our affairs which I think alarming, others think prosperous. Time will determine which of these opinions is right. But supposing the latter to be so, no harm can arise from any representations which have a tendency to put us on our guard.

I have bestowed particular attention on the observations in the third section of this second part;

and I think the ſubject of this ſection ſo important, that it is probable, I ſhould not have reſolved on the preſent publication, had it not been for the opportunity it gives me to lay the obſervations it contains before the public.——An intimation of them was given in the Introduction to the third edition of the Treatiſe on *Reverſionary Payments.* The nation being now once more got into a courſe of borrowing; and our firſt ſtep having been a return to a mode of borrowing, which had appeared to me abſurd and detrimental, I was induced to reſume the ſubject, and to examine it with more care. And the reſult of an examination of only a *part* of the public loans, will be found to be, "that a capital of more than "TWENTY MILLIONS has been a needleſs addition "to the public debt, for which no money, or any "ſort of equivalent has been received; and which "might have been avoided, together with a great "expence of intereſt, by only forming differently "the ſchemes of the public loans."

The intention of the firſt ſection of the THIRD PART is to give, in as ſhort a compaſs as poſſible, a view of the progreſs of our *foreign trade*, and its effect on the nation, from the beginning of this century; and, particularly, to point out an unfavourable change which ſeems to have taken place ſince 1764.

In the ſecond ſection of this part, an explanation and analyſis are given of all the different articles

articles of the national debt, which will probably inform every perſon of moſt that he can wiſh to know concerning them.—I have added a general account of the debts and reſources of FRANCE. This is a ſubject at preſent particularly intereſting to this country; and, having been informed of ſome important facts relating to it, I have thought proper to lay them before the public, with ſuch reflexions as have offered themſelves in mentioning them.

The laſt ſection contains ſuch of the calculations in the APPENDIX to the *Obſervations on Civil Liberty* as were neceſſary to be reprinted, in order to introduce the remarks I have added on ſome particulars in the ſtate of the *public income and expenditure*, publiſhed not long ago by the *Earl of Stair*. I have alſo meant to accommodate the purchaſers of the different editions of the *Obſervations on Civil Liberty*, who will be enabled, by this ſection, to poſſeſs themſelves of all the material alterations and improvements which were made in that pamphlet after its firſt publication.—The accounts, in the latter part of this tract, are ſo various and extenſive, that it is ſcarcely poſſible there ſhould not be ſome incorrectneſſes in them. But the pains I have taken, and the means of information which I have poſſeſſed have been ſuch, that I cannot ſuſpect that I have fallen into any miſtakes of conſequence. Should, however, any ſuch have eſcaped me, it will be kind in any

3 perſon

perſon to point them out with candour; and to aſſiſt in making thoſe accounts ſo correct and perfect, as that they may ſerve for a baſis to all future accounts of the ſame kind.

The following note in Mr. *Hume*'s Hiſtory of *England* was written by him a little before his death, and left with other additions to be inſerted in the new edition of that hiſtory juſt publiſhed. It contains, therefore, a kind of dying warning from Mr. *Hume* to this kingdom; and I have thought proper to tranſcribe it, and to inſert it in this place, as a confirmation of ſimilar ſentiments frequently expreſſed in theſe tracts.

"The ſupplies granted Queen *Elizabeth*, du-
" ring a reign of FORTY-FIVE YEARS, amounted
" to three millions. The miniſter, in the war
" which begun in 1754, was, in ſome periods,
" allowed to laviſh a ſum equal to this in TWO
" MONTHS. The extreme frivolous object of
" the late war, and the great importance of hers,
" ſet this matter in ſtill a ſtronger light. Money
" too was in moſt particulars of the ſame value
" in both periods: ſhe paid eight-pence a day
" to every foot ſoldier;—but our LATE DELU-
" SIONS have much exceeded any thing known
" in hiſtory, not even excepting thoſe of the

" Cruſades.

" Crusades. For, I suppose, there is no mathe-
" matical, still less an arithmetical demonstration,
" that the road to the holy land was not the road
" to Paradise; as there is, that the endless in-
" crease of national debt is the direct road to
" national ruin. But having now completely
" reached that goal, it is needless at present to
" reflect on the past. It will be found in the
" present year (1776) that all the revenues of
" this island, north of the *Trent*, and west of
" *Reading*, are mortgaged or anticipated for
" ever. Could the small remainder be in a
" worse condition, were these provinces seized
" by *Austria* and *Prussia?* There is only this
" difference, that some event might happen in
" *Europe*, which would oblige those great mo-
" narchs to disgorge their acquisitions. But no
" imagination can figure a situation which will
" induce our creditors to relinquish their claims,
" or the public to seize their revenues.——So
" egregious, indeed, has been our folly, that
" we have even lost all title to compassion, un-
" der the numberless calamities that are waiting
" us."——Mr. *Hume*'s History, vol. 5th, page
475.

# PART I.

## SUPPLEMENTAL OBSERVATIONS

ON THE

## NATURE and VALUE of CIVIL LIBERTY and FREE GOVERNMENT.

---

### SECT. I.

*Of the Nature of Civil Liberty, and the Essentials of a Free Government.*

WITH respect to Liberty in general there are two questions to be considered: First, What it is?—And Secondly, How far it is of value?

There is no difficulty in answering the first of these questions.—To be FREE, is "to be able to "act or to forbear acting, as we think best;" or "to be masters of our own resolutions and con- "duct."——It may be pretended, that it is not desirable to be thus free; but, without doubt, this it is to be *free*; and this is what all mean when they ſay of themſelves or others that they are *free*.

I have obſerved, that all the different kinds of Liberty run up into the general idea of ſelf-government (*a*).——The Liberty of men as *agents* is that power of ſelf-determination which all agents, as ſuch, poſſeſs.—Their Liberty as *moral* agents is their power of ſelf-government in their *moral* conduct.—Their Liberty as *religious* agents is their power of ſelf-government in *religion*.——And their Liberty, as members of communities aſſociated for the purpoſes of civil government, is their power of ſelf-government in all their civil concerns. It is Liberty, in the laſt of theſe views of it, that is the ſubject of my preſent enquiry; and it may, in other words, be defined to be "the power of a ſtate to govern itſelf by its own "will."——In order, therefore, to determine whether a ſtate is free, no more is neceſſary than to determine whether there is any will, different from its own, to which it is ſubject.

When we ſpeak of a ſtate, we mean the *whole* ſtate, and not any *part* of it; and the will of the ſtate, therefore, is the will of the whole.——There are two ways in which this will may be expreſſed. Firſt, by the ſuffrages of all the members given in perſon. Or ſecondly, by the ſuf-

(*a*) See Obſervations on Civil Liberty, Part I. ſect. 1.

frages of a body of Repreſentatives, in appointing whom all the members have voices.——A ſtate governed by its own will in the firſt of theſe ways enjoys the moſt complete and perfect Liberty; but ſuch a government being impracticable, except in very ſmall ſtates, it is neceſſary that civil communities in general ſhould ſatisfy themſelves with that degree of Liberty which can be obtained in the laſt of theſe ways; and Liberty ſo obtained may be ſufficiently ample, and at the ſame time is capable of being extended to the largeſt ſtates (*a*).

But here, before I proceed, I muſt deſire, that an obſervation may be attended to, which appears to me of conſiderable conſequence.——A diſtinction ſhould be made between the *Liberty* of a ſtate, and its not ſuffering oppreſſion; or between a free government, and a government under which freedom is enjoyed. Under the moſt deſpotic government liberty may happen to be enjoyed. But being derived from a will over which the ſtate has no controul, and not from its own will; or from an accidental mildneſs in the *adminiſtration*, and not from a *conſtitution* of government; it is nothing but an indulgence of a precarious nature, and of little importance.——Individuals in pri-

(*a*) See Obſervations, Part I. ſect. 2.

vate life, while held under the power of masters, cannot be denominated free, however equitably and kindly they may be treated. This is strictly true of *communities* as well as of *individuals*.—— Civil Liberty (it should be remembered) must be enjoyed as a right derived from the Author of nature only, or it cannot be the blessing which merits this name. If there is any human power which is considered as *giving* it, on which it depends, and which can invade or recall it at pleasure, it changes its nature, and becomes a species of slavery.

But to return——The force superseding self-government in a state, or the power destroying its Liberty, is of two kinds. It may be either a power *without* itself, or a power *within* itself. The former constitutes what may be properly called *external*, and the latter *internal* slavery.— Were there any distant state which had acquired a sovereignty over this country, and exercised the power of making its laws and disposing its property, we should be in the first kind of slavery; and, if not totally depraved by a habit of subjection to such a power, we should think ourselves in a miserable condition; and an advocate for such a power would be considered as insulting us, who should attempt to reconcile us to it by telling us, that we were *one* community with that distant

state,

ſtate, though deſtitute of a ſingle voice in its legiſlature; and, on this ground, ſhould maintain, that all reſiſtance to it was no leſs criminal than any reſiſtance *within* a ſtate to the authority of that ſtate.—In ſhort, every ſtate, not incorporated with another by an equal repreſentation, and yet ſubject to its dominion, is enſlaved in this ſenſe.—Such was the ſlavery of the provinces ſubject to antient *Rome*; and ſuch is the ſlavery of every community, as far as any other community is maſter of it; or as far as, in reſpect of taxation and internal legiſlation, it is not independent of every other community. Nor does it make any difference to ſuch a community, that it enjoys within itſelf a free conſtitution of government, if that conſtitution is itſelf liable to be altered, ſuſpended or over-ruled at the diſcretion of the ſtate which poſſeſſes the ſovereignty over it.

But the ſlavery moſt prevalent in the world has been internal ſlavery.——In order better to explain this, it is proper to obſerve, that all civil government being either the government of a *whole* by *itſelf*, or of a *whole* by a *power extraneous* to it, or of a *whole* by a *part*; the firſt *alone* is LIBERTY, and the two laſt are TYRANNY, producing the two ſorts of ſlavery which I have mentioned. Internal ſlavery, therefore, takes place wherever a whole community is governed by a *part*; and this, perhaps, is the moſt conciſe and comprehensive account that can be given of it.— The part that governs may be either a *single* man, as in *absolute Monarchies*; or, a body of grandees, as in *Aristocracies*. In both these cases the powers of government are commonly held for life without delegation, and descend from father to son; and the people governed are in the same situation with cattle upon an estate, which descends by inheritance from one owner to another.—— But farther. A community may be governed by a body of delegates, and yet be enslaved.—— Though government by representation alone is free, unless when carried on by the personal suffrages of all the members of a state, yet *all* such government is by no means free. In order to render it so, the following requisites are necessary.

First, The representation must be *complete*. No state, a *part* of which only is represented in the Legislature that governs it, is *self*-governed. Had *Scotland* no representatives in the Parliament of *Britain*, it would not be free; nor would it be proper to call *Britain* free, though *England*, its other part, were adequately represented. The like is true, in general, of every country subject to a Legislature in which *some* of its parts, or some classes of men in it, are represented, and others not.

Secondly, The representatives of a free state must be *freely* chosen. If this is not the case, they

are

are not at all repreſentatives; and government by them degenerates into government by a junto of men in the community, who happen to have power or wealth enough to command or purchaſe their offices.

Thirdly, After being *freely* choſen, they muſt be themſelves *free*. If there is any higher will which directs their reſolutions, and on which they are dependent, they become the inſtruments of that will; and it is that will alone that in reality governs the ſtate.

Fourthly, They muſt be choſen for ſhort terms; and, in all their acts, be accountable to their conſtituents. Without this a people will have no controul over their repreſentatives; and, in chuſing them, they will give up entirely their Liberty; and only enjoy the poor privilege of naming, at certain intervals, a ſet of men whom they are to *ſerve*, and who are to diſpoſe, at their diſcretion, of their property and lives.

The cauſes of internal ſlavery now mentioned prevail, ſome of them more and others leſs, in different communities. With reſpect, in particular, to a government by repreſentation; it is evident, that it deviates more or leſs from Liberty, in proportion as the repreſentation is more or leſs imperfect. And, if imperfect in every one of the inſtances I have recited; that is, if inadequate and partial; ſubject to no controul from the

 people;

people; corruptly chosen for long terms; and, after being chosen, venal and dependent;—in these circumstances, a representation becomes an imposition and a nusance; and government by it is as inconsistent with true Liberty as the most arbitrary and despotic government.

I have been so much misunderstood (*a*) on this subject, that it is necessary I should particularly observe here, that my intention in this account has been merely to shew what is requisite to constitute a state or a government free, and not at all to define the best form of government. These are two very different points. The first is attended with few difficulties. A free state is a state self-governed in the manner I have described. But it may be free, and yet not enjoy the best constitution of government. Liberty, though the most essential requisite in government, is not the only one. Wisdom, union, dispatch, secresy, and vigour are likewise requisite; and that is the best form of government which best unites all these qualities; or which, to an equal and perfect Liberty, adds the greatest

(*a*) The greatest part of Mr. *Goodricke*'s remarks are founded on this misunderstanding. He is so candid that I know he did not mean to misrepresent me; and yet I cannot help thinking it hard, after repeated declarations of my preference of such a constitution as our own, to be considered as an advocate for a pure Democracy. See *Observations on Dr. Price's Theory and Principles of Civil Liberty and Government*, by Mr. Goodricke.

wisdom

wiſdom in deliberating and reſolving, and the greateſt union, force and expedition in executing (*a*).

In ſhort, my whole meaning is, that the will of the Community alone ought to govern; but that there are different methods of obtaining and executing this will; of which thoſe are the beſt which collect into it moſt of the knowledge and experience of the community, and at the ſame time carry it into execution with moſt diſpatch and vigour.

It has been the employment of the wiſeſt men in all ages to contrive plans for this purpoſe; and the happineſs of ſociety depends ſo much on civil government, that it is not poſſible the human underſtanding ſhould be better employed.

I have ſaid in the Obſervations on Civil Liberty, that "in a free ſtate every man is his own legiſlator."—I have been happy in ſince finding the (*b*) ſame aſſertion in *Monteſquieu*, and alſo in

(*a*) One of the beſt plans of this kind has been with much ability, deſcribed by Mr. De Lolme, in his account of the Conſtitution of England.

(*b*) "As in a free ſtate, every man who is ſuppoſed a free "agent, ought to be his own governor; ſo the legiſlative "power ſhould reſide in the whole body of the people." *Spirit of Laws*, Book XI. chap. vi. See likewiſe Juſtice Blackſtone's Commentaries on the Laws of England, page 158. 1ſt Vol. oct. edition.——*Demoſthenes* ſpeaking in his firſt Philippic, ſect. 3d. of certain free ſtates, calls them *their own legiſlators*, αυτονομυμένα καὶ ελευθερα.

Mr.

Mr. Juſtice *Blackſtone*'s Commentaries. It expreſſes the fundamental principle of our conſtitution; and the meaning of it is plainly, that every independent agent in a free ſtate ought to have a ſhare in the government of it, either by himſelf *perſonally*, or by a body of repreſentatives, in chuſing whom he has a free vote, and therefore all the concern and weight which are poſſible, and conſiſtent with the equal rights of every other member of the ſtate.——But though the meaning of this aſſertion is ſo obvious, and the truth of it undeniable, it has been much exclaimed againſt, and occaſioned no ſmall part of the oppoſition which has been made to the principles advanced in the *Obſervations on Civil Liberty.*——One even of the moſt candid, as well as the ableſt of my opponents, (whoſe difference of opinion from me I ſincerely lament) has intimated, that it implies, that, in a free ſtate, *(a) thieves and pick-pockets have a right to make laws for themſelves.*——The public will not, I hope, wonder that I chuſe to take little notice of ſuch objections.

It has been ſaid, that the liberty for which I have pleaded, is " a right or power in every one

(*a*) See *Remarks*, printed for Mr. Cadell, *on a pamphlet publiſhed by Dr. Price. In a letter from a gentleman in the country to a member of parliament*, page 10.

" to

" to act as he likes without any restraint."——However unfairly this representation has been given of my account of liberty, I am ready to adopt it, provided it is understood with a few limitations.——MORAL LIBERTY, in particular, cannot be better defined than by calling it " a " power in every one to do as he likes." My opponents in general seem to be greatly puzzled with this; and I am afraid it will signify little to attempt explaining it to them by saying, that every man's will, if perfectly free from restraint, would carry him invariably to rectitude and virtue; and that no one who acts wickedly acts as he *likes*, but is conscious of a tyranny within him overpowering his judgment, and carrying him into a conduct, for which he condemns and hates himself. *The things that he would he does not*; *(a) and the things that he would not, those he does.* He is, therefore, a slave in the properest sense.

RELIGIOUS LIBERTY, likewise, is a power of acting as we *like* in religion; or of professing and practising that mode of religious worship which we think most acceptable to the Deity.——But here the limitation to which I have referred must be attended to. ALL have the same unalienable right to this Liberty; and consequently, no one has a right to such a use of it as shall take it from others.

(*a*) Rom. vii.

Within

Within this limit, or as far as he does not encroach on the equal liberty of others, every one has a right to do as he pleaſes in religion.—— That the right to religious Liberty goes as far as this every one muſt allow, who is not a friend to perſecution; and that it cannot go farther, is ſelf-evident; for if it did, there would be a contradiction in the natures of things; and it would be true, that every one had a right to enjoy what every one had a right to deſtroy.——If, therefore, the religious faith of any perſon leads him to hurt another becauſe he profeſſes a different faith; or if it carries him, in any inſtances, to intolerance, Liberty itſelf requires he ſhould be reſtrained, and that, in ſuch inſtances, he ſhould loſe his liberty.

All this is equally applicable to the Liberty of man in his *civil* capacity; and it is a maxim true univerſally, "that as far as any one does not "moleſt *others*, others ought not to moleſt *him*." ——All have a right to the free and undiſturbed poſſeſſion of their good names, properties and lives; and it is the right all have to this that gives the right to eſtabliſh civil government, which is or ought to be nothing but an inſtitution (by laws and proviſions made with *common* conſent) for guarding this right againſt invaſion; for giving to every one, in *temporals* and *ſpirituals*, the power of commanding his own conduct; or, of acting

acting as he pleases, and going where he will, provided he does not run foul of others.——Just government, therefore, does not *infringe* liberty, but *establish* it.——It does not *take away* the rights of mankind, but *protect* and *confirm* them.——I will add, that it does not even create any new subordinations of particular men to one another, but only gives security in those several stations, whether of authority and pre-eminence, or of subordination and dependence, which nature has established, and which must have arisen among mankind whether civil government had been instituted or not. But this goes beyond my purpose in this place, and more will be said of it presently.

To sum up the whole—Our ideas of Civil Liberty will be rendered more distinct by considering it under the three following views:—The Liberty of the *citizen*—The liberty of the *government*—And the liberty of the *community*.——A *citizen* is free when the power of commanding his own conduct and the quiet possession of his life, person, property and good name are *secured* to him by being his own legislator in the sense explained in page 10 (*a*).——A *government* is free when constituted

(*a*) Dr. PRIESTLY, in his Essay on the *first principles of Government*, makes a distinction between *civil* Liberty and *political* Liberty; the former of which he defines to be "the "power constituted in such a manner as to give this *security*.——And the freedom of a community or nation is the same among nations, that the freedom of a citizen is among his fellow-citizens.——It is not, therefore, as observed in page 3, the mere possession of Liberty that denominates a citizen or a community free; but that *security* for the possession of it which arises from such a free government as I have described; and which takes place, when there exists no power that can take it away.——It is in the same sense that the mere performance of virtuous actions is not what denominates an agent virtuous; but the temper and habits from whence they spring; or that *inward constitution*, and right balance of the affections, which *secure* the practice of virtue, produce stability of conduct, and constitute a *character*.

I cannot imagine how it can be disputed whether this is a just account of the nature of Liberty. It has been already given more briefly in the Observations on Civil Liberty; and it is with reluctance I have repeated so much of what has

" power which the members of a state ought to enjoy over " their actions;" and the latter, " their power of arriving at " public offices, or, at least, of having votes in the nomina- " tion of those who fill them."—This distinction forms a very proper subdivision of *the liberty of the citizen* here mentioned; and it may be accommodated to all I have said on this subject, by only giving some less general name to that which Dr. Priestly calls *civil* Liberty.

has been there ſaid. But the wrong apprehenſions which have been entertained of my ſentiments have rendered this neceſſary. And, for the ſame reaſon, I am obliged to go on to the ſubject of the next ſection.

## SECT. II.

### *Of the* VALUE *of Liberty, and the* EXCELLENCE *of a Free Government.*

HAVING ſhewn in the preceding ſection "what Liberty is;" the next queſtion to be conſidered is, "how far it is valuable."

Nothing need be ſaid to ſhew the value of the three kinds of liberty which I have diſtinguiſhed under the names of *Phyſical*, *Moral*, and *Religious* Liberty. They are, without doubt, the foundation of all the happineſs and dignity of men, as reaſonable and moral agents, and the ſubjects of the Deity.—It is, in like manner, true of *Civil* Liberty, that it is the foundation of the whole happineſs and dignity of men as members of civil ſociety, and the ſubjects of civil government.

Firſt. It is Civil Liberty, or ſuch free government as I have deſcribed, that alone can give juſt ſecurity againſt oppreſſion. One government is better than another in proportion as it gives more of this ſecurity. It is, on this account, that the ſupreme government of the Deity is perfect. There

There is not a poſſibility of being oppreſſed or aggrieved by it. Subjection to it is the ſame with complete freedom.

Were there any men on whoſe ſuperior wiſdom and goodneſs we might abſolutely depend, they could not poſſeſs too much power; and the love of liberty itſelf would engage us to fly to them, and to put ourſelves under their direction. But ſuch are the principles that govern human nature; ſuch the weakneſs and folly of men; ſuch their love of domination, ſelfiſhneſs, and depravity; that none of them can be raiſed to an elevation above others without the utmoſt danger. The conſtant experience of the world has verified this; and proved, that nothing intoxicates the human mind ſo much as power, and that men, when they have got poſſeſſion of it, have ſeldom failed to employ it in grinding their fellow-men, and gratifying the vileſt paſſions.—In the eſtabliſhment, therefore, of civil government, it would be prepoſterous to rely on the diſcretion of any men. If a people would obtain ſecurity againſt oppreſſion, they muſt ſeek it in *themſelves*, and never part with the powers of government out *of their own* hands. It is there only they can be ſafe.—A people will never oppreſs themſelves, or invade their own rights. But if they truſt the arbitrary will of any body or ſucceſſion of men, they truſt

ENEMIES,

ENEMIES, and it may be depended on that the worſt evils will follow.

It follows from hence, that a free government is the only government which is conſiſtent with the ends of government.——Men combine into communities and inſtitute government to obtain the peaceable enjoyment of their rights, and to defend themſelves againſt injuſtice and violence: And when they endeavour to ſecure theſe ends by ſuch a free government as I have deſcribed, improved by ſuch arrangements as may have a tendency to preſerve it from confuſion, and to concentrate in it as much as poſſible of the wiſdom and force of the community; In this caſe, it is a moſt rational and important inſtitution.——But when the contrary is done; and the benefits of government are ſought by eſtabliſhing a government of *men*, and not of *laws* made with common conſent; it becomes a moſt abſurd inſtitution.—It is ſeeking a remedy for oppreſſion in *one* quarter, by eſtabliſhing it in *another*; and avoiding the outrages of *little* plunderers, by conſtituting a ſet of *great* plunderers.——It is, in ſhort, the folly of *giving up* liberty in order to *maintain* Liberty; and, in the very act of endeavouring to ſecure the moſt valuable rights, to arm a body of enemies with power to deſtroy them.

I can eaſily believe, that mankind, in the firſt and rude ſtate of ſociety, might act thus irrationally. Abſolute governments, being the ſimpleſt forms of government, might be the firſt that were eſtabliſhed. A people having experienced the happy effects of the wiſdom or the valour of particular men, might be led to truſt them with unlimited power as their rulers and legiſlators. But they would ſoon find reaſon to repent: And the time, I hope, may come, when mankind in general, taught by long and dear experience, and *weary* of the abuſes of power under *ſlaviſh* governments, will learn to deteſt them, and never to give up that SELF-GOVERNMENT, which, whether we conſider men in their private or collective capacities, is the firſt of all the bleſſings they can poſſeſs.

Again. Free governments are the only governments which give ſcope to the exertion of the powers of men, and are favourable to their improvement.——The members of free ſtates, knowing their rights to be ſecure, and that they ſhall enjoy without moleſtation the fruits of every acquiſition they can make, are encouraged and incited to induſtry. Being at liberty to puſh their reſearches as far as they can into all ſubjects, and to guide themſelves by their own judgments in all their religious and civil concerns, while they

allow

allow others to do the ſame; error and ſuperſtition muſt loſe ground. Conſcious of being their own governors, bound to obey no laws except ſuch as they have given their conſent to, and ſubject to no controul from the arbitrary will of any of their fellow-citizens; they poſſeſs an elevation and force of mind which muſt make them great and happy.——How different is the ſituation of the vaſſals of deſpotic power?——Like cattle inured to the yoke, they are driven on in one track, afraid of ſpeaking or even thinking on the moſt intereſting points; looking up continually to a poor creature who is their maſter; their powers fettered; and ſome of the nobleſt ſprings of action in human nature rendered uſeleſs within them. There is nothing indeed more humiliating than that debaſement of mankind which takes place in ſuch ſituations.

It has been obſerved of free governments, that they are often torn by violent conteſts, which render them dreadful ſcenes of diſtreſs and anarchy. But it ought to be conſidered, that this has not been owing to the *nature* of ſuch governments; but to their having been ill-modelled, and wanted thoſe arrangements and ſupplemental checks which are neceſſary to conſtitute a wiſe form of government.——There is no reaſon to doubt, but that free governments may be ſo contrived, as to exclude the greateſt part of the ſtruggles and tumults which have arisen in free ſtates; and, as far as they cannot be excluded, they will do more good than harm. They will occaſion the diſplay of powers, and produce exertions which can never be ſeen in the *ſtill* ſcenes of life. They are the active efforts of health and vigour; and always tend to preſerve and purify. Whereas, on the contrary, the *quiet* which prevails under ſlaviſh governments, and which may ſeem to be a recommendation of them, proceeds from an ignominious tameneſs, and ſtagnation of the human faculties. It is the ſame with the *ſtillneſs* of midnight, or the *ſilence* and torpor of death.

Further. Free governments are the only governments which are conſiſtent with the natural equality of mankind. This is a principle which, in my opinion, has been aſſumed, with the greateſt reaſon, by ſome of the beſt writers on government. But the meaning of it is not, that all the ſubordinations in human life owe their exiſtence to the inſtitution of civil government. The ſuperiorities and diſtinctions ariſing from the relation of parents to their children; from the differences in the perſonal qualities and abilities of men; and from ſervitudes founded on voluntary compacts, muſt have exiſted in a ſtate of nature, and would now take place were all men ſo virtuous as to leave no occaſion for civil government.——The maxim,

 therefore,

therefore, "that all men are naturally equal," refers to their ſtate when grown up to maturity, and become independent agents, capable of acquiring property, and of directing their own conduct. And the ſenſe of it is, that no one of them is conſtituted by the author of nature the vaſſal or ſubject of another, or has any right to give law to him, or, without his conſent, to take away any part of his property, or to abridge him of his liberty.——In a ſtate of nature, one man may have received benefits from another; and this would lay the perſon obliged under an obligation of gratitude, but it would not make his *benefactor* his *maſter*; or give him a right to judge for him what grateful returns he ought to make, and to extort theſe from him.——In a ſtate of nature, alſo, one man may poſſeſs more ſtrength, or more knowledge, or more property than another; and this would give him weight and influence; but it would not give him any degree of authority. There would not be one human being who would be bound to *obey* him.——A perſon likewiſe, in a ſtate of nature, might let out his labour, or give up to another, on certain ſtipulated terms, the direction of his conduct; and this would ſo far bring him into the ſtation of a *ſervant*; but being done by himſelf, and on ſuch terms only as he chuſes to conſent to, it is an *inſtance* of his liberty;

 and

and he will always have it in his power to quit the service he has chosen, or to enter into another.

This equality or independence of men is one of their essential rights. (*a*) It is the same with that equality or independence which now actually takes place among the different states or kingdoms of the world with respect to one another. Mankind came with this right from the hands of their Maker.——But all governments, which are not free, are totally inconsistent with it. They imply, that there are some of mankind who are born with an inherent right of dominion; and that the rest are born under an obligation to subjection; and that civil government, instead of being founded on any compact, is nothing but the exercise of this right. Some such sentiments seem to be now reviving in this country, and even to be growing fashionable. Most of the writers against the *Observations on Civil Liberty* argue on the supposition of a right in the *few* to govern the *many* (*b*), independently

(*a*) See on this Subject an excellent Sermon entitled, *The Principles of the* REVOLUTION *vindicated.* By Dr. Watson, Regius Professor of Divinity, at Cambridge.

(*b*) Some who maintain this doctrine concerning government, overthrow their own system by acknowledging the right of resistance in certain cases. For, if there is such a right, the people must be judges *when* it ought to be exercised; a right to resist only when civil governors *think* there is reason, being a gross absurdity and nullity.——The right of resistance,

pendently of their own choice. Some of these writers have gone so far as to assert, in plain language, that civil governors derive their power immediately from the Deity; and are *his* agents or representatives, accountable to him only. And one courtly writer, in particular, has honoured them with the appellation of OUR POLITICAL GODS. ——Probably, this is the idea of civil governors entertained by the author of the *Remarks on the Acts of the Thirteenth Parliament of Great Britain*: for it is not easy to imagine on what other ground he can assert, that *property* and *civil rights* are derived from civil governors, and their *gifts* to mankind (*a*).

sistance, therefore, cannot mean less than a right in the people, whenever they think it necessary, to change their governors, and to limit their power. And from the moment this is done, government becomes the work of the people, and governors become their trustees or agents.

(*a*) It has been commonly reckoned, that it is the end of civil government and civil laws to protect the *property* and *rights* of men; but, according to this writer, civil government and civil laws create *property* and *rights*. It follows therefore, that, antecedently to civil laws, men could have no *property* or *rights*; and that civil governors, being the makers of civil laws, it is a contradiction to suppose, that mankind can have any property or rights which are valid against the claims of their governors. See Three Letters to Dr. *Price*, p. 21, &c. And Remarks on the principal Acts of the 13th Parliament of Great-Britain, p. 58, &c. and p. 191.

If these sentiments are just, civil governors are indeed an awful order of beings; and it becomes us to enquire with anxiety who they are, and how we may distinguish them from the rest of mankind.——Shall we take for such all, whether *men* or *women*, whom we find in actual possession of civil power, whatever may be their characters; or however they may have acquired their power?—This is too extravagant to be asserted. It would legalize the *American* Congress.——There must then be some *pretenders* among civil governors; and it is necessary we should know how to discover them. It is incredible, that the Deity should not have made this easy to us, by some particular marks and distinctions, which point out to our notice his *real* vicegerents; just as he has pointed out man, by his figure and superior powers, to be the governor of the lower creatures.——In particular; these persons must be possessed of wisdom and goodness superior to those of the rest of mankind (*a*); for, without this, a grant of the powers they are supposed to possess would be nothing but a grant of power to injure and oppress, without remedy and without bounds. But this is a test by which they cannot be tryed. It would leave but few of them in possession of the places they

(*a*) This has been done in a lower instance. Parents have been furnished with a particular affection for their children, in order to prevent any abuse of their power over them.

hold

hold and the rights they claim. It is not in the high ranks of life, or among the great and mighty, that we are to ſeek wiſdom and goodneſs. Theſe love the ſhade, and fly from obſervation. They are to be found chiefly in the middle ranks of life, and among the contemplative and philoſophical, who decline public employments, and look down with pity on the ſcramble for power among mankind, and the reſtleſſneſs and miſery of ambition.——It is proper to add, that it has never been hitherto underſtood that any ſuperiority in intellectual and moral qualifications lays the foundation of a claim to *dominion.*

It is not then, by their ſuperior endowments, that the Deity intended to point out to us the *few* whom he has deſtined to command the *many.* —But in what other manner could they be diſtinguiſhed?——Muſt we embrace Sir *Robert Filmer*'s *Patriarchal* ſcheme? One would have thought, that Mr. *Locke* has ſaid more than enough to expoſe this ſtupid ſcheme. One of my opponents, however, has adopted it; and the neceſſary inference from it is that, as there is but now one lineal deſcendent from Adam's eldeſt ſon, there can be but one rightful monarch of the world.— But I will not abuſe my reader's patience by ſaying more on this ſubject. I am ſorry that in this country there ſhould be any occaſion for taking notice of principles ſo abſurd, and at the

ſame

ſame time ſo pernicious (*a*). I ſay, PERNICIOUS; for they imply, that King *James* the Second was depoſed at the Revolution unlawfully and impiouſly; that the preſent King is an uſurper; and that the preſent government, being derived from rebellion and treaſon, has no right to our allegiance.

Without all doubt, it is the choice of the people that makes civil governors.—The people are the ſpring of all civil power, and they have a right to modify it as they pleaſe.

(*a*) "In ages of darkneſs, and too often alſo in thoſe of "greater knowledge, by the perfidious arts of deſigning "princes, and by the baſe ſervility of too many eccleſiaſtics, "who managed the ſuperſtition of the populace, by the violent reſtraints put upon divulging any juſter ſentiments "about the rights of mankind, the natural notions of polity "were eraſed out of the minds of men; and they were filled "with ſome confuſed imaginations of ſomething adorable in "monarchs, ſome repreſentation of the Divinity; and that "even in the worſt of them; and of ſome certain Divine "claims in certain families.——No wonder this! that millions thus look upon themſelves as a piece of property to "one of their fellows as ſilly and worthleſs as the meaneſt "of them; when the like arts of ſuperſtition have made millions, nay the very artificers themſelves, fall down before "the block or ſtone they had ſet up; or adore monkies, cats, "and crocodiles, as the ſovereign diſpoſers of their fortunes." See Dr. HUTCHESON's Syſtem of Moral Philoſophy. Vol. ii. p. 280.

Mankind

Mankind being naturally equal according to the foregoing explanation, civil government, *in its genuine intention*, is an inſtitution for maintaining that equality, by defending it againſt the encroachments of violence and tyranny. All the ſubordinations and diſtinctions in ſociety previous to its eſtabliſhment, it leaves as it found them, only confirming and protecting them. It makes no man *maſter* of another. It elevates no perſon above his fellow citizens. On the contrary, it levels all by fixing all in a ſtate of ſubjection to one common authority.——The authority of the laws.—The will of the community.——TAXES are *given*; not *impoſed*. LAWS are regulations of common choice; not injunctions of ſuperior power.——The authority of magiſtrates is the authority of the State; and their ſalaries are wages paid by the State for executing its will and doing its buſineſs. *They* do not govern the *State*. It is the *State* governs *them*; and had they juſt ideas of their own ſtations, they would conſider themſelves as no leſs properly *ſervants* of the Public, than the labourers who work upon its roads, or the ſoldiers who fight its battles.——A KING, in particular, is only the firſt executive officer; the creature of the law; and as much accountable and ſubject to the law as the meaneſt peaſant (*a*). And were Kings properly attentive

(*a*) " Let not, therefore, theſe *pretended maſters* of the " people be allowed even to do good againſt the general " conſent.

to their duty, and as anxious as they ſhould be about performing it, they could not eaſily avoid ſinking under the weight of their charge.

The account now given is, I am fully perſuaded, in every particular, a true account of what civil government *ought* to be; and it teaches us plainly the great importance and excellence of FREE Government.——It is this only that anſwers the deſcription I have given of government; that ſecures againſt oppreſſion; that gives room for that elevation of ſpirit and that exertion of the human powers which is neceſſary to human improvement; or that is conſiſtent with the ends of government, with the rights of mankind, and their natural equality and independence. *Free* Government, therefore, only, is *juſt* and *legitimate* government.

It follows farther from the preceding account, that no people can lawfully ſurrender or cede their Liberty. This muſt appear to any one

" conſent.———Let it be conſidered, that the condition of " rulers is exactly the ſame as that of the Cacique, who being " aſked whether he had any ſlaves, anſwered; *Slaves? I* " *know but one ſlave in all my diſtrict, and that is myſelf.*" See the Philoſophical and Political Hiſtory of the Settlements and Trade of the *Europeans* in the EAST AND WEST INDIES. Tranſlated from the French of the Abbe *Raynal,* by Mr. *Juſtamond.* Vol. v. page 414.

who

who will consider, that when a people make such a cession, and the extensive powers of government are trusted to the discretion of any man or body of men, they part with the powers of life and death, and give themselves up a prey to oppression; that they make themselves the instruments of any injustice in which their rulers may chuse to employ them, by arming them against neighbouring states; and also, that they do this not only for *themselves*, but for their *posterity*.——I will add, that if such a cession has been made; or if through any causes, a people have lost their Liberty, they must have a right to emancipate themselves as soon as they can (*a*). In attempting this, indeed, they ought to consider the sufferings which may attend the struggle, and the evils which may arise from a defeat. But at the same time, it will be proper to consider, that the sufferings attending such a struggle must be temporary, whereas the evils to be avoided are permanent; and that Liberty is a blessing so inestimable, "that whenever there appears any pro-"bability of recovering it, a people should be "willing to run many hazards, and even not to

(*a*) See Obs. p. 25. "The rights of mankind are so sacred "that no prescription of tyranny or arbitrary power can have "authority enough to abolish them." Mr. *Hume*'s Essays, vol. iii. Essay on the Coalition of Parties.

"repine

" repine at the greateſt expence of blood or trea-
" ſure." (*a*)

I am very ſenſible, that civil government, as it actually exiſts in the world, by no means anſwers to the account I have given of it.——Inſtead of being an inſtitution for guarding the weak againſt the ſtrong, we find it an inſtitution which makes the ſtrong yet ſtronger, and gives them a ſyſtematical power of oppreſſing. Inſtead of promoting virtue and reſtraining vice, encouraging free enquiry, eſtabliſhing Liberty, and protecting alike all peaceable perſons in the enjoyment of their civil and religious rights; we ſee a ſavage deſpotiſm, under its name, laying waſte the earth, unreaſonably elevating ſome and depreſſing others, diſcouraging improvement, and trampling upon every human right. That force of ſtates, which ought to be applied only to their own defence, we ſee continually applied to the purpoſe of attack, and uſed to extend dominion by conquering neighbouring communities.——Civil governors conſider not themſelves as *ſervants* but as *maſters*. Their ſtations they think they hold in their own right. The people they reckon their property;

(*a*) " Mankind have been generally a great deal too tract-
" able; and hence ſo many wretched forms of power have
" always enſlaved nine tenths of the nations of the world,
" where they have the fulleſt right to make all efforts for a
" change." Dr. *Hutcheſon*'s Moral Philoſophy. Vol. ii. p. 280.

 and

and their poſſeſſions, a common *ſtock* from which they have a right to take what (*a*) they will, and of which no more belongs to any individual than they are pleaſed to *leave* him.

What a miſerable perverſion is this of a moſt important inſtitution? What a grievance is government ſo degenerated?——But this perverſion furniſhes no juſt argument againſt the truth of the account I have given. Similar degeneracies have prevailed in other inſtances of no leſs importance.

Reaſon in man, like the will of the community in the political world, was intended to give law to his whole conduct, and to be the ſupreme controuling power within him. The paſſions are ſubordinate powers, or an *executive force* under the direction of reaſon, kindly given to be, as it were, wind and tide to the veſſel of life in its courſe through this world to future honour and felicity.——How different from this is the *actual* ſtate of man?——Thoſe powers which were deſtined to *govern* are made to *ſerve*; and thoſe powers which were deſtined to *ſerve*, are allowed to *govern*. Paſſion guides human life; and moſt

(*a*) See Remarks on the Acts of the Thirteenth Parliament of *Great Britain*. P. 34, &c.——"Is not the ſame reaſoning "applicable to taxes paid for the ſupport of civil government? "Are not theſe too the property of the civil magiſtrate?" Ibid. p. 56.——If I underſtand this writer, his meaning is, not only that the taxes which the civil magiſtrate *has* impoſed are his property; but alſo, *any* which he ſhall pleaſe to impoſe.

men

men make no other uſe of their reaſon than to juſtify whatever their intereſt or their inclinations determine them to do.

RELIGION likewiſe (the perfection of REASON) is, in its true nature, the inſpirer of humanity and joy, and the ſpring of all that can be great and worthy in a character; and were we to ſee its genuine effects among mankind, we ſhould ſee nothing but peace and hope and juſtice and kindneſs, founded on that regard to God and to his will, which is the nobleſt principle of action.—But how different an aſpect does religion actually wear? What is it, too generally, in the practice of mankind, but a gloomy and cruel ſuperſtition, rendering them ſevere and ſour; teaching them to compound for wickedneſs by punctuality in religious forms; and prompting them to harraſs, perſecute and exterminate one another?

The ſame perverſion has taken place ſtill more remarkably in CHRISTIANITY; the perfection of RELIGION.—JESUS CHRIST has eſtabliſhed among Chriſtians an abſolute equality. He has declared, that they have but *one* maſter, even himſelf; and that they are all *brethren*; and, therefore, has commanded them not to be called *maſters*; and, inſtead of aſſuming authority over one another, to be ready to *waſh one another's feet* (*a*). The

(*a*) Matth. xxiii. 8—12.——John xiii. 14.

princes

princes of the Gentiles, he ſays, exerciſe lordſhip over them, and are flattered with (*a*) high titles; but he has ordained, that it ſhall not be ſo amongſt his followers; and that if any one of them would be *chief*, he muſt be the *ſervant* of all.——The clergy in his church are, by his appointment, no more than a body of men, choſen by the different ſocieties of Chriſtians, to conduct their worſhip, and to promote their ſpiritual improvement, without any other powers than thoſe of perſuaſion and inſtruction. It is expreſsly directed, that they ſhall not make themſelves Lordsof *God's heritage*, or exerciſe dominion over the faith of Chriſtians, but be *helpers of their joy* (*b*).——Who can, without aſtoniſhment, compare theſe appointments of Chriſtianity, with the events which have happened in the Chriſtian church?——That religion which thus inculcates humility and forbids all domination, and the end of which was to produce *peace on earth, and good-will among men*, has been turned into an occaſion of animoſities the moſt dreadful, and of ambition the moſt deſtructive. Notwithſtanding its mildneſs and benignity, and the tendency it has to extinguiſh in the human breaſt pride and malevolence; it has been the means of arming the ſpirits of men with unrelenting fury

(*a*) Luke xxii. 25, &c. (*b*) 1 Pet. v. 3.——2 Cor. i. 24.

 against

againſt one another. Inſtead of *peace*, it has brought a *ſword*; and its profeſſors, inſtead of waſhing one another's feet, have endeavoured to tread on one another's necks.——The miniſters, in particular, of Chriſtianity, became, ſoon after its eſtabliſhment, an independent body of ſpiritual rulers, nominating one another in perpetual ſucceſſion; claiming, by divine right, the higheſt powers; and forming a HIERARCHY, which by degrees produced a deſpotiſm more extravagant than any that ever before exiſted on this earth.

A conſiderate perſon muſt find difficulties in enquiring into the cauſes and reaſons of that depravity of human nature which has produced theſe evils, and rendered the beſt inſtitutions liable to be ſo corrupted. This enquiry is much the ſame with the enquiry into the origin of moral evil, which has in all ages puzzled human wiſdom. I have at preſent nothing to do with it. It is enough for my purpoſe in theſe obſervations, that the facts I have mentioned prove undeniably, that the ſtate of civil government in the world affords no reaſon for concluding, that I have not given a juſt account of its true nature and origin.

I have ſhewn at the beginning of this ſection, that it is free government alone that can preſerve from oppreſſion, give ſecurity to the rights of a people,

people, and anſwer the ends of government. It is neceſſary I ſhould here obſerve, that I would not be underſtood to mean, that there can be no *kind* or *degree* of ſecurity for the rights of a people, under any government which cannot be denominated free. Even under an abſolute Monarchy or an Ariſtrocracy, there may be laws and cuſtoms which, having gained ſacredneſs by time, may reſtrain oppreſſion, and afford ſome important ſecurities.——Under governments by repreſentation, there muſt be ſtill greater checks on oppreſſion, provided the repreſentation, though partial, is uncorrupt, and alſo frequently changed. In theſe circumſtances, there may be ſo much of a common intereſt between the body of repreſentatives and the people, and they may ſtand ſo much on one ground, that there will be no temptations to oppreſſion.——The taxes which the repreſentative body impoſe, they will be obliged themſelves to pay; and the laws they make, they will make with the proſpect of ſoon returning to the ſituation of thoſe for whom they make them, and of being themſelves governed by them.

It ſeems particularly worth notice here, that as far as there are any ſuch checks under any government, they are the conſequence of its partaking ſo far of Liberty, and that the ſecurity attending them is more or leſs in proportion as a government partakes more or leſs of Liberty.

If, under an abſolute government, fundamental laws and long eſtabliſhed inſtitutions give ſecurity in any inſtances, it is becauſe they are held ſo ſacred that a deſpot is afraid to violate them; or, in other words, becauſe a people, not being completely ſubdued, have ſtill ſome controul over the government.——The like is more evidently true under mixed governments of which a houſe of repreſentatives, fairly choſen and freely deliberating and reſolving, forms a part; and it is one of the higheſt recommendations of ſuch governments that, even when the repreſentation is moſt imperfect, they have a tendency to give more ſecurity than any other governments.——Under other governments, it is the fear of exciting inſurrections by contradicting eſtabliſhed maxims, that reſtrains oppreſſion. But, as, in general, a people will bear much, and are ſeldom driven to reſiſtance till grievances become intolerable, their rulers can venture far without danger; and therefore, under ſuch governments, are very imperfectly reſtrained. On the contrary; If there is an honeſt repreſentation, veſted with powers like to thoſe of our *Houſe of Commons*, the redreſs of grievances, as ſoon as they appear, will be always eaſily attainable, and the rulers of a ſtate will be under a neceſſity of regarding the firſt beginnings of diſcontent.—Such, and greater than can be eaſily deſcribed, are the advantages of of even an *imperfect representation* in a government. How great then must be the blessing of a COMPLETE REPRESENTATION?——(a) It is this only gives full security; and that can properly denominate a people free.

It deserves to be added here, that as there can be no private character so abandoned as to want *all* virtue; so there can be no government so slavish, as to exclude *every* restraint upon oppression.——The most slavish and, therefore, the worst governments are those under which there is nothing to set bounds to oppression, besides the *discretion* and *humanity* of those who govern.——Of this kind are the following governments.

First, All governments *purely* despotic. These may be either monarchical, or aristocratical. The latter are the worst, agreeably to a common observation, that it is better to have *one* master than *many*. The appetites of a single despot may be easily satiated; but this may be impossible where there is a multitude.

Secondly, All provincial governments.—The history of mankind proves these to be the worst of all governments; and that no oppression is equal

(a) He who wants to be convinced of the *practicability*, even in this country, of a complete representation, should read a pamphlet lately published, the title of which is, TAKE YOUR CHOICE.

to that which one people are capable of practiſing towards another. I have mentioned ſome of the reaſons of this in the *Obſervations on Civil Liberty*, Part I. ſect. 3. Bodies of men do not feel for one another as individuals do. The *odium* of a cruel action, when ſhared among many, is not regarded. The maſter of ſlaves working on a plantation, though he may keep them down to prevent their becoming ſtrong enough to emancipate themſelves, yet is led by *intereſt*, as well as *humanity*, to govern them with ſuch moderation, as to preſerve their uſe: But theſe cauſes will produce more of this good effect, when the ſlaves are under the eye of their proprietor, and form a part of his family, than when they are ſettled on a diſtant plantation, where he can know little of them, and is obliged to truſt them to the management of rapacious ſervants.

It is particularly obſervable here, that *free* governments, though happier in themſelves, are more oppreſſive to their provinces than deſpotic governments. Or, in other words, that the *ſubjects* of free (*a*) ſtates are worſe ſlaves than the ſubjects of ſtates not free. This is one of the obſervations which Mr. HUME repreſents as an univerſal axiom in politicks (*b*).——" Though,

(*a*) " A *free* ſubject of a free ſtate" is a contradiction in terms. See the Proclamation for a Faſt.

(*b*) Mr. Hume's Eſſays. Vol. i. Eſſay iv. p. 31.

" ſays

" ſays he, free governments have been commonly
" the moſt happy for thoſe who partake of their
" freedom, yet are they the moſt oppreſſive and
" ruinous to their provinces; and this obſervation
" may be fixed as an univerſal axiom in politics.
" What cruel tyrants were the Romans over the
" world during the time of their commonwealth?
" ——After the diſſolution of the commonwealth
" the Roman yoke became eaſier upon the pro-
" vinces, as *Tacitus* informs us; and it may be
" obſerved, that many of the worſt Emperors
" (*Domitian*, for inſtance) were very careful to
" prevent all oppreſſion of the provinces.——
" The oppreſſion and tyranny of the *Carthaginians*
" over their ſubject ſtates in *Africa* went ſo far,
as we learn from *Polybius* (Lib. 1. cap. 72.)
" that not content with exacting the *half* of all
" the produce of the ground, which of itſelf was a
" very high rent, they alſo loaded them with many
" other taxes.—If we paſs from antient to modern
" times we ſhall always find the obſervation to
" hold. The provinces of abſolute monarchies
" are always better treated than thoſe of free
" ſtates."

Thirdly, Among the worſt ſorts of govern-ments I reckon all governments by a corrupt re-preſentation.——There is no inſtance in which the trite obſervation is more true than in this, " that the beſt things when corrupted become the

 " worſt."

" worſt." A corrupt repreſentation is ſo far from being any *defence* againſt oppreſſion, that it is a *ſupport* to it. Long eſtabliſhed cuſtoms, in this caſe, afford no ſecurity, becauſe, under the ſanction of ſuch a repreſentation, they may be eaſily undermined or counteracted; nor is there any injury to a people which, with the help of ſuch an inſtrument, may not be committed with ſafety. It is not, however, every degree of corruption, that will deſtroy the uſe of a repreſentation, and turn it into an evil ſo dreadful. In order to this, corruption muſt paſs a certain limit. But *every degree* of it *tends* to this, ſaps the foundation of Liberty, and poiſons the fountain of Legiſlation. And when it gets to its laſt ſtage, and has proceeded its utmoſt length: When, in particular, the means by which candidates get themſelves choſen are ſuch as admit the *worſt*, but exclude the *beſt* men; a Houſe of Repreſentatives becomes little better than a ſink into which is collected all that is moſt worthleſs and vile in a kingdom.—— There cannot be a greater calamity than ſuch a government.——It is impoſſible there ſhould be a condition more wretched than that of a nation, once free, ſo degenerated.

# CONCLUSION.

IT is time to difmifs this fubject. But I cannot take a final leave of it, (and probably of all fubjects of this kind) without adding the following reflections on our own ftate in this kingdom.

It is well known, that MONTESQUIEU has paid the higheft compliment to this country, by defcribing its conftitution of government, in giving an account of a perfect government; and by drawing the character of its inhabitants, in giving an account of the manners and characters of a free people.——
" All (he fays) having, in free ftates, a fhare in
" government, and the laws not being made for
" fome more than others, they confider themfelves
" as *monarchs*, and are more properly *confederates*
" *than fellow-fubjects.*——No one citizen being
" fubject to another, each fets a greater value on
" his Liberty than on the glory of any of his fel-
" low-citizens.——Being independent, they are
" proud; for the pride of kings is founded on
" their independence.——They are in a conftant
" ferment, and believe themfelves in danger,
" even in thofe moments when they are moft
" fafe.——They reafon; but it is indifferent whe-
" ther they reafon well or ill. It is fufficient
" that

"that they *do* reaſon. Hence ſprings that Li-
"berty which is their ſecurity.——This ſtate,
"however, will loſe its Liberty. It will periſh,
"when the *Legiſlative* power ſhall become more
"corrupt than the *executive*." (*a*)

Such is the account which this great writer gave, many years ago, of the *Britiſh* conſtitution and people. We may learn from it, that we have nothing to fear from that diſpoſition to examine every public meaſure, to cenſure miniſters of ſtate, and to be reſtleſs and clamorous, which has hitherto characterized us.——On the contrary; we ſhall have every thing to fear, when this diſpoſition is loſt. As ſoon as a people grow ſecure, and ceaſe to be quick in taking alarms, they are undone. A free conſtitution of government cannot be preſerved without an earneſt and unremitting jealouſy. OUR Conſtitution, in particular, is ſo excellent, that it is the propereſt object of ſuch a jealouſy. For my own part, I admire ſo much the general frame and principles of it, that I could be almoſt ſatisfied with that repreſentation of the kingdom, which forms the moſt important part of it, had I no other objection to this repreſentation than its *inadequateneſs*. Did it conſiſt of a body of men, fairly elected for a ſhort term, by a number of independent perſons, of all orders in every part of the king-

(*a*) Spirit of Laws. Book xix. ch. 27.

dom,

dom, equal to the number of the preſent voters; and were it, after being elected, under no undue influence; it would be a ſecurity of ſuch importance, that I ſhould be leſs diſpoſed to complain of the injuſtice done, by its inadequateneſs, to the greateſt part of the kingdom by depriving them of one their natural and unalienable rights. To ſuch a body of repreſentatives we might commit, with confidence, the guardianſhip of our rights, knowing, that having one intereſt with the reſt of the ſtate, they could not violate them; or that if they ever did, a little time would bring the power of gaining redreſs without tumult or violence.——Happy the people ſo bleſſed.—— If wiſe, they will endeavour, by every poſſible method, to preſerve the purity of their repreſentation; and, ſhould it have degenerated, they will loſe no time in effecting a reformation of it.—— But if, unhappily, infection ſhould have pervaded the whole maſs of the ſtate, and there ſhould be no room to hope for any reformation, it will be ſtill ſome conſolation to reflect, that ſlavery, in all its rigour, will not immediately follow. Between the time in which the ſecurities of Liberty are undermined, and its final ſubverſion, there is commonly a flattering interval during which the *enjoyment* of Liberty may be continued, in conſequence of fundamental laws and rooted habits which cannot be at once exterminated. And this

interval

interval is longer or ſhorter, according as the progreſs of corruption is more or leſs rapid; and men in power more or leſs attentive to improve favourable opportunities. —— The government of this country, in particular, is ſo well balanced, and the inſtitutions of our common law are ſo admirable, and have taken ſuch deep root, that we can bear much decay before our liberties fall. ——Fall, however, they muſt, if our public affairs do not ſoon take a new turn. That very evil, which, according to the great writer I have quoted, is to produce our ruin, we ſee working every where and increaſing every day.——The following facts, among many others, ſhew too plainly whither we are tending and how far we are advanced.

Firſt. It ſeems to me, that a general indifference is gaining ground faſt among us.——This is the neceſſary effect of increaſing luxury and diſſipation; but there is another cauſe of it, which I think of with particular regret.—In conſequence of having been often duped by falſe patriots; and found, that the leaders of oppoſition, when they get into places, forget all their former declarations; the nation has been led to a conviction, that all patriotiſm is impoſture, and all oppoſition to the meaſures of government nothing but a ſtruggle for power and its emoluments. The honeſt and independent part of the nation entertain at preſent

moſt

moſt of this conviction; and, therefore, having few public men to whom they can look with confidence, they give up all zeal, and ſink into inactivity and deſpondence.

Secondly. At the Revolution, the Houſe of Commons acquired its juſt weight in the conſtitution; and, for ſome years afterwards, it was often giving much trouble to men in power. Of late, it is well known, that means have been tryed and a ſyſtem adopted for quieting it.——I will not ſay with what ſucceſs——But I muſt ſay, that the men whoſe policy this has been, have ſtruck at the very *heart* of public liberty, and are the worſt traitors this kingdom ever ſaw.——" If ever, " (ſays Judge *Blackſtone*) it ſhould happen, that " the independency of any one of the three " branches of our legiſlature ſhould be loſt; or " that it ſhould become ſubſervient to the views " of either of the other two, there would ſoon be " an end of our conſtitution. The legiſlature " would be changed from that which was originally ſet up by the general conſent and fundamental act of the ſociety; and ſuch a change, " however effected, is according to Mr. *Locke* " (who perhaps carries his theory too far) at " once an entire diſſolution of the bands of " government, and the people are thereby " reduced to a ſtate of anarchy, with liberty " to "to conſtitute to themſelves a new legiſlative "power." (a)

Thirdly. Soon after the REVOLUTION, bills for triennial parliaments paſſed both Houſes, in oppoſition to the court (b). At the ACCESSION, ſeptennial parliaments were eſtabliſhed. Since this laſt period, many attempts have been made, by the friends of the conſtitution, to reſtore triennial parliaments; and, formerly, it was not without difficulty that the miniſtry were able to defeat theſe attempts. The diviſion in the Houſe of Commons in 1735, on a bill for this purpoſe, was 247 to 184.——I need not ſay, that *now* all ſuch attempts drop of themſelves. So much are the ſentiments of our repreſentatives changed in this inſtance, that the motion for ſuch a bill, annually made by a worthy member of the Houſe of Commons, can ſcarcely produce a ſerious debate, or gain the leaſt attention.——For ſeveral years, at the beginning of the laſt reign, the HOUSE OF COMMONS conſtantly paſſed *penſion* and *place* bills, which were as conſtantly rejected by the HOUSE OF LORDS. At preſent, no one is ſo romantic as ever to think of introducing any ſuch bills into the Houſe of Commons.

(a) Introduction to the Commentaries on the Laws of England, p. 48. See alſo Book i. ch. 8,

(b) In 1692 King William rejected a bill for triennial Parliaments, after it had paſſed both Houſes. But in a following year he thought proper to give his aſſent to it.

7 Fourthly,

Fourthly. Standing armies have in all ages been destructive to the Liberties of the states into which they have been admitted.—MONTESQUIEU (*a*) observes, that the preservation of Liberty in ENGLAND requires, that it should have no land forces.——Dr. FERGUSON calls the establishment of standing armies "A FATAL REFINEMENT in "the present state of civil government." (*b*)——Mr. *Hume* pronounces "our standing army a "mortal distemper in the British constitution, of "which it must *inevitably* perish." (*c*)—Formerly, the nation was apprehensive of this danger; and the *standing army* was a constant subject of warm debate in both Houses of Parliament. The principal reason then assigned for continuing it was, the security of the House of HANOVER against the friends of the *Pretender*. This is a reason which now exists no more; the House of *Hanover* being so well established as not to want any such security.——The standing army also is now more numerous and formidable than ever; and yet all opposition to it is lost, and it is become in a manner a part of the constitution.

Fifthly. For many years after the accession the national debt was thought an evil so alarming, that the reduction of it was recommended every

(*a*) Spirit of Laws. Book xix. ch. 27.
(*b*) History of Civil Society. Part vi. sect. 5.
(*c*) *Political* Discourses. Essay xii. p. 301.

year

year from the throne to the attention of Parliament as an object of the last importance. The FUND appropriated to this purpose was called the ONLY HOPE of the kingdom; and when the practice of alienating it begun, it was reckoned a kind of sacrilege, and zealously opposed in the House of *Commons*, and protested against in the House of *Lords*. But now, though the debt is almost *tripled*, we sit under it with perfect indifference; and the sacred fund, which repeated laws had ordered to be applied *to no other purpose* than the redemption of it, is always alienated of course, and become a constant part of the current supplies, and much more an encouragement to dissipation than a preservative from bankruptcy.

Sixthly. Nothing is more the duty of the representatives of a nation than to keep a strict eye over the expenditure of the money granted for public services.—In the reign of King William, the House of Commons passed almost every year bills for appointing commissioners for taking, stating and examining the public accounts; and, particularly, the army and navy debts and contracts. In the reign of Queen Ann such bills became less frequent. But since the accession, only two motions have been made for such bills; one in 1715, and the other in 1741; and both were rejected.

Seventhly.

Seventhly. I hope I may add, that there was a time when the kingdom could not have been brought to acquiefce in what was done in the cafe of the *Middlefex* election. This is a precedent which, by giving the Houfe of Commons the power of excluding its members at difcretion, and of introducing others in their room on a minority of votes, has a tendency to make it a felf-created Houfe, and to deftroy entirely the right of reprefentation: And a few more fuch precedents would completely overthrow the conftitution.

Laftly. I cannot help mentioning here the addition which has been lately made to the power of the Crown, by throwing into its hands the *Eaft-India Company*. Nothing more unfavourable to the fecurity of public Liberty has been done fince the REVOLUTION: And fhould our ftatefmen, thus ftrengthened by the patronage of the EAST, be farther ftrengthened by the conqueft and patronage of the WEST, they will indeed have no fmall reafon for triumph; and there will be little left to protect us againft the encroachments and ufurpations of power. ROME funk into flavery, in confequence of enlarging its territories, and becoming the center of the wealth of conquered provinces, and the feat of univerfal empire. It feems the appointment of Providence, that free ftates, when, not contented with *felf*-government,



and

and prompted by the love of domination, they make themſelves maſters of other ſtates, ſhall loſe Liberty at the ſame time that they take it away; and, by ſubduing, be themſelves ſubdued. Diſtant and dependent provinces can be governed only by a military force. And a military force which governs abroad, will ſoon govern at home. The *Romans* were ſo ſenſible of this, that they made it treaſon for any of their generals to march their armies over the *Rubicon* into *Italy*. CÆSAR, therefore, when he came to this river, heſitated; but he paſſed it, and enſlaved his country.

" Among the circumſtances (ſays Dr. FERGU-
" SON) which in the event of national proſperity
" and in the reſult of commercial arts, lead to
" the eſtabliſhment of deſpotiſm, there is none
" perhaps that arrives at this termination with ſo
" ſure an aim as the perpetual enlargement of ter-
" ritory. In every ſtate the freedom of its mem-
" bers depends on the balance and adjuſtment of
" its interior parts; and the exiſtence of any ſuch
" freedom among mankind depends on the ba-
" lance of nations. In the progreſs of conqueſt
" thoſe who are ſubdued are ſaid to have loſt their
" liberties. But, from the hiſtory of mankind,
" to conquer or to be conquered has appeared in
" effect the ſame." (*a*)

(*a*) Hiſtory of Civil Society. Part iv. ſect. 5.

Many

Many more facts of this kind might easily be enumerated; but these are sufficient.——They shew, with sad evidence, how fast we have, for some time, been advancing towards the greatest of all public calamities.

We may, also, infer from the preceding observations, that there is only one way in which our deliverance is possible; and that is, by RESTORING OUR GRAND NATIONAL SECURITY. This is the object which our great men in opposition ought to hold forth to the kingdom, and to bind themselves by some decisive tests to do all they can to obtain. That patriotism must be spurious which does not carry its views principally to this. Without it, nothing is of great importance to the kingdom; and even an accommodation with *America* would only preserve a limb, and save from present danger, while a gangrene was left to consume the vitals.

But, probably, we are gone too far; and corruption has struck its roots too deep to leave us much room for hope.——Mr. HUME has observed, (*a*) that as the affairs of this country are not likely to take a turn favourable to the establishment of a perfect plan of Liberty, "an absolute monarchy is the easiest death, the true "EUTHANASIA of the British constitution."—

(*a*) See Mr. Hume's Essays. Vol. i. p. 91.



If

If this observation is just, our constitution (should no great calamity intervene) is likely, in some future period, to receive a very quiet dissolution. ——At present, however, it must be acknowledged, that we enjoy a degree of Liberty, civil and religious, which has seldom been paralleled among mankind. We ought to rejoice in this happiness; and to be grateful to that benevolent disposer of all events who blesses us with it. But, at the same time, our hearts must bleed when we reflect, that, the supports of it having given way, it is little more than a *sufferance* which we owe to the temper of the times; the lenity of our governors; and some awe, in which the friends of despotism are still held, by the voice and spirit of the uncorrupted part of the kingdom.——May these causes, if no better securities can be hoped for, long delay our fate.

It must not be forgotten, that all I have now said is meant on the supposition, that our affairs will proceed smoothly till, by a common and natural progress, we have gone the round of other nations once free, and are brought to their end. ——But it is possible this may not happen.—— Our circumstances are singular; and give us reason to fear, that we have before us a death which will not be easy or common.

PART

# PART II.

CONTAINING

REMARKS on ſome Particulars in a SPEECH at opening the BUDGET in *April* 1776.

## SECT. I.

*Supplemental Obſervations on the Surplus of the Revenue; the Quantity of Coin in the Kingdom; and Paper-Credit.*

IT is well known, that the great miniſter who preſides over our finances, took occaſion, at opening the Budget in April laſt, to enter into a particular account of the ſtate of the nation. In this account, he repreſented us as in a condition the moſt ſound and happy; our trade and revenue flouriſhing; our common people well provided for; our debts and taxes light; our current ſpecie ſufficiently ample; our paper-circulation ſafe; and the BANK, in particular, as little leſs firm and durable than the world.

This account, ſo encouraging and flattering, was generally underſtood to be given in deſigned oppoſition to another account very different, which had been given in the *Obſervations on Civil Liberty.*——It cannot, therefore, I hope, be thought too preſuming in me to offer the following remarks in my own defence.

I have grounded my opinion of the hazardous ſtate of the kingdom, partly on the ſmallneſs of the ſurplus in the revenue, and the nature and circumſtances of our paper-circulation, compared with the quantity of *ſpecie* in the kingdom, and the weight of our debts and taxes.

The ſurplus of the revenue I have made out in two different methods; and by a deduction ſo minute, that it is, I think, ſcarcely poſſible it ſhould be materially wrong. One of theſe methods brings it out 338,759*l. per ann.* (*a*): and the other, 300,000*l. per ann.* ſuppoſing the expence of calling in the gold coin, and the profits of lotteries excluded; the land-tax at three ſhillings in the pound; and the peace eſtabliſhment the ſame that it has been at a medium for eleven years, from 1764 to 1775.

Nothing more was ſaid in oppoſition to this, than a general intimation, that had it not been for the war with *America*, the peace-eſtabliſhment for

(*a*) See the concluſion of the Third Part.

5 the

the navy would have been reduced, and a ſufficient ſurplus gained (including lotteries) to enable parliament to pay off a million every year of the public debt.

I am very ſenſible that reductions of the public expences and improvements in the revenue are practicable, which would give ſuch a ſurplus. But I am afraid, they will never take place. Nor can I think it proper, in determining what permanent ſurplus we poſſeſs, to include thoſe pernicious profits of lotteries, by which infinitely more is upon the whole loſt than gained; or, to form our judgment of the expence of *future* years, by any other rule than the medium expence of *paſt* years. ——It would, however, give little conſolation, were there a certainty that, had peace continued, a MILLION annually of the public debt would have been diſcharged. This would have made a very ſlow progreſs in diſcharging our debts. A million every year diſcharged in peace, and eight or ten millions every year added in war, would leave us under the neceſſity of breaking at laſt. But hitherto we have not proceeded in a courſe ſo favourable. The great perſon to whom I refer, muſt know, that in 1772, he announced in the *Houſe of Commons*, his intention to pay off a *million and a half* every year, and SEVENTEEN MILLIONS in ten years; that yet only 2.800,000*l.* was paid off in the three ſubſequent years; and that, on account of the increaſe of the *navy* and *civil-liſt* debts, there has not been in fact the ability (without the help of lotteries) to pay half that ſum.

In page 74th of the *Obſervations on Civil Liberty*, I have ſaid, " that it has appeared lately, " that the gold ſpecie of the kingdom, is no " more than about TWELVE MILLIONS AND A " HALF."——This aſſertion has been much controverted; and it is therefore neceſſary I ſhould give a diſtinct account of the reaſons on which it was grounded.

I had learnt from unqueſtionable authority, that the quantity of gold coin brought into the mint, by the Acts of Parliament and Proclamations in 1773 and 1774, was about NINE MILLIONS (*a*); or as much as, when recoined, amounted nearly to that ſum.——I find alſo, that it was expected by the beſt judges, that the proclamation lately iſſued would bring in about *three* millions. Theſe two ſums make up *twelve* millions; and they include the gold coin of *Ireland*. Let this be eſtimated at a (*b*) million; and the whole gold coin

(*a*) This was confirmed by the account of the noble Lord at opening the laſt Budget.

(*b*) I have mentioned this ſum at random. It is not of great conſequence whether it is half a million too little or half a million too much.

of

of *Britain*, to be brought in by all the calls, will be ELEVEN millions; and none will remain, except that part which was deficient leſs than a grain in a guinea, and remained in the kingdom, at the time the coin Act took effect in June 1773. We are here left entirely to conjecture. But it ſhould be remembered, that for many years before 1773, the heavy coin was catched up as ſoon as iſſued, and either clipped, or melted down and exported; and that from hence aroſe ſuch a ſcarcity of heavy coin, that, in ſome counties, heavy guineas might be diſpoſed of at a premium.——In ſuch circumſtances, an allowance of about a million and a half, for the coin deficient leſs than a grain in a guinea before the coin Act in 1773, ſeems to be ſufficient; and therefore, it might, I think, with reaſon be ſaid, that it appeared that the gold coin of the kingdom was about TWELVE MILLIONS AND A HALF.

But there is another reaſon, by which I have been convinced, that this is a moderate eſtimate.

The quantity of gold coin, deficient between three and ſix grains in a guinea, was 4.800,000*l.* and this, when recoined, made 4.600,000*l.*—— The coin deficient leſs than three grains could not have been ſo much, for the following reaſons. Firſt, new coin being rougher, wears faſter than old coin; and therefore, does not remain ſo long

in

in any given degree of deficiency.—Secondly, coin, deficient less than three grains, is subject to several peculiar causes of diminution and destruction.—Clipping and sweating remove part of it to greater degrees of deficiency; and part is destroyed by being melted down and exported; whereas, lighter coin is diminished only by being worn (*a*).

(*a*) The quantity of coin within all equal degrees of deficiency would be equal, were equal quantities issued every year, and were there also no cause which diminished or destroyed it, except the *uniform* operation of time in wearing it. Any cause, therefore, which destroys it more, or diminishes it faster at first than at last, must render the quantity less in the first degrees of deficiency. And the same must be the consequence of a greater proportion issued formerly, in any given time, than of late.——The causes of diminution never probably operated so much on the gold coin as they did for about twelve years before 1773; and this will balance the greater proportion coined during that time. The very reason of the increase of coinage in those years was, a necessity created by the loss of the new coin, and never before felt in an equal degree. The coinage, however, in those years, was not so much more than usual as some may imagine. In ten years before 1770, eight millions and a half were coined; and in twelve years after the *Accession*, the same quantity was coined; and in twenty-seven years after the *Accession*, more was coined than in twenty-seven years before 1770. See *Considerations on Money, Bullion*, &c. p. 2.——The whole quantity of gold coined from the Accession to 1770, was near 29 millions; more than one half of which must have been melted and exported; and, the greatest part of the remainder must have been precipitated in its progress towards deficiency by being clipped and sweated.

These

Theſe reaſons ſeem to prove, that if the gold coin, deficient in June 1773 leſs than three grains, is eſtimated at *five millions*, (that is, at a little more than the coin deficient between three and ſix grains) it will be rated rather too high; and the concluſion will be, that the whole of our gold coin (excluſive of the *Iriſh)* might poſſibly be *leſs*, but could nöt have been *much more*, than the ſum at which I have reckoned it.

Such have been the facts and arguments by which my judgment has been determined in this inſtance.——But it muſt not be overlooked, that it helps only to aſcertain the quantity of *circulating* ſpecie in the kingdom, as diſtinguiſhed from that which is *hoarded*. When the *Obſervations on Civil Liberty* were publiſhed, I did not apprehend, that this part of the coin could be conſiderable enough to deſerve regard. But the contrary has lately appeared. The Proclamation iſſued laſt ſummer, and which it was expected would bring in about three millions, has, I am informed, brought in about *ſix millions and a half*. This exceeds the ſum at which I have been led to ſtate the *whole* gold coin deficient leſs than three grains; and proves, that ſeveral millions muſt have been hoarded (*a*). Nor, I think,

(*a*) When the ſilver *ſpecie* was recoined in King William's time, it appeared, that a great treaſure had been hoarded before

I think, will this appear incredible, when it is recollected, that only gold coin under three grains of deficiency is likely to be hoarded; and alſo, that diſtruſt of the *Funds* and of Paper-money has a particular tendency to increaſe the practice of hoarding.

Aſſiſted, therefore, by this new light, I would now ſtate the *circulating* gold coin of the kingdom before 1773, nearly as I did before; and call it TWELVE or THIRTEEN MILLIONS. But the whole gold coin (including the hoarded part) I would reckon at SIXTEEN or SEVENTEEN MILLIONS (*b*).

An account very different from this was given at opening the Budget; the ſubſtance of which I will ſtate as faithfully as my memory will enable me; and juſt as I underſtood it.

" From the beginning of the year 1772, to " the 23d of April laſt, 13.200,000*l.* had been " coined at the Tower; and on that day there " was 600,000*l.* more ready to be coined.——

before the *Revolution*, in conſequence of the danger of public liberty at that time. See Davenant's Works, Vol. I. p. 439, &c.

In *Ruſſia* it is reckoned, that as much money lies buried under ground, as exiſts above ground.

(*b*) In theſe ſums is included all the coin which the late Proclamations have brought in from HOLLAND and other foreign countries; and which, I think, ought not to be deemed a part of the reſting ſtock of the kingdom.

All

" All this, (it was intimated) is now left in the
" kingdom. The laſt Proclamation, it was ex-
" pected, would bring in three millions more;
" which, added to the coin deficient leſs than a
" grain reſting in the kingdom at the time of the
" Coin Act in 1773, and iſſued before 1772,
" will make the whole, EIGHTEEN OR NINETEEN
" MILLIONS (*a*)."

On this account I would obſerve,

Firſt. That if juſt, it proves that, in 1773, a *third* at leaſt of the *circulating* coin was in the beſt ſtate poſſible. For the late calls having ſhewn, that there was then, in *Britain* and *Ireland*, no more than about twelve *millions* deficient *more* than a grain; ſix millions (that is, a third of eighteen millions) or ſeven millions (that is, more than a third of nineteen millions) muſt have been deficient *leſs* than a grain. (*b*)—It will alſo follow,

(*a*) Or deducting a million for the *Iriſh* coin, ſeventeen or eighteen millions.

(*b*) This is ſaid on the ſuppoſition, that the laſt call would bring in no more than was expected, or about three millions. Its having brought in above double this ſum makes little difference. For it proves, that the whole quantity of gold coin muſt have been (according to Lord NORTH's method of computing) 21 or 22 millions; and the quantity deficient more than a grain about 15 millions; and, conſequently, ſix or ſeven millions (that is, near a *third*) will ſtill remain to be the quantity deficient leſs than a grain.

(ſince

(ſince the quantity brought in by the firſt call is known to have been 4,900,000 l.) that but little more than a *fourth* could have been deficient ſo much as ſix grains, or a ſhilling in a guinea.—— No perſon can think this credible who recollects the diſtreſs of traffic, and the complaints of the kingdom before 1773.

Secondly. The truth of the account I have ſtated depends, in a great meaſure, on the ſuppoſition, that all the gold coined ſince the beginning of 1772 is now in the kingdom. I cannot conceive on what grounds this was taken for granted. ——From the beginning of 1772 to June 1773, the practice of clipping was more prevalent than it had ever been. During the greateſt part of 1772, the price of gold was ſo much above mint price, that a profit, from 2 to 4 *per cent.* might be got by melting heavy guineas (a). And, in February in that year, the price of gold was at

(a) It has been thought very ſtrange, that a piece of metal ſhould bear a higher price, merely becauſe it wants the ſtamp of the mint. But the reaſon is, that bullion alone being exportable in any conſiderable quantity, the price of it muſt vary as the demand for it varies; or, in other words, as the *balance of payment* between us and the reſt of the world is favourable or unfavourable.——This will be explained at the beginning of the Third Part, where it will appear that, in conſequence of the increaſe of luxury and the national debt, this balance has been generally againſt us ever ſince the end of the laſt war.

4l. 1s.

4l. 1s. 6d. per ounce; and 4 ½ *per cent.* might be got by melting heavy guineas. Inſtead, therefore, of believing, that all the gold coined ſince the beginning of 1772 remains with us; I think it almoſt certain, that the greateſt part of all coined during the firſt year and a half of this period, has been either clipped or melted into bullion. That part which was clipped has been recoined; and that part which was melted has been either recoined or exported; and, therefore, neither has made any addition to the coin of the kingdom.

Theſe obſervations demonſtrate, that the amount of the gold coin at the time of the Coin Act in 1773, muſt have been near the ſum at which I have reckoned it. There may, for ought I know, have been an increaſe ſince; but I ſhall not believe there has, till I know, whether the coin brought in by the laſt proclamation has been all recoined and iſſued. But this cannot be expected; for ſhould it be done, FOUR MILLIONS (*a*) more will have been coined and iſſued, than has been brought in.——The truth, therefore, may be, that the coinage, ſince June 1773, has been car-

(*a*) The coin brought in laſt Summer, added to near 14 millions coined from the beginning of 1772 to the time of the laſt call, amounts to about 20 millions and a half; but only 16 millions and a half have been brought in, including the coin from *Ireland* and foreign countries.

ried,

ried on only to provide a ſupply of new coin to be exchanged for old; in which caſe, the quantity of coin in the kingdom, even according to this method of computing it, will come out nearly the ſame with that which I have given.

After all, let the *ſpecie* of the kingdom, including the ſilver, be allowed to be as conſiderable as ſome have aſſerted; or about four millions more than I have reckoned it; the difference ariſing from hence will not be of particular conſequence; and it will be ſtill true, that notwithſtanding all our increaſe of trade and apparent opulence, the *ſpecie* of the kingdom (*a*) is not much more than it was at the *Revolution*.——What then is all the reſt of our circulating caſh? What is it keeps up rents; feeds our luxury; pays our taxes; ſupplies the revenue, and ſupports government? —Paper, chiefly, emitted, not only at the Bank, but by tradeſmen, merchants, and bankers in every corner of the kingdom.——And is this a ſolid

(*a*) Or EIGHTEEN MILLIONS AND A HALF. See Dr. DAVENANT's Works, Vol. i. p. 363, &c. 443, &c. A great part of this ſpecie was carried out of the nation in King WILLIAM's wars; and the conſequence was, that the taxes became unproductive; and that Government fell under great difficulties, from which it was afterwards relieved by the eſtabliſhment of the *Bank* and the increaſe of trade. See the beginning of the Third Part.

and permanent ſupport? (*b*) Is there, in the annals of the world, another inſtance of a great kingdom ſo ſupported?——The cauſes are numberleſs which may ſuddenly deſtroy it; and were this

(*b*) The paper currency of the Colonies is one of the greateſt diſadvantages under which they labour; but it is of a more ſafe and permanent nature than ours. Were it not ſo, it could not have been of the leaſt uſe to them for the laſt year and a half. He who doubts this, need only conſider what our paper would be worth were we now invaded as they are.

This difference depends chiefly, on the following circumſtances.——Their paper is not payable on demand.—It is a legal tender.——It repreſents fixed property which is mortgaged for it.——It does not ſupport ſuch a monſtrous debt as ours.—And when public emergencies require any extraordinary emiſſions, they are generally ſunk by taxes in four or five years.——It is the firſt of theſe circumſtances that gives our paper its currency; and it is alſo this circumſtance that creates the danger attending it, by rendering it incapable of ſuſtaining any great ſhock or panic.——The poſſeſſion of ſecurities equal in nominal value to the amount of the paper emitted, or the debts contracted, is of little conſequence when the value of theſe ſecurities depends on the paper, and is created by it; that is, in other words, when the debts themſelves are the very caſh which muſt pay the debts.——Nothing can be more unnatural than ſuch a ſtate of things; and it may hereafter be a curious object of enquiry, how it could be ever poſſible that it ſhould ſubſiſt any long time.

In page 78 of the *Obſervations on Civil Liberty*, I have ſaid, "that the kingdom of FRANCE has no ſuch dependence as "we have on paper-credit; and that its ſpecie amounts to "67 millions ſterling." In mentioning this ſum I took the

this to happen, we ſhould fall at once, with a debt of 140 millions upon us, to the ſtate we were in before the REVOLUTION.——Imagination cannot paint to itſelf the ſhock this would give.——

loweſt of different accounts which I had then received from different authorities. I have ſince received accounts which make it 87 millions and a half; or 2000 millions of *livres*. This, in particular, is the account of an author whom all know to be likely to be well informed on this ſubject; I mean the author of the Treatiſe on the *Legiſlation* and *Commerce of Corn*, Part I. chap. v.——In the ſame treatiſe it is ſaid, (Part I. chap. viii,) that it appears, from the returns made by the intendants of the different Provinces, that the number of *annual* deaths in the whole kingdom of France, for three yeats ended in 1772, was 780,040. I have been informed by the ingenious author, that this account may be depended on; and if ſo, *France* muſt contain 26 millions of inhabitants; for the beſt obſervations prove, that no more than a thirty-third part of a whole kingdom dies annually. See Obſervations on Reverſionary Payments, page 200.—In *Sweden*, though a nineteenth part die in the capital every year, only a thirty-fifth part die in the whole kingdom. See Philoſophical Tranſactions, Vol. lxv. for 1775, p. 426. The particulars now mentioned, added to the nature of the debts of FRANCE as mentioned in page 78 of the *Obſervations on Civil Liberty*, form a ſtriking contraſt between the ſtate of that kingdom and ours. Nothing gives us our ſuperiority but the advantages we derive from our RELIGION, and our LIBERTY. Even in theſe reſpects, however, they ſeem to be improving, while we are declining. *Monteſquieu*, *Abbe Raynal*, and others of their moſt admired writers, inculcate principles of government, and breathe a ſpirit of Liberty, which, to the ſhame of this country, are become offenſive in it.

I muſt

I must repeat here what I have said in the *Observations on Civil Liberty*, page 73, &c. that we should think of nothing but guarding ourselves against the danger of such a situation, by restricting our paper currency, and gradually discharging our public debts.——In giving this admonition, I look upon myself as doing my country one of the best offices in my power; and acting in the character of one who calls to another to awake who is sleeping over a precipice.——But I know I call in vain.——The great minister who directs our finances has assured us all is well; and, under this persuasion, we are advancing, with unsuspicious and careless speed, to the catastrophe I have pointed out; and pursuing measures which must increase the difficulty of avoiding it, and the distress attending it.

Among these measures I have mentioned the present new coinage.——Before this coinage, I have observed, the light money always remained, because nothing could be got by melting and exporting it. But now, as soon as gold rises to the price it bore for many years before 1773, the melters and exporters of coin will be saved the trouble of selection; and every piece on which they can lay their hands will be proper for their purpose.——It seems, therefore, obvious, that, in consequence of this measure, all our coin may be carried away, and the whole superstructure of paper ſupported by it, break down, before we are aware of any danger.

I will take this opportunity to add, that this meaſure will at the ſame time increaſe our paper. This has been the conſequence of the two former calls; but it will probably be more the conſequence of the laſt call. For, as no coin is now to be current which is more than a grain deficient; and as alſo a great deal of it is already at or near that limit; the vexation attending it will be ſo intolerable, that it will be generally cried down, and paper ſubſtituted in its room.—— Certain it is, that nothing can prevent this evil, but another evil; I mean, the deficient coin forcing itſelf again into circulation, and furniſhing clippers with more employment than ever; and, conſequently, a return, with increaſed violence, of the confuſion and diſtreſs which took place before the Coin Act in 1773.——This, indeed, will be much the leaſt of the two evils; nor, in my opinion, are there any methods of preventing the diminution of the coin, which will not produce greater evils, except ſuch alterations in its form (*a*) as ſhall render clipping leſs practicable, joined to the execution of ſevere laws againſt clippers, and a ſtrict vigilance in detecting them.

Upon the whole. It ſeems to me, that enough had been done by the firſt coin act to reſtore the

(*a*) See the propoſals and obſervations in a pamphlet lately publiſhed by Lord Viſcount MAHON on this ſubject.

gold

gold coin; and that all which has been done ſince, at the expence of about 650,000l. has been nothing but a preparation of the coin for melters and exporters, to the dreadful hazard of the kingdom.——Theſe are my preſent views of this ſubject. But I muſt ſay, that I ſuſpect my own judgment in this inſtance. The noble Lord, who is furniſhed with infinitely more of the means of information than I am, intimated, if I remember rightly, that there is no ſuch danger: And though I did not underſtand the reaſon he aſſigned for this aſſertion, I muſt believe, that, in a matter ſo particularly intereſting to the kingdom, he has gone upon the beſt evidence.

## S E C T. II.

### *Of the State of the Nation; and the War with America.*

AT the beginning of the preceding ſection, I have taken notice of the flattering account which was given, at opening the Budget in April laſt, of the ſtate of the kingdom with reſpect to its commerce, revenue, and opulence. On that account I ſhall beg leave to offer the following reflections.

Firſt. The obſervations in the laſt ſection prove, I think, that it is not ſo well ſuppotted by facts, as there

there is reaſon to wiſh. I am ſenſible, indeed, that we never made a more gay and ſplendid appearance. But no conſiderate perſon will draw much encouragement from hence. That pride and ſecurity; that luxury, venality and diſſipation which give us this appearance, are melancholy ſymptoms; and have hitherto been the forerunners of diſtreſs and calamity.

Secondly. When this account was given there was a particular end to be anſwered by it. Additional taxes were to be impoſed; and it was neceſſary to reconcile the public to the proſpect of a great increaſe of its burthens, in order to carry on the war with *America*.——On other occaſions, different accounts had been given. In order to prove the juſtice of taxing the *Americans*, the weight of our own taxes had been often inſiſted upon; and the difficulty of raiſing a ſufficient force among ourſelves to reduce them, had been urged as a reaſon for ſeeking and employing, at a great expence, the aſſiſtance of foreign powers. On ſuch occaſions, I have heard our unhappy and embarraſſed ſituation mentioned; and, at the end of the laſt ſeſſion of Parliament, one of our greateſt men, whoſe opinion in favour of coercion, had contributed to bring us into our preſent ſituation, acknowledged the diſtreſs attending it, and repreſented the veſſel of the ſtate as having never before rode in ſo dangerous a ſtorm.

a ſtorm.——This is, without doubt, the truth. But, if the account on which I am remarking was juſt, we were then ſafe and happy; nor was the veſſel of the ſtate ever wafted by more gentle and proſperous gales.

But the reflection which, on this occaſion, has given me moſt pain is the following.

If, without *America*, we can be in a ſtate ſo flouriſhing, a war to reduce *America* muſt be totally inexcuſeable. I wiſh I could engage attention to this. War is a dreadful evil; and thoſe who involve a people in it *needleſsly*, will find they have much to anſwer for. Nothing can ever juſtify it, but the neceſſity of it to ſecure ſome *eſſential* intereſt againſt unjuſt attacks. But, it ſeems, there is no intereſt to be ſecured by the preſent war. The revenue has never flouriſhed ſo much, as ſince *America* has been rendered hoſtile to us; and it is now reckoned by many a decided point, that little depends on the *American* trade. It follows then, that if the end of the preſent war is to "obtain a revenue," it is a revenue we do not want; if "to maintain authority," it is an authority of no uſe to us.——Muſt not humanity ſhudder at ſuch a war?——Why not let *America* alone, if we can ſubſiſt without it?——Why carry fire and ſword into a happy country to do ourſelves no good?

Some of the very persons who depreciate the value of the colonies, as a support to our revenue and finances, yet say, that we are now under a necessity of reducing them, or perishing. I wish such persons would give an account of the causes which, according to their ideas, create this dreadful necessity. Is it the same that led *Haman* of old to reckon all his honours and treasures nothing to him, while *Mordecai* the Jew would not bow to him?——Or, are we become so luxurious, that luxury even in the revenue is become necessary to us; and so depraved, that, like many individuals in private life, having lost *self*-dominion, we cannot subsist without dominion over *others?*

It must not be forgotten, that I speak here on the supposition, that it is possible for this country to be as safe and prosperous without *America* as some have asserted, and as was implied in what was said at opening the last Budget.——This is far from being my own opinion.—Some time or other we shall, in all probability, feel severely, in our commerce and finances, the loss of the colonies. As a source of revenue they are, I think, of great importance to us; but they are still more important as supports to our navy, and an aid to us in our wars. It appears now, that there is a force among them so formidable and so growing, hat, with its assistance, any of the great *European* powers may soon make themselves masters

of

of all the *West-Indies* and *North-America*; and nothing ought to be more alarming to us than that our natural enemies see this, and are influenced by it.——With the colonies united to us, we might be the greatest and happiest nation that ever existed. But with the colonies separated from us, and in alliance with *France* and *Spain*, we are no more a people.——They appear, therefore, to be indeed worth any price.——Our existence depends on keeping them.——But now are they to be kept?——Most certainly, not by forcing them to unconditional submission at the expence of many millions of money and rivers of blood. The resolution to attempt this, is a melancholy instance of that infatuation, which sometimes influences the councils of kingdoms. It is attempting to keep them by a method, which, if it succeeds, will destroy their use, and make them not worth the having; and which, if it does *not* succeed, will throw them into the scale of rival powers, kindle a general war, and undo the empire.

The extension of our territories in *America*, during the last war, increased the expence of our *peace*-establishment, from 2.400,000 l. *per ann.* to four millions *per ann.*—Almost all the provinces in *America*, which used to be ours, are now to be conquered. Let the expence of this be stated at 25 or 30 millions; or, at a capital bearing a million

lion *per annum* intereſt.——*America* recovered by the ſword muſt be kept by the ſword, and forts and garriſons muſt be maintained in every province to awe the wretched inhabitants, and to hold them in ſubjection. This will create another addition of expence; and both together cannot, I ſuppoſe, be ſtated at leſs than two millions *per annum.*——But how is ſuch an increaſe of revenue to be procured?——The colonies, deſolated and impoveriſhed, will yield no revenue.—The ſurpluſſes of the ſinking fund have, for many years, formed a neceſſary part of the current and ordinary ſupplies.——It muſt, therefore, be drawn from *new* taxes.——But can the kingdom bear ſuch an increaſe of taxes? Or, if it can, where ſhall we find a ſurplus for diſcharging an enormous debt of above 160 millions? And what will be our condition, when the next foreign war ſhall add two millions *per annum* more to our expences?——Indeed this is a frightful proſpect. But it will be rendered infinitely more frightful by carrying our views to that increaſe of the power of the Crown which will ariſe from the increaſe of the army, from the diſpoſal of new places without number, and the patronage of the whole continent of *North-America.*

Theſe conſequences have been ſtated moderately on the ſuppoſition, that we ſhall ſucceed in ſubduing *America*; and that, while we are doing it,

our

our natural enemies will neglect the opportunity offered them, and continue to ſatisfy themſelves with aſſiſting *America indirectly.*——But ſhould the contrary happen.——I need not ſay what will follow.

Some time ago this horrid danger might have been avoided, and the colonies kept by the eaſieſt means.——By a prudent lenity and moderation.——By receiving their petitions.——By giving up the right we claim to diſpoſe of their property, and to alter their governments.——By guarantying to them, in theſe reſpects, a legiſlative independence; (*a*) and eſtabliſhing them in the

(*a*) "There is ſomething (ſays a great writer) ſo unnatural "in ſuppoſing a large ſociety, ſufficient for all the good pur- "poſes of an independent political union, remaining ſubject "to the direction and government of a diſtant body of men "who know not ſufficiently the circumſtances and exigencies "of this ſociety; or in ſuppoſing this ſociety obliged to be "governed ſolely for the benefit of a diſtant country; that it "is not eaſy to imagine there can be any foundation for it "in juſtice or equity. The inſiſting on *old claims* and *tacit* "*conventions*, to extend civil power over diſtant nations, and "form grand unwieldy empires, without regard to the ob- "vious maxims of humanity, has been one great ſource of "human miſery." *Syſtem of Moral Philoſophy*, by Dr. HUTCHESON, vol. ii. p. 309. In the ſection from whence this quotation is taken, Dr. HUTCHESON diſcuſſes the queſtion, "When colonies have a right to be releaſed from the domi- "nion of the parent ſtate?" And his general ſentiment ſeems

 to

the poſſeſſion of equal liberty with ourſelves.——This a great and magnanimous nation ſhould have done. This, ſince the commencement of hoſtilities, would have brought them back to their former habits of reſpect and ſubordination; and might have bound them to us for ever.

MONTESQUIEU has obſerved, that ENGLAND, in planting colonies, ſhould have *commerce*, not *dominion*, in view; the increaſe of dominion being incompatible with the ſecurity of public liberty.—Every advantage that could ariſe from commerce they have offered us without reſerve; and their language to us has been——" Reſtrict us, as much " as you pleaſe, in *acquiring* property by regu- " lating our trade for your advantage; but claim " not the diſpoſal of that property after it has " been acquired.—Be ſatisfied with the authority " you exerciſed over us before the preſent reign.— " PLACE US WHERE WE WERE IN 1763."——On theſe terms they have repeatedly ſued for a reconciliation. In return, we have denounced them *Rebels*; and with our fleets in their ports,

to be, that they acquire ſuch a right, " Whenever they are " ſo increaſed in numbers and ſtrength, as to be ſufficient by " themſelves for all the good ends of a political union."——Such a deciſion given by a wiſe man, long before we had any diſputes with the colonies, deſerves, I think, particular notice.

 and

and our bayonets at their breasts, have left them no other alternative than to acknowledge our supremacy, and give up rights they think most sacred; or stand on the defensive, and appeal to heaven.—They have chosen the latter.

In this situation, if our feelings for *others* do not make us tremble, our feelings for *ourselves* soon may.——Should we suffer the consequences I have intimated, our pride will be humbled.——We shall admire the plans of moderation and equity which, without bloodshed or danger, would have kept *America*.——We shall wish for the happiness of former times; and remember, with anguish, the measures which many of us lately offered their lives and fortunes to support.

I must not conclude these observations, without taking particular notice of a charge against the colonies, which has been much insisted on.—" They have, it is said, always had independency " in view; and it is this, chiefly, that has pro-" duced their present resistance."——It is scarcely possible there should be a more unreasonable charge. Without all doubt, our connexion with them might have been preserved for ages to come, (perhaps *for ever*) by wise and liberal treatment. Let any one read a pamphlet published in 1761, by Dr. *Franklin*, and entitled, *The*

*The interest of Great Britain with respect to her Colonies*; and let him deny this if he can.—Before the present quarrel, there prevailed among them the purest affection for this country, and the warmest attachment to the House of HANOVER. And since the present quarrel begun, and not longer ago than the beginning of last winter, independency was generally dreaded among them. There is the fullest evidence for this; and all who are best acquainted with *America*, must know it to be true. As a specimen of this evidence, and of the temper of *America* till the period I have mentioned, I will just recite the following facts.

In the resolutions of the *Assembly*, which met at *Philadelphia*, July 15, 1774, after making the strongest professions of affection to *Britain*, and duty to their sovereign, they declare their abhorrence of every idea of an unconstitutional independence on the parent state.——An assembly of delegates from all the towns of the county of *Suffolk* (of which *Boston* is the capital) delivered in September 1774, to General Gage, a remonstrance against fortifying *Boston-neck*. In this remonstrance, they totally disclaim every wish of independence.——The same is done in the instructions given by the several colonies to the first deputies chosen for a general Congress.——In the petition of the first Congress to the King, they declare they

they ſhall always, carefully and zealouſly, endeavour to ſupport and maintain their connexion with *Great Britain.* In the memorial of the ſame Congreſs to the people of this country, they repeat this aſſurance.——In the order of the *Congreſs*, which met in May 1775, for a general faſt, they call upon all *America* to unite in beſeeching the Almighty to avert the judgments with which they were threatened, and *to bleſs their rightful Sovereign*, that ſo *a reconciliation might be brought about with the parent ſtate.*——And in their declaration ſetting forth the cauſes of their taking arms, they warn us, " that, ſhould they " find it neceſſary, foreign aſſiſtance was undoubt- " edly attainable ;" but at the ſame time declare, " that they did not mean to diſſolve the union " which had ſo long and ſo happily ſubſiſted " between them and this country ; that neceſſity " had not yet driven them to that deſperate " meaſure, or induced them to excite any other " nation to war againſt us ; and that they had " not raiſed armies with ambitious deſigns of " forming independent ſtates, but ſolely for the " protection of their property againſt violence, " and the defence of that freedom which was their " birth-right."——In the inſtructions, delivered Nov. 9, 1775, by a committee of the repreſentatives of the province of *Penſylvania*, to their delegates in the third general congreſs ; they enjoin

join them, in behalf of the province, "utterly to "reject any propositions, should such be made, "that might lead to a separation from the mother "country."

What reason can there be for thinking the colonies not sincere in all these declarations?—— In truth; it was not possible they should be otherwise than sincere; for so little did they think of war, at the time when most of these declarations were made, that they were totally unprepared for it: And, even when hostilities were begun at LEXINGTON in April 1775, they were so destitute of every instrument of defence, particularly ammunition, that *half* the force which is now invading them, would have been sufficient to conquer them at once.

I will beg leave to add on this occasion, the following extracts from letters, written by some leading persons at NEW-YORK, the genuineness of which may be depended on.

*New-York, August* 3d. 1775.——"I am "sensible of the many artifices and falshoods "which have been used to biass the minds of "your countrymen, who believe evil reports of "us; and, particularly, that we are aiming at "independence.——Of this be assured, that even "HANCOCK and ADAMS are averse to inde- "pendence. There was a lye current last week, "that the congress had finally agreed upon inde-

"pendence

" pendence to take place the 10th of March
" next, ſhould not our grievances be redreſſed
" before that time. I wrote to one of our
" delegates, to enquire whether this report
" was true. In his anſwer he declares, upon
" his honour, that he believed there was not
" one man in the Congreſs who would dare to
" make a motion tending to independence; or,
" that if any one did, two could not be found
" to ſupport the motion.——None but thoſe
" who are on the ſpot can conceive what a ſpirit
" is gone forth among all ranks and degrees of
" men.——We deſerve to be free. It is a heavy
" ſacrifice we are making. Trade is at an end.
" We expect our city to be knocked about our
" ears. But I declare ſolemnly, I will ſubmit to
" all, and die in a log-houſe in the wilds of
" America, and be free; rather than flouriſh in
" ſervitude."———In a ſubſequent letter, dated
NEW-YORK, Jan. 3d. 1776, the ſame perſon writes
as follows: —— " It is in the power of the
" miniſtry to annihilate all our diſputes, by re-
" ſtoring us to the ſituation we were in at the
" concluſion of the laſt war. If this is done, we
" ſhall immediately return to our allegiance.
" But if not, be aſſured, that an awful ſcene will
" be opened in the ſpring. Let me repeat a
" caution to you; believe not the inſinuations

" of our enemies, who would make you all believe " that *independence* is what *America* aims at. It " is an insidious falshood. Madmen will be " found in all large societies. It would be " singular, were there none such to be found " in a body of three millions of people and " upwards. But they are like a grain of sand on " the sea shore."

Another person writes thus.——NEW-YORK, Nov. 2d. 1775. " We love and honour our " King. He has no subjects in all his dominions " more attached to his person, family and govern- " ment, notwithstanding the epithet of rebels be- " stowed upon us. No charge is more unjust " than the charge that we desire an independence " on *Great Britain*. Ninety-nine in a hundred " of the inhabitants of this country deprecate " this as the heaviest of evils. But if administra- " tion will persist in their present measures, this " will and must inevitably be the event; for " submit to the present claims of the British par- " liament, while unrepresented in it, you may be " assured they never will. And what deserves " notice is, that all the violence of *Britain* only " unites the *Americans* still more firmly together, " and renders them more determined to be free " or die. This spirit is unconquerable by vio- " lence; but they may be easily won by kindness.

" Serious

" ——Serious people of all denominations among
" us, episcopal and non-episcopal, are much em-
" ployed in prayer to God for the success of the
" present struggles of *America*. They consider
" their cause as the cause of God; and as such,
" they humbly commit it to him, confident of
" success in the end, whatever blood or treasure
" it may cost them.

Since these letters were written, the sentiments of *America*, with respect to *independence*, have been much altered. But it should be remembered, that this alteration has been owing entirely to OURSELVES; I mean, to the measures of the last winter and summer, and particularly the following.

First. The rejection of the petition from the Congress brought over by Governor PENN. In this petition they professed, in strong language, that they still retained their loyalty to the King and attachment to this country; and only prayed, " that they might be directed to some mode by " which the united applications of the Colonies " might be improved into a happy reconciliation; " and that, in the mean time, some measures " might be taken for preventing their farther de- " struction, and for repealing such statutes as " more immediately distressed them."——The Colonies had often petitioned before without being heard. They had, therefore, little hope

 from

from this application; and meant that, if rejected, it should be their last.

Secondly. The last prohibitory bill, by which our protection of them was withdrawn; their ships and effects confiscated; and open war declared against them.

Thirdly. Employing *foreign* troops to subdue them. This produced a greater effect in *America* than is commonly imagined. And it is remarkable, that even the writers in *America* who answered the pamphlet entitled COMMON SENSE, acknowledge, that should the *British* ministry have recourse to foreign aid, it might become (*a*) proper to follow their example, and to embrace the necessity of resolving upon *independence*.

I have, further, reason to believe, that the answer to the last petition of the City of London, presented in March 1776, (*b*) had no small share in producing the same effect.

By these measures, and others of the same kind, those Colonists who had all along most dreaded and abhorred independence, were at last reconciled to it.——I can, however, say from

(*a*) See COMMON SENSE, and PLAIN TRUTH, p. 44. Published for Mr. *Almon*.

(*b*) The Colonies, I am assured, were not perfectly unanimous till they saw this answer.

particular

particular information, that even ſo lately as the month of June laſt, an accommodation might have been obtained with the Colonies, on a reaſonable and moderate plan; without giving up any one of the rights claimed by this country, except that of altering their charters and diſpoſing of their property.——And, as it would have reſtored peace and prevented the deſolating calamities into which *America* and *Britain* are now plunged, no friend to humanity can avoid regretting that ſuch a plan, when offered, was not adopted. But our rulers preferred coercion and conqueſt: And the conſequence has been, that the Colonies, after being goaded and irritated to the utmoſt, reſolved to diſengage themſelves, and directed the CONGRESS to declare them Independent States; which was accordingly done, as is well-known, on the 4th of July laſt. Since that time, they have, probably, been making applications to foreign powers; and it is to be feared, that *now* we may in vain offer them the very terms for which they once ſued.——All this is the neceſſary conſequence of the principles by which human nature is governed.——There was a time when, perhaps, we ſhould ourſelves have acted with more violence; and, inſtead of remonſtrating and praying, as *America* has done, have refuſed the moſt advantageous terms when offered with defiance, and under an awe from a military

 force.

force. Had King WILLIAM, inſtead of coming over by invitation to deliver us, invaded us; and, at the head of an army, offered us the BILL OF RIGHTS; we ſhould, perhaps, have ſpurned at it; and conſidered LIBERTY itſelf as no better than SLAVERY, when enjoyed as a boon from an inſolent conqueror.——But we have all along acted as if we thought the people of *America* did not poſſeſs the feelings and paſſions of *men*, much leſs of *Engliſhmen.*——It is indeed ſtrange our miniſters did not long ago ſee, that they had miſtaken the proper method of treating the Colonies; and that though they might be gradually *influenced* to any thing, they could be dragooned to nothing.—Had King *James the Second* avoided violence; and been a little more patient and ſecret in purſuing his views, he might have gained all he wiſhed for. But an eager haſte and an open avowal of the odious claims of prerogative ruined him.——This has been ſince conſidered; and a plan both here and in *Ireland*, (*a*) leſs *expeditious* indeed, but more *ſure*, has been purſued.

(*a*) I am ſorry to differ from thoſe reſpectable perſons who have propoſed placing *America* on the ſame ground with *Ireland*. If the ſame ground of LAW is meant, it is already done; for our laws give us the ſame power over *Ireland*, that we claim over *America*. If the ſame ground of PRACTICE is meant; it has been moſt unfortunate for *Ireland*, and would be equally ſo for *America*.

And

And had the ſame plan been purſued in *America*, the whole empire might in time have been brought, without a ſtruggle, to reſt itſelf quietly in the lap of corruption and ſlavery. It may, therefore, in the iſſue prove happy to the Colonies, that they have not been thought worthy of any ſuch cautious treatment. Our coercive meaſures have done all for them that their warmeſt patriots could have deſired. They have united them among themſelves, and bound them together under one government. They have checked them in the career of vicious luxury; guarded them againſt any farther infection from hence; taught them to ſeek all their reſources within themſelves; inſtructed them in the uſe of arms; and led them to form a naval and military power which may, perhaps, in time, become ſuperior to any force that can attack them, and prove the means of preſerving from invaſion and violence, a government of juſtice and virtue, to which the oppreſſed in every quarter of the globe may fly, and find peace, protection, and liberty.——In ſhort. Theſe meaſures have, in all probability, haſtened that diſruption of the *new* from the *old* world, which will begin a new *æra* in the annals of mankind; (*a*) and produce a revolution more

(*a*) See the Abbe RAYNAL's Reflections on this ſubject at the end of the 18th book of his Hiſtory of the *European Settlements* in the Eaſt and Weſt-Indies.——" Is it not likely, " ſays

important, perhaps, than any that has happened in human affairs.——As a friend, therefore, to the general interest of mankind, I ought, probably, to rejoice in these measures; and to bless that all-governing Providence, which, often, out of the evil intended by wretched mortals, brings the greatest good.——But when I consider the *present* sufferings which these measures must occasion, and the *catastrophe* with which they threaten GREAT-BRITAIN; I am shocked; and feel myself incapable of looking forward, without distress, to the fate of an empire, once united and happy, but now torn to pieces, and falling a sacrifice to despotic violence and blindness. Under the impression of these sentiments, and dreading the

" says this writer, that the distrust and hatred which have of " late taken place of that regard and attachment which the " *English* Colonies felt for the parent country, may hasten their " separation from one another? Every thing conspires to pro- " duce this great disruption; the æra of which it is impos- " sible to know.——Every thing tends to this point: The " progress of good in the new hemisphere, and the progress " of evil in the old.——In proportion as our people are " weakened, and resign themselves to each other's dominion, " population and agriculture will flourish in *America*; and " the arts make a rapid progress: And that country rising out " nothing, will be fired with the ambition of appearing with " glory in its turn on the face of the globe——O posterity! " ye, peradventure, will be more happy than your unfortunate " and contemptible ancestors."——Mr. *Justamond*'s Translation.

awful *crisis* before us, I cannot help, however impotent my voice, crying out to this country——"Make no longer war against *yourselves*. Withdraw your armies from your Colonies. Offer your power to them as a *protecting*, not a *destroying* power. Grant the security they desire to their property and charters; and renounce those notions of dignity, which lead you to prefer the exactions of force to the offerings of gratitude, and to hazard *every thing* to gain *nothing*.——By such wisdom and equity *America* may, perhaps, be still preserved; and that dreadful breach healed, which your enemies are viewing with triumph, and all *Europe* with astonishment."

But what am I doing?——At the moment I am writing this, the possibility of a reconciliation may be lost.——*America* may have formed an alliance with FRANCE——And the die may be cast.

## SECT. III.

### *Of Schemes for raising Money by Public Loans.*

THE following observations were occasioned by the scheme for the public loan of last year, proposed to the *House of Commons* at opening the *Budget*, and afterwards agreed to. I have thought

thought proper, therefore, to introduce these observations here; and, as they appear to me of some importance, I shall endeavour to explain them with as much care and perspicuity as possible.

In order to raise *two millions*, the Legislature created last year a new capital in the 3 *per cent.* consolidated annuities, of 2.150,000l. Every share of 77l. 10s. in this new capital was valued at 65l. 17s. 6d. or every 100l. *stock* at 85l. For the whole new capital, therefore, Government has received in money, 1.827,500l.— The remaining sum, necessary to make up *two millions*, was a compensation advanced to Government for relinquishing the profits of a Lottery, consisting of 60,000 tickets, each of the same value with 10l. *three per cent. stock*; and might have been obtained, without annexing the Lottery to the annuities.——This new capital the public may be obliged to redeem at *par*; in which case, 322,500l. (being the difference between 1.827,500 and 2.150,000l.) that is 17 $\frac{1}{2}$ *per cent.* will be paid by the public more than it has received.——In this transaction, therefore, Government has acted as a private person would act, who, in order to raise 850l. on a mortgage, should promise for it 30l. *per ann.* (or 3 $\frac{1}{2}$ *per cent.* interest) and 150l. (that is 17 $\frac{1}{2}$ *per cent.*

 nearly)

nearly) over and above the principal, when the mortgage came to be discharged.——Such a *premium* (should the mortgage be discharged soon) would be very extravagant; but, if *never* to be discharged, would be insignificant: Nor would it be possible to account for such a bargain, except by supposing, that the borrower, instead of meaning to repay the sum he borrowed, chose to continue *always* paying interest for it, or returning 30l. annually for 850l. once advanced; and to subject his estate, for that purpose, to an eternal incumbrance.

The public, I have said, may be obliged to discharge the new capital, lately created, at *par*; and, consequently, to suffer a loss by this year's loan of 322,500l. This will, undoubtedly, happen, should the nation prosper, and the public debts be put into a regular and fixed course of redemption; for the 3 *per cents.* would then soon rise to *par*.

The extravagance I have pointed out is the more to be regretted, because it was entirely needless; for the same sum might as well have been borrowed by schemes, which would not have subjected the public to the necessity of paying, when the loan came to be discharged, more money than had been received.——For instance. The sum advanced for the new capital of 2,150,000l. *three per cent.* annuities, might have been

been procured by offering 3 ½ *per cent.* on a capital equal to the sum advanced; or on 1.827,500 l. And the remainder, necessary to make up *two millions*, might have been obtained by the profits of a Lottery, consisting of 60,000 tickets each worth 10l. in Money. This scheme would have differed but little in value from the other; and the interest, or the annuity payable by the public, would have been 63,962 l. at 3 ½ *per cent.* on a capital of 1.827,500; (*a*) instead of 64,500l. at 3 *per cent.* on a capital of 2.150,000l.

When a 100l. *stock* in the 3 *per cent.* annuities is sold at 85 ¾, purchasers get 3 ½ *per cent.* interest for their money. When, therefore, the 3 *per cents* are at this price, 3 ½ *per cents* would be at *par*; and a capital of 1.827,500l. might be redeemed by the public, (without losing any advantage arising from its debts being at a discount,) by paying this sum; or by returning the money borrowed (*b*). But in the same circumstances, a capital

(*a*) Had this interest been insufficient, it might have been increased a 16th or even an 8th *per cent.* without any material difference; or, (which would have been better) 3 ½ *per cent.* might have been offered for *four fifths* of the sum borrowed, and 4 *per cent.* for the remainder; in which case, the annuity payable by the public would have been 65,790 l.

(*b*) It should be remembered here, that tho' Government, when its debts are at a discount, may be able, with the consent

capital of 2.150,000l. in the 3 *per cent.* annuities, for which 85l. *per cent.* or, in the whole, 1.827,500l. had been received, could not be redeemed without offering 86 or 87 *per cent.* for it; nor, therefore, without paying *more* than the original ſum borrowed.——When the 3 *per cents* are near *par*, there would be a loſs of 322,500l. in redeeming the ſame capital; whereas, the former annuities, for which the ſame ſum had been advanced, might be always diſcharged by either paying the very ſum (*a*) advanced, or a *leſs ſum.* In

ſent of the creditors, to redeem a given capital by paying a leſs ſum than that capital; yet it can never be obliged to pay *more.* ——In other words; a 100l. capital in the 3 *per cents*; 3 ½ *per cents*; or 4, or 5 *per cents*, Government is always at liberty to redeem by paying 100l. whatever the market price of it may be, and whether the creditors will conſent or not.

(*a*) There is another very great advantage which would attend theſe annuities.——One and the ſame *ſurplus* would diſcharge a given capital in leſs time. For example. A ſurplus of a million *per ann.* invariably applied, and the firſt payment to be made immediately, would diſcharge a capital of a *hundred millions* bearing 3 *per cent.* intereſt in 46 years. But if the ſame capital bore 3 ½ *per cent.* intereſt, it would be diſcharged in 43 ½ years; if 4 *per cent.* in 40 years; if 5 *per cent.* in 37 ¼ years.——A capital *leſs* than a 100 millions, in the ſame proportion that the intereſt is *more* than 3 *per cent.* and for which, therefore, the ſame annuity is paid, (as in the preſent caſe) the ſame ſurplus would diſcharge in 39 years, if the intereſt is 3 ½; in 34 ¼ years, if the intereſt is 4 *per cent.*

——In all poſſible circumſtances, therefore, theſe annuities would have the advantage.——But we never, when contracting debts, carry our views to the diſcharge of the principal; and the conſequences muſt prove fatal.

It

*cent.* in 27¼ years if the intereſt is 5 *per cent.*——Suppoſing, therefore, 75 millions borrowed in the manner of our Government, by creating a capital of a 100 millions bearing 3 *per cent.* (that is, by ſelling 3 *per cent.* ſtock for 75l. in money) which might have been borrowed by creating a capital of only 75 millions bearing 4 *per cent.* (that is by ſelling 4 *per cent.* ſtock at 100) there will not only be a loſs of 25 millions by a needleſs increaſe of the capital; but alſo a loſs of 14 millions, by an increaſe of the time in which one and the ſame ſaving will diſcharge the two capitals.——This may be proved in the following manner.——A million *per ann.* will, in 34 years and a quarter, very nearly diſcharge a debt of 75 millions bearing intereſt at 4 *per cent*; but the ſame ſaving will, in the ſame time, diſcharge only a capital of 61 millions, if it bears intereſt at 3 *per cent.* When, therefore, ſuch a ſaving has compleated the redemption of the *one* capital, there will remain unpaid of the other, 39 millions.——What has been now applied to a large ſum holds true in proportion of any ſmaller ſums.

It appears from hence to be a very wrong obſervation which ſome have made; "that provided the annual charge is the ſame, "it ſignifies little what the *principal* of the public debt is."——As there is no way of removing the annual charge but by paying the *principal*, it is of juſt as much conſequence what it is, as whether it is practicable or impracticable, to remove a burden which weakens and cripples, and muſt in time ſink the public. An annuity of SIX MILLIONS, if the principal is

a HUN-

It is neceſſary I ſhould obſerve, in juſtice to our preſent miniſters, that in adopting the ſcheme on which I have made theſe remarks, they have only followed the example of former miniſters; and that, however needleſs a waſte it occaſions of public money, there is reaſon to fear it will be followed by future miniſters; for the increaſe of difficulty and expence in redeeming the public debts, which ſuch ſchemes create, being to be felt *hereafter*, it makes no impreſſion, and is little regarded.

In 1759, the fifth year of the laſt war, the lenders of 6.600,000 l. were granted a capital in the 3 *per cents* of 7,590,000 l. together with the profits of the Lottery. Subtract from the ſum advanced, 150,000l. for the profits of the Lottery; and it will appear, that, in this inſtance, 1.140,000l. was *needleſsly* added to the capital; there being no reaſon to doubt, but that lenders would then have

a HUNDRED MILLIONS borrowed at 6 *per cent.* might be redeemed in 33 years with a million *per ann.* ſurplus. But if the principal is TWO HUNDRED MILLIONS bearing 3 *per cent.* the ſame ſurplus would, in the ſame time, pay off only 56 millions; and but little more than a *quarter* of the annuity would be redeemed. If, therefore, the ſame ſum might as well have been obtained by creating a principal of a hundred millions bearing 6 *per cent.* as by creating a capital of two hundred millions bearing 3 *per cent.* there will be a needleſs expence, in diſcharging the debt, of 144 millions.

readily

readily advanced 6.600,000l. for a capital of 6.450,000l. bearing 3 ½ *per cent.* (*a*) intereſt, provided the profits of a Lottery were annexed; inſtead of advancing the ſame ſum for a nominal capital near 18 *per cent.* greater, but bearing 3 *per cent* intereſt.

Again. In 1762, in order to raiſe 12 millions, every contributor of 80 l. was entitled to a capital of 100l. to bear 4 *per cent.* intereſt for 19 years; and afterwards to become redeemable, and to bear intereſt at 3 *per cent.* And for the remaining 20 l. neceſſary to make up a 100l. contributors were entitled to an annuity of 1 l. for 98 years.——This was the ſame with promiſing, for every 60l. advanced, a 100l. capital in the 3 *per cent.* annuities, not redeemable for 19 years; and, for the remaining 40 l. neceſſary to make up 100l. an annuity of 2 l. for 19 years; and, after that, of 1 l. for 79 years.

By this ſcheme no leſs a ſum than 4.800,000l. was needleſsly added to the capital of the public debts. For, had 5 *per cent.* been offered for for every 60l. advanced; (*b*) and, for the remaining

(*a*) The price of the 3 *per cents* at the time of this loan (in the beginning of Feb. 1759) was 88 ½ and 89.

(*b*) The 3 *per cents* juſt before this loan were at 69 l. and, conſequently, 5 *per cent.* intereſt, (or 3 l. *per ann.* for 60l.) would

maining 40 l. an annuity of 2 l. during 19 years, and afterwards of 1 l. for 79 years; equal encouragement might have been given (as will appear presently) to contributors; the annuity payable by the public would have been the same; and the new capital would have been 7.200,000 l. bearing 5 *per cent.* interest; which might, at any time, have been redeemed with a saving of a quarter of a million *per ann.* (the first payment to be made immediately) in 17 years and two months: Whereas now, this debt will not become redeemable till 1781; and then, it will form a capital of 12 millions, not capable of being redeemed with the same saving, in less than twenty years. Above six millions, therefore, will be wasted. (*a*)

The capital of 12 millions four *per cent.* annuities created this year, were made irredeemable for 19 years, to guard against the effects of an apprehension then unavoidable, that an interest of 4 *per cent.* would, if the capitals were redeemable, be reduced, whenever peace came, to 3 *per cent.*

would have afforded subscribers a profit of 9 l. for every 60 l. advanced. The long annuity was worth, as the stocks then stood, 21 years purchase, and the short annuity, 13 years purchase. Upon the whole loan, therefore, the profit would have been 3 *per cent.*

(*a*) That is, the difference between 12 millions, and the sum bearing interest at 3 *per cent.* which a quarter of a million *per ann.* would pay off in 17 years

as had been done in the preceding peace.—But this end would have been anſwered, with equal effect and more advantage to the public, by ſubjecting the redemption of any new capitals bearing high intereſt, to ſuch a regulation as the following; namely, "that the intereſt of them ſhould be for "ever irreducible, and no part of the principal ca-"pable of being redeemed without at the ſame time "redeeming three times or four times more of the "3 *per cent.* or ſome other ſtocks."(*a*) This would have placed ſuch capitals ſo nearly on the ſame footing with the 3 *per cent.* annuities as to render it poſſible, without increaſing the annual charge, to obtain for them ſums equal to or even greater than the capitals themſelves.——In the preſent inſtance, particularly, it ſeems probable that (100l. three *per cent.* ſtock being at 69) a greater ſum than 100l. would be given for 100l. FIVE *per cent.* ſtock, ſuppoſing it not redeemable except under the reſtriction I have mentioned; and conſequently, that as much money might be given for a capital of 7.200,000l. bearing the latter intereſt, as for 12 millions bearing the former. This would be to exchange an irreducible annuity of 360,000l. (the intereſt of 12 millions) not redeemable for 19 years, for an equal annuity irreducible

(*a*) For a farther account, and a more diſtinct explanation of the whole ſubject of this Section, I muſt beg leave to refer to the Supplement at the end of this Tract.

alſo, but the intereſt of 7.200,000l. redeemable in ſome degree at any time.——It is manifeſt that the amount of intereſt on both capitals being the ſame, many millions would be ſaved without incurring any loſs. Had there however been a neceſſity of granting a *quarter* or a *half per cent* more intereſt on the ſmaller capital, the advantage of the exchange would ſtill have been very conſiderable.

Again. In January 1760, eight millions were borrowed by offering for this ſum a capital of eight millions to carry 4 *per cent.* intereſt for 21 years, and afterwards 3 *per cent.* together with a *premium* of 240,000l. ſtock carrying the ſame intereſt, and divided into 80,000l. lottery tickets, each 3l. ſtock.——This was the ſame with offering, for 80l. of every 100l. advanced, a capital of 100l. in the 3 *per cent.* annuities, not redeemable for 21 years; and for the remainder, beſides a lottery ticket, an annuity of 1l. for 21 years.——The ſame ſum, with the help of the regulation I have propoſed, (*a*) might have

(*a*) The 3 *per cents.* being at this time at 80l. an annuity of 3l. equally durable, purchaſed for 75l. would have produced a profit of 5l. Therefore theſe ſchemes are of exactly the ſame value. But they are too narrow; and the ſubſcription this year fell immediately to one *per cent.* diſcount. But in the ſcheme I have propoſed this might have been prevented by only offering 4 *per cent.* for 77l. or 78l. (inſtead of 75l.) of every 100l.

 been

been raiſed by offering 4 *per cent.* for 75l. of every 100l. advanced, and for the remaining 25l. an annuity of 1 l. for 21 years, together with a lottery ticket.——In this caſe, the new capital, inſtead of 8.240,000 l. bearing 3 *per cent.* not ſubject to redemption, and having an annuity of 82,400 l. annexed for 21 years, would have been 6.000,000 l. bearing 4 *per cent.* with the ſame annuity annexed, but redeemable at *any* time; and 240,000 l. (*a*) bearing 4 *per cent.* for 21 years, and afterwards 3 *per cent.*

By the ſcheme likewiſe in 1761, for borrowing 11.400,000l. a capital of 100l. bearing 3 *per cent. intereſt*, was given for part of every 100l. advanced; and for the other part, an annuity of 1l. 2s. 6d. for 99 years. Had, in this caſe, 75 l. FOUR *per cent.* STOCK, ſubject to the reſtriction at redemption before propoſed, been offered for 75 l. in *money*; and, for the remaining 25 l. neceſſary to make up 100 l. the ſaid annuity of 1 l. 2 s. 6 d. for 99 years; (*b*) the whole annual charge would

(*a*) It is plain, that this capital, as well as the former, might have been a quarter (or 60,000 l.) leſs, which would have made the whole ſaving of capital 2.060,000 l.

(*b*) At the time of this loan, the 3 *per cents.* were above 75; and, therefore. a perpetual annuity of 3 l. could not be purchaſed for 75 l. and an annuity of 1 l. 2s. 6d. for 99 years, was worth at leaſt 27 l. This, therefore, would have been a ſcheme very profitable to ſubſcribers.

have

have been the ſame; ſubſcribers could not have been ſenſible of any difference in the encouragement offered them; and the public, in paying its debts, would have ſaved 2.850,000 l.

There was alſo this year 600,000 l. received by government for 600,000 l. ſtock, carrying 3 *per cent.* intereſt, and divided into 60,000 lottery tickets, each worth 10 l. in ſtock.—As 150,000 l. of this ſum was paid for the profits of the lottery; and as 4 *per cent.* could not at this time be made of money laid out in the funds, it is out of doubt, that the ſame ſum (or 600,000 l.) would have been given for 450,000 l. ſtock, carrying 4 per *cent.* and divided into 60,000 lottery tickets, each of the ſame value with 7l. 10s. four *per cent.* ſtock; and thus 150,000 l. more would have been ſaved.

In like manner; it will appear, that *three millions*, raiſed in 1757, by creating a capital of *three millions* bearing 3 *per cent.* intereſt, (*a*) with a life annuity

(*a*) Suppoſing the life-annuity granted in this caſe worth no more than 14 years purchaſe; a capital of 100l. in the 3 *per cents.* was ſold for 84l. or a capital of three millions, for 2.520,000l.———A premium, therefore, was granted of 480,000l. and this was done without the leaſt reaſon. For the 3 *per cents.* being at that time at 87 and 88, 2.520,000l. would have been lent at $3\frac{1}{2}$ *per cent.* intereſt; and the remaining 480,000l. neceſſary to make up three millions, would have been given for the life annuities; in which caſe, the annual charge occaſioned by the new capital would have been ſomewhat

annuity annexed of 1 l. 2 s. 6 d. for every 100 l. advanced; and alſo, *four millions and a half* raiſed in 1758, by creating a capital of *four millions and a half*, bearing 3 *per cent.* with an annuity of a *half per cent.* annexed for 24 years; might have been raiſed by creating, in the former caſe, a capital of two millions and a half, and, in the latter, a capital of four millions, bearing 3½ *per cent.* intereſt, with the ſame annuities annexed.

In 1758, the additional ſum of half a million was borrowed at 3 *per cent.* by a lottery, conſiſting of 50,000 tickets, each of the ſame real value with 10 l. *ſtock*, but ſold to the ſubſcribers for 10 l. in *money* (*a*). As the 3 *per cents.* were now at 94, 3¼ *per*

what leſs; and 480,000 l. would have been ſaved, together with the additional expence occaſioned by the longer time which a given ſurplus would require to diſcharge a debt bearing 3 *per cent.* intereſt, as explained in the note, p. 94.

(*a*) It is a general and certain maxim "that whenever "money is borrowed by a lottery which gives a right to *ſtock* "equal to the ſum advanced, there is a loſs equal to the ſum "which might have been received for the profits of the lot-"tery."——When the three *per cents.* are at 76 or 77, half a million might be borrowed by a lottery, conſiſting of 50,000 tickets, each of the ſame value with 10 l. three *per cent.* ſtock: and hitherto ſuch a method of borrowing has been reckoned advantageous. But it only gives a fallacious appearance of borrowing at 3 *per cent.* It is the ſame with ſelling the profits of

3¼ *per cent.* could not be made of money laid out in the funds. Therefore, 350,000l. of this half million

of a lottery, and at the ſame time abſurdly converting the purchaſe-money into a debt due to the purchaſer.——Since the laſt war we have had ſeven of theſe lotteries, including two in 1763; and above a million has been loſt by them.

In Queen *Anne*'s time, there were ſeveral lotteries, conſiſting of all *prizes* and no *blanks*. This is ſo curious, and moſt perſons may be ſo much at a loſs to conceive of the poſſibility of it, that I cannot help explaining it.

A capital, equal to the whole money advanced, was diſtributed *equally* among all the tickets in the lottery; and, in order to make them prizes of different values, there was farther diſtributed among them different ſhares of an additional capital, to which a right was given, though no money had been paid for it.——For example——In 1711, two millions were raiſed by a lottery of this kind, called a claſs lottery. The whole ſum advanced was divided into 20,000 tickets, each 100l. ſtock bearing 6 *per cent.* intereſt. This capital was increaſed by a gratuitous capital of 602,200l. bearing the ſame intereſt, and divided into ſhares which were added to the tickets, in order to form prizes.—This was the ſame with giving near 8 *per cent.* for money, beſides a *premium* at redemption of 30 *per cent.*—As the intereſt of money was at this time 6 *per cent.* the ſum borrowed would moſt certainly have been advanced at 8 *per cent.* without any *premium*; but it was, I ſuppoſe, reckoned neceſſary that government ſhould not *ſeem* to give ſuch high intereſt.——In the ſame year, 1.500,000l. was borrowed by another ſuch lottery, and creating a capital of 1.928,570l. And in 1712, 3.600,000l. was borrowed by two more ſuch lotteries, and creating a capital of 4.683,080l.



——The

million might have been raiſed at $3\frac{1}{2}$ *per cent.* intereſt, and the remaining 150,000l. might have been procured for the profits of the lottery. Or (which is the ſame) 10 l. each would have been given for 50,000 tickets, of the ſame value taken all together, with 350,000l. carrying $3\frac{1}{2}$ *per cent.* intereſt; and a capital of 150,000l. would have been ſaved.

The ſame is true of the lottery, by which half a million was borrowed in 1756.——A million and a half alſo borrowed in this year carrying $3\frac{1}{2}$ *per cent.* irredeemable for 15 years, might have been procured by creating a capital of only 1.400,000 l. bearing $3\frac{1}{4}$ *per cent.* intereſt. But I will not examine any more of theſe loans. Let us next conſider how detrimental they have been to the public.

The

——The greateſt part of the debts contracted by theſe lotteries (amounting to 9.213,850 l. though only 7.100,000l. was advanced) remains at this hour an incumbrance on the public; and the duties conſtituting the *general fund* are charged with the intereſt of it.

In 1714, the national intereſt was reduced to 5 *per cent.* But in that very year 1.400,000l. was borrowed by a lottery, which gave a right to a capital of 1.876,000 l. bearing 4 *per cent.* that is, by giving near $5\frac{1}{2}$ *per cent.* intereſt, beſides a *premium* of 34 *per cent.*——Thus have our debts been increaſed. But even worſe has been done. The taxes charged with the intereſt of the public debts proving often deficient, the ſhorteſt

way

The attentive reader must have observed, as I have gone along, that the extravagance on which I have insisted, has been the consequence of not separating, in the schemes for raising money, the premiums from the perpetual annuities, and requiring them to be distinctly paid for; and also of not considering how important a difference there is between selling an *Annuity*, and selling the *Stock* for which that annuity is paid.

Would any one, in selling any part of his property, offer to make the purchase-money an outstanding principal which he shall be bound to return? This is what government has uniformly done in its proposals for raising money.—Were I to desire any sum to be lent me *without* interest, offering as a *compensation* or *premium* a short or long or life annuity, or an advantageous contract; the proposal would not be accepted, unless the annuity or the contract was worth the sum to be lent; and I should make myself a debtor to the purchaser for the very thing which I sold to him. (*a*)

——The

way of discharging the arrears has been taken, by adding them to the principal, and paying *compound* interest for money.——Is it a wonder, that a nation which has been so careless in contracting debts, should have done so little towards discharging them?

(*a*) The expectation of receiving back some time or other the purchase-money would probably, in private loans, influence

——The absurdity would be the same, if instead of borrowing *without* interest, I should in the same way borrow at a *low* interest. In every such bargain, I should bring upon myself a needless debt, equal to the value of the *premium*.

I am afraid I have tired my reader's attention on this subject. But as much depends upon a right understanding of it, I wish to shew it in every possible light. In hopes, therefore, of being attended to a little longer, I shall endeavour to give a yet fuller view of this subject, and to prove its importance, by recapitulating some of the foregoing remarks, and comparing the *present* state of our public debts, with that which would have been their state, had the errors I have pointed out in the schemes of the public loans during the last war, been avoided.

The sum of 12 millions, borrowed in 1762, would have left, at the end of the war, a redeemable capital of 7.200,000l. carrying 5 *per cent.* interest, with an annuity added of 120,000l. for 18 years from January 1763, instead of an *ir*-redeemable capital of 12 millions carrying 4 *per cent.* for 18 years, and afterwards 3 *per cent.* See page 95, &c.

ence a purchaser. But in the cases to which I allude, this certainly was not considered, and did not influence. And if it had influenced, the observations I have made as I have gone along, demonstrate that the same loans might have been obtained without giving any such expectation.

The

The ſum of 12 millions, borrowed in 1761, would have left a redeemable capital of 9 millions bearing 4 *per cent.* intereſt, with a long annuity annexed; inſtead of 12 millions with the ſame annuity annexed. Page 100.

The ſum of 8 millions, borrowed in 1760, would have left a redeemable capital of 6.180,000l. carrying 4 *per cent.* with an annuity of 82,400l. for 18 years from January 1763; inſtead of 8.240,000l. *ir*-redeemable, and carrying 4 *per cent.* for 18 years, and afterwards 3 *per cent.* Page 99.

The ſum of 6.600,000l. borrowed in 1759, would have left a capital of 6.450,000l. carrying 3½ *per cent.* inſtead of a capital of 7.590,000l. carrying 3 *per cent.* Page 95.

The ſum of five millions, borrowed in 1758, would have left a redeemable capital of 4.350,000l. bearing 3½ *per cent.* intereſt, with an annuity added of 22,500l. for 19 years from Midſummer 1763; inſtead of a capital of five millions irredeemable, and carrying 3½ *per cent.* for 19 years, and afterwards 3 *per cent.* Page 101, 102, &c.

The ſum of three millions, borrowed in 1757, would have left a capital of two millions and a half bearing 3½ *per cent.* intereſt, inſtead of three millions bearing 3 *per cent.* intereſt.——And two millions, borrowed in 1756, inſtead of leaving a capital of two millions, would have left a capital of only 1.750,000l. Page 104.

It

It will appear from the POSTSCRIPT at the end of this tract, that all the savings and surplus monies of the kingdom, ordinary and extraordinary, from 1763 to 1775, have amounted to no more than 10.739,793 l. It follows, therefore, that the whole surplus of the revenue for 12 years has not been sufficient to discharge the capital to which in the last war a right was given without receiving any money for it, or obtaining the least advantage by it. I will add, that had it not been for this mistake, the *annual charge* as well as the *capital* of the public debts would now have been considerably less than it is; for the greatest part of the money which has been applied since the last war to the discharge of our debts, having been applied to the discharge of debts bearing 3 and 3½ *per cent.* interest, would have been applied to the discharge of debts bearing 3½, 4 and 5 *per cent.* interest. (*a*)

The result, therefore, is, that the whole capital of the public debts, would have been, at the end of the last war, near TWELVE MILLIONS AND A HALF less than it was; and at the same time, the annual charge not greater.

(*a*) The regulation proposed in P. 98 is here supposed to have been applied separately to all the loans of the war, in consequence of which the whole of all surplus monies would be left free to be applied to the redemption of those loans preferably to any loans bearing lower interest.

4 In

In these obſervations I have confined my enquiries to the loans of the laſt war. Had I extended them to all our loans, it would have appeared, that a greater ſum than moſt perſons can think credible, (*b*) has been ſuch a needleſs addition to our debts as I have explained; or, " a pure and un-" compenſated loſs, which might have been " avoided by only framing differently the ſchemes " of the public loans."

(*b*) SIXTEEN MILLIONS have been ſpecified. It will come in my way to mention ſeveral MILLIONS more in the ſecond ſection of the next part. See note 1, p. 125; note 12, p. 132; note 15, p. 134; and a note in p. 137.

# PART III.

## SECT. I.

ABSTRACT of the EXPORTS from and IMPORTS to GREAT-BRITAIN from 1697 to 1773, with REMARKS.

| ANNUAL MEDIUM. | IMPORTS. | EXPORTS. | EXCESS of EXPORTS. | |
|---|---|---|---|---|
| | £. | £. | £. | |
| for FOUR Years ended at 1700 — | 4.956,975 — | 6.034,724 — | 1.077,749 | or $\frac{10}{56}$ of the exports. |
| For FIVE Years ended at 1710 — | 5.321,717 — | 6.713,246 — | 1.391,529 | or $\frac{10}{48}$ of the exports. |
| at 1715 — | 5.304,343 — | 7.401,946 — | 2.097,603 | or $\frac{10}{35}$ of the exports. |
| at 1725 — | 6.628,279 — | 9.663,527 — | 3.035,248 | or $\frac{10}{32}$ of the exports. |
| at 1735 — | 7.470,454 — | 11.855,226 — | 4.384,772 | or $\frac{10}{27}$ of the exports. |
| at 1745 — | 7.363,079 — | 11.922,982 — | 4.559,903 | or $\frac{10}{26}$ of the exports. |
| at 1750 — | 7.429,739 — | 12.877,129 — | 5.447,390 | or $\frac{10}{24}$ of the exports. |
| at 1755 — | 8.264,834 — | 13.406,530 — | 5.141,696 | or $\frac{10}{26}$ of the exports. |
| at 1760 — | 8.877,144 — | 14.253,377 — | 5.376,233 | or $\frac{10}{26}$ of the exports. |
| For FOUR Years ended at 1764 — | 10.110,870 — | 15.793,158 — | 5.682,228 | or $\frac{10}{28}$ of the exports. |
| For NINE Years ended at 1773 — | 11.996,769 — | 14.814,074 — | 2.817,305 | or $\frac{10}{53}$ of the exports. |



This

This ABSTRACT has been formed from the accounts delivered annually to the HOUSE OF COMMONS, and lately publiſhed by Sir CHARLES WHITWORTH.

In order to draw juſt inferences from it, the following particulars ſhould be remembered.——Firſt. The EXPORTS in the *Cuſtom-Houſe* entries are, for reaſons well known, too high. This exceſs has, by ſome of the beſt judges, been reckoned at a million *per ann.*——Secondly. The IMPORTS are too low, no ſmuggled commodities being included in them. This deficiency has been eſtimated at another million *per ann.* But, in order to be ſure of keeping within bounds, I will take both at a *million and a half per ann.*——Thirdly. The intereſt of the national debt paid to foreigners; the money ſpent in foreign countries by *Engliſh* travellers; the bullion conſumed in manufactures; and the wear of the current coin, cannot, perhaps, amount to much leſs than two millions *per ann.* I will, however, take them at no more than the annual ſum which has been commonly ſuppoſed to be due to foreigners from our funds; or, a *million and a half.*——In order, therefore, to find the GRAND BALANCE OF PAYMENT between *Britain* and the reſt of the world *ſince* the laſt war, all theſe ſums (making up THREE MILLIONS) muſt be deducted from the exceſs of the exports. ——But, in order to find the ſame balance *before* the end of the laſt war, leſs muſt be deducted, in proportion as the national debt and the foreign trade were *then* leſs than they are *now*.

If the foregoing Abſtract is examined with a due regard to this rule, it will be found that, from (*a*) 1710 to 1764, the BALANCE OF PAYMENT muſt have been in favour of *Britain*; and that conſequently, there muſt have been, during that period, an influx of money into the kingdom.—It was this, together with the increaſe of our paper, that produced the rapid fall of intereſt which began a few years before the *Acceſſion*. And it was this alſo that enabled us to bear the great expence of the two laſt wars, and the loſs of thoſe enormous ſums which were ſent out of the kingdom to pay foreign ſubſidies, and to ſupport armies on the continent.

Before 1710 it appears to be doubtful, whether the exceſs of the exports was ſuch as brought any money into the kingdom; but it ſeems certain, that it could not have been ſuch as in any degree compenſated that drain of the public caſh, which was occaſioned by the continental wars of King

(*a*) In the exports, as delivered to the *Houſe of Commons*, is included bullion exported. If this, as well as the other ſums I have mentioned, is deducted, there will be ſtill a balance left in favour of *Britain* during this period. Since 1764, it does not appear, from the accounts laid before the *Houſe of Commons*, as publiſhed by Sir *Charles Whitworth*, that any bullion has been entered for exportation.

*William* and Queen *Ann*. In consequence of this, the quantity of *specie* in the kingdom must have been greatly diminished; and Dr. *Davenant* computes that in 1711 it was nine millions less than at the *Revolution*. Hence proceeded the high rate of interest; the unproductiveness of the taxes; and the difficulties which government met with in raising money during those two wars: And there is reason to believe, these difficulties would have been insurmountable, had not a substitute for *specie* been provided by the establishment of the *Bank*.

In the interval of peace between the two last wars, or from 1748 to 1755, the balance in favour of *Britain* was at the highest; and this contributed to raise the stocks (*a*) to such a price, as enabled government to reduce the interest of the public debts from 4 to 3 *per cent*.

But the observation I here intended principally to make is, that the *balance*, since the year 1764, appears, from the preceding abstract, to have been *against* BRITAIN; and that this accounts for the high price of bullion, the scarcity of specie, and the distress of the *Bank* from that year to 1773.

(*a*) The 3 *per cent*. annuities were then at 105; and, during the first five years of the war which began in 1755, they were higher than they have generally been *since* the war.

It deſerves farther to be obſerved that, while the exports were decreaſing from 1764 to 1773, the IMPORTS appear to have increaſed faſter than ever: And the fact is, that ſince 1760, a greater addition has been made to them, than had been made during the whole time from the *Acceſſion* to that year.——This is a ſtriking proof that luxury has been for ſome years increaſing with rapidity among us; and it is worth adding, that the productiveneſs of the taxes has kept pace, as might have been expected, with this increaſe of luxury, both the CUSTOMS and EXCISES having brought in lately, near 250,000l. *per ann.* each, more than they did twelve years ago.——It ſhould be attended to, that this improvement of the revenue muſt be the effect ſolely of an increaſed conſumption occaſioned by luxury; the taxes, ever ſince the end of the laſt war, having been nearly the ſame.

The *exports* from 1710 to 1764 went on increaſing conſtantly. I have obſerved, that from 1764 to 1773 they have decreaſed. One reaſon of this has been, the decline of the PORTUGAL trade; the exports to that country having fallen, ſince 1760, from 1.200,000l. *per ann.* to 600,000l. *per ann.*——Another reaſon has been the check which a wretched policy has been giving, ever ſince 1763, to our trade with the Colonies. This trade had for many years contributed more than any

 other

other trade towards raiſing our *exports*; and even in the period between 1763 and 1774, notwithſtanding the checks it received, it went on increaſing, and produced a balance in our favour of a million and a half *per ann.* But ſince 1774 it has been entirely loſt. *Before* this loſs, the balance of payment between us and the reſt of the world was, according to the account I have given, *againſt* us. Undoubtedly then, it was a loſs we could by no means have ſuſtained, had it not been for the ſeaſonable interpoſition of ſome very particular cauſes. Time will ſhew whether theſe cauſes are of a permanent nature, or temporary and accidental.

# SECT. II.

## HISTORICAL DEDUCTION *and* ANALYSIS *of the* PUBLIC DEBTS.

---

### STATE *and* AMOUNT *of the* NATIONAL DEBT, *at Midsummer*, 1775, *with the Charges of Management.*

### CAPITALS and ANNUITIES transferrable at the BANK OF ENGLAND.

| | Principal. £. | Interest. £. |
|---|---|---|
| CAPITAL of their original Fund—See Note (1) p. 125 — — | 3.200,000 | 96,000 |
| EXCHEQUER bills, by 3d of *Geo.* I. c. 8th, bearing originally 5 *per cent.* interest, but reduced to 4 *per cent.* in 1727, and to 3 *per cent.* by 23d *George* II. 1749. See Note (2) p. 126 - | 500,000 | 15,000 |
| Purchased of the SOUTH SEA COMPANY in 1722, —reduced from 6 to 5 *per cent.* interest in 1717; from 5 to 4 *per cent.* in 1727; and to 3 *per cent.* by 23d of *George* II. 1749.—See Note (3) — — | 4.000,000 | 120,000 |
| Carried over | 7.700,000 | 231,000 |

 Lent

| | Principal. £. | Interest. £. |
|---|---|---|
| Brought over — | 7.700,000 | 231,000 |
| Lent to government at 4 *per cent.* in 1728, charged on the surplus of the fund for the lottery in 1714, and reduced to 3 *per cent.* by 23d *George* II. 1749 | 1.250,000 | 37,500 |
| Lent at 4 *per cent.* in 1727; charged on the duties on coals; and reduced to 3 *per cent.* by 23d of *George* II. 1749 — — | 1.750,000 | 52,500 |
| Lent at 4 *per cent.* in 1746; charged on licences for retailing spirituous liquors; and reduced to 3 *per cent.* by 23d *Geo.* II. 1749 — | 986,800 | 29,604 |
| Amount of Bank capital £. | 11.686,800 | 350,604 |
| See Note (4) p. 126. | | |
| Charge of management 5,898 *l.* *per ann.* | | |
| BANK ANNUITIES. | | |
| Consolidated 4 *per cent.* annuities due *April* 5, and *October* 10—See Note (5) — — | 18,986,300 | 759,452 |
| Carried over £ | 30.673,100 | 1.110,056 |

These annuities fall to 3 *per cent.* in *January*, 1781.

Charge of management 10,680 *l.* *per ann.*

Annuities

| | Principal. | Interest, |
|---|---|---|
| Brought over — | £.30.673,100 | 1.110,056 |
| Annuities at 3½ *per cent.* 1758, due *Jan.* 5, and *July* 5.—These annuities fall to 3 *per cent.* in 1782 — — | 4.500,000 | 157,500 |
| See an account of them in p. 101. | | |
| Charge of management 2,805*l. per ann.* including management on half a million raised at the same time by a lottery, and made a part of the consolidated 3 *per cents.* | | |
| CONSOLIDATED 3 *per cent.* annuities due *Jan.* 5, and *July* 5. See Note (6) | 38.251,696 | 1.147,551 |
| Management 21,087 *l. per ann.* | | |
| REDUCED 3 *per cent.* annuities, due *April* 5, and *Oct.* 10. See Note (7) | 18.353,774 | 550,613 |
| Charge of management 10,324*l. per ann.* | | |
| Three *per cent.* 1726, due *Jan.* 5, and *July* 5, charged on the deduction of 6*d. per* pound on all pensions from the civil list; and on all payments from the crown, except to the navy and army—See Note (8) p. 128 — | 1.000,000 | 30,000 |
| Carried over £. | 92.778,560 | 2.995,720 |

Management 360*l. per ann.*

Long

| | Principal. £. | Interest. £. |
|---|---|---|
| Brought over — | 92.778,560 | 2.995,720 |
| Long annuity due *Jan.* 5, and *July* 5 — — | 6.702,750 | 248,250 |
| The remaining term from *Jan.* 1776, is 84 years— See Note (9) p. 128. | | |
| Management 3,491 *l. per ann.* | | |
| CAPITALS and ANNUITIES transferrable at the SOUTH SEA HOUSE. | | |
| SOUTH SEA STOCK — | 3.662,784 | 109,884 |
| The dividend on this ſtock, at $3\frac{1}{2}$ *per cent.* is 128,197*l.* 9*s.*—Due *Jan.* 5, and *July* 5. | | |
| SOUTH SEA 3 *per cent.* OLD Annuities due *April* 5, and *Oct.* 10 | 11.907,470 | 357,224 |
| Three *per cent.* NEW Annuities due *Jan.* 5, and *July* 5 — — | 8.494,830 | 254,845 |
| Three *per cent.* 1751, due *Jan.* 5, and *July* 5 — | 1.919,600 | 57,588 |
| Charge of management on *South Sea* Stock and Annuities 15,100*l. per ann.*—See Note (10). | | |
| Carried over £. | 125.465,994 | 4.023,511 |

| | Principal. £. | Interest. £. |
|---|---|---|
| Brought over — | 125.465,994 | 4.023,511 |
| CAPITAL and ANNUITIES transferrable at the INDIA HOUSE. | | |
| EAST INDIA STOCK — Interest 3 *per cent.* *Dividend* 7 *per cent.* 224,000*l.* due *Jan.* 5, and *July* 5.——— See Note (11). | 3.200,000 | 96,000 |
| Charge of management 1.285*l.* 14*s.* 4*d.* | | |
| EAST INDIA Annuity due *April* 5, and *Oct.* 10, charged on the surplus of a tax on spirituous liquors. See Note (12) | 1.000,000 | 30,000 |
| Management 401*l.* 15*s.* 8*d.* *per ann.* | | |
| ANNUITIES payable at the EXCHEQUER. | | |
| ANNUITIES for 96 and 99 years, from various dates, in the time of King *William* and Queen *Anne*—See Note (13) — — | 1.836,276 | 131,203 |
| Salaries to Exchequer officers, and management—5,250*l.* *per ann.* | | |
| Annuities for lives, with benefit of survivorship, granted by the 4th of | | |
| Carried over £. | 131.502,270 | 4.280,714 |

William

| | Principal. £. | Interest. £ |
|---|---|---|
| Brought over — | 131.502,270 | 4.280,714 |
| *William* and *Mary*, 1693.—These annuities are not yet extinct, and they are valued at three years purchase | 22,781 | 7,567 |
| Annuities for lives, with benefit of survivorship, by an Act of the 5th of *Geo.* III. 1765—See Note (14) — — | 18,000 | 540 |
| Annuities for two or three lives, granted in 1694.—Also, Annuities on single lives 1745, 1746, and 1757.—See Note (15)—Their original amount, taken all together, was very nearly 124,000*l.* but they are now reduced by deaths to near 80,000*l.* and their value is here taken at 10 years purchase — | 800,000 | 80,000 |
| Unfunded Debt, consisting of Exchequer bills, (1.250,000*l.*) Navy debt, (1.850,000*l.*) and Civil list debt, supposed 500,000*l.*—The interest is reckoned at 2 *per cent.*—See Note (16) | 3.600,000 | 72,000 |
| Salaries to Exchequer bill officers 650*l.* *per ann.* | | |
| Total of the principal and interest of the National Debt at *Midsummer* 1775. | £. 135.943,051 | 4.440,821 |

# NOTES *containing an* EXPLANATION *and* HISTORY *of the different Articles in the foregoing Account.*

NOTE (1)——BANK OLD CAPITAL. See Page 119.——The BANK was eſtabliſhed in 1694. Their original capital was 1.200,000*l.* bearing 8 *per cent.* intereſt, charged on 5/7ths. of 9*d. per* barrel exciſe, with 4000*l. per ann.* for management.——In 1709, they lent to government 400,000*l.* without intereſt, which increaſed their old capital to 1.600,000*l.* bearing 6 *per cent.* intereſt. In 1742, they again lent to government 1.600,000l. without intereſt; and thereby increaſed this capital to its preſent amount, or to 3.200,000*l.* bearing 3 *per cent.* with the ſame annual ſum for management.——It is of particular importance to obſerve with reſpect to the ſums of 400,000*l.* and of 1.600,000*l.* juſt mentioned, that they were properly a compenſation from the *Bank* to the public for continuing their excluſive privileges; and would have been advanced, or at leaſt the greateſt part of them, though government had not bound itſelf to return the purchaſe money, by making it a part of the principal due to the *Bank*, provided the ſame intereſt had been continued for ſome time on their former principal, and the ſame liberty granted to increaſe their *ſtock.*——The like is true of 1.200,000*l.* advanced by the *India* Company without intereſt in 1708.—In theſe inſtances, therefore, a needleſs addition was made to the public debt of 3.200,000*l.* which, had it been avoided, the public would have had not only a principal ſo much leſs to pay; but it would have ſaved in intereſt at leaſt 96000*l. per ann.* for the old capital of the *Bank* and the capital of the *Eaſt India* Company would have formed, in this caſe, between them, a debt of only 3.200,000*l.* (inſtead of 6.400,000*l.*) the intereſt of which might long ago have been reduced at leaſt one half; or from 8 *per cent.* the original intereſt, to 4 *per cent.*

NOTE

NOTE (2)——*Half a million*, part of the BANK CAPITAL. See Page 119.——This part of the Bank capital consisted originally of two millions in *Exchequer* bills, cancelled for government by an act of the 3d of *Geo.* I. But half a million was discharged in 1729; and a million in 1738.

NOTE (3)——FOUR MILLIONS purchased of the SOUTH-SEA COMPANY; part of the BANK Capital. See Page 119. ——In order to procure this money, the *Bank* sold new stock at 18 *per cent.* premium. This produced a saving of 610,169*l.* the sale of 3.389,831*l.* *stock* having produced four millions in *money*. And, consequently, though by this transaction the capital for which they received interest was increased four millions, yet the *stock* on which they made their dividends was increased only 3.389,831*l.*

NOTE (4)——BANK STOCK and DIVIDEND.——The *stock* on which the *Bank* divides is only 10,780,000*l.* This dividend varies as their profits vary; but for several years it has been 5½ *per cent.* payable half-yearly at *Lady-day* and *Michaelmas.* Their whole annual dividend is, therefore, 592,900*l.* which subtracted from 350,604*l.* the interest paid by government, makes their clear annual profit 242,296*l.* ——Besides interest, they receive for management of their capital 4000*l.* *per ann.* on account of their old capital, and 1,898*l.* *per ann.* on account of four millions purchased of the South Sea Company; in all, 5,898*l.* *per ann.*——The *Bank* receives farther the sums specified in the foregoing account, towards bearing the expences of managing the annuities commonly called *Bank Annuities.* All these expences, including the sums granted for managing their capital, amount to 54,645*l.* *per ann.*

NOTE (5)——CONSOLIDATED 4 *per cent.* BANK ANNUITIES. See Page 120.——The capital of these Annuities consists of two loans, one in 1760, and the other in 1762, consolidated

solidated into one stock, and charged on the additional duty of 3 *d.* per bushel on malt, the surplus of the duties on spirituous liquors, and the additional duties on windows; all which duties were ordered by 2d Geo. III. to be carried to the Sinking Fund, and the interest with which they were charged to be paid out of that fund.——I have made some remarks on these loans in page 96, and page 99. They amounted to 20.240,000 *l.* But 1.253,700*l.* of this capital was changed in 1770, from an interest of 4 to 3 *per cent.* and the capital reduced to the present sum.——A more full account of these annuities may be found in Mr. *Ashmore's* Analysis of the several Bank Annuities, p. 17.

NOTE (6)——CONSOLIDATED 3 *per cent.* BANK ANNUITIES. See page 121.—The capital of these annuities is made a distnct stock from that of the annuities called *Reduced*, because it never bore a higher interest than 3 *per cent.*—It consisted originally of the following loans—37,821 *l.* remaining in 1727, of 3 *per cent.* annuities, granted in lieu of St. *Christopher's* and *Nevis* debentures—800,000*l.* borrowed in 1731—600,000*l.* borrowed in 1736——300,000*l.* in 1738——6.400,000*l.* in 1742, 1743, 1744 and 1745, and charged on additional duties on spirituous liquors, wines, vinegar, &c.——1.000,000*l.* borrowed in 1750——24.490,000*l.* borrowed in the course of the last war, and funded on the additional duties on beer, houses, stamps, &c.——4.900,000*l.* borrowed in 1766, 1767 and 1768——And 1.253,700*l.* of the 4 *per cent.* annuities, subscribed into the 3 *per cent.* annuities in 1770.

All these loans were by 25 Geo. II. 1751, and several subsequent Acts of Parliament, consolidated into one joint stock; and carried, with the duties for paying the interest, to the *Sinking Fund.* And in 1770, they formed a capital of 39.781,521*l.* which has been since reduced, by the payments mentioned in the *Postscript* at the end of this tract, to the sum specified in the account to which this note refers.—See a more full

full account in Mr. Ashmore's Analysis, &c. from page 5 to page 11.

NOTE (7)——REDUCED 3 *per cent.* BANK ANNUITIES. See page 121.—The capital of these annuities consisted, in 1749, of loans in 1746, 1747, and 1748, and navy, ordnance and transport debts funded in 1749, amounting to 18.402,472*l.* and all bearing 4 *per cent.* interest.——By the 23d of Geo. II. 1749, these loans were reduced to an interest of 3 *per cent.* and by the great consolidating Act in 1751, they were converted into one stock, and carried into the Sinking Fund with the duties on carriages, and the additional duties on glass, spirituous liquors, houses, windows, stamps, merchandize imported, &c. which had been granted for paying the interest.—In 1751, certain exchequer tallies and orders, amounting to 129,750*l.* were subscribed into this stock; and in 1765, navy bills to the amount of 1,482,000*l.* were subscribed into it, which made its whole original amount 20.014.222*l.*——In 1751, there was paid off 830,898*l.* being stock which had not been subscribed agreeably to the Act in 1749 for reducing interest; and in 1772, 1774, and 1775, so much more of this stock was paid off as reduced it to its present amount.—See Mr. Ashmore's Analysis, p. 12—16.

NOTE (8)——CIVIL LIST MILLION. See page 121.—The income settled upon King George I. for his civil list, was 700,000*l.*——In 1720, there had been granted him besides, from the *Royal Exchange* and *London* Assurance companies, 300,000*l.* And in 1726, this million was farther granted towards paying off his debts.

NOTE (9)——BANK LONG ANNUITY. See page 122.——This annuity consists of 128,250*l. per ann.* for 99 years, given in 1761, as a *premium* to the subscribers of 11.400,000*l.* at 3 *per cent*; and of 120,000*l. per ann.* for 98 years, given in 1762, as a premium to the lenders of twelve millions at 4 *per*

*cent.*

*cent.* See page 95 and 100. It is charged, together with the loans to which it was annexed, on the *Sinking Fund.* ——— Its value in the Alley is about 25 years purchase; but the remaining term is really worth 27 years purchase, reckoning interest at $3\frac{1}{2}$, (or the 3 *per cents.* being at $85\frac{3}{4}$.) But when interest is at 4 *per cent.* or the 3 *per cents.* are at 75, it is worth only 24 years purchase.——When this annuity is called a *premium*, it must not be imagined, that no compensation was given for it. Government received the value of it; but, at the same time, made itself a debtor for that value. And, what is very surprizing, this has been uniformly practised with respect to all the premiums or douceurs granted by government; and the consequence has been, that great and needless increase of the public debt explained in the 3d section of the 2d Part.

NOTE (10).—SOUTH-SEA STOCK AND ANNUITIES. See page 122.—These four capitals amounting to 25.984,684*l.* 13*s.* consist almost entirely of the remainder of debts contracted in the reigns of *King William* and Queen *Anne*. The following account will probably give sufficient information concerning them.

In 1711, Lord Oxford being minister, the proprietors of certain navy, army, ordnance and transport debts, to the amount of 9.177,968*l.* including arrears of interest, and half a million for the current supplies, were incorporated into a company for trading to the *South-seas*. They were allowed 6 *per cent.* interest for this debt, with 8000*l.* *per ann.* for management; and the duties on wine, tobacco, *East-India* goods, candles, &c. were made perpetual, and granted as a *Fund* (ever since called the *South-sea Company's Fund)* for paying the interest. This kept up public credit at the time, and has been called the *Earl of Oxford's* master-piece.——By the 1st of Geo. I. 822,032*l.* consisting chiefly of interest payable on the Company's capital, was added to the capital, in consequence of which it was increased to TEN MILLIONS, (ever since called their *original capital)* bearing 6 *per cent.* interest,

interest.——In 1717, they agreed to take 5 *per cent*; and this was the first great reduction of interest, which in conjunction with the same reduction of the other redeemable debts almost all carrying 6 *per cent.* laid the foundation of the SINKING FUND established in this year. But it is remarkable, that so fast did interest fall at this time, that the price of *South-sea stock*, notwithstanding this reduction, rose from 101 to 111.—In 1719, the *South-sea* capital was increased to 11.746,844*l.* bearing 5 *per cent.* interest (with an addition of 1,397*l.* 9*s.* to their former allowance for management) by advancing to government 544,142*l.* and by the proprietors of 94,329*l.* 12*s.* lottery annuities for 32 years granted in 1710, accepting in lieu of them 1.202,702*l.* *South Sea stock.*——In 1720, the agreement was made by government with the South Sea Company, which produced the great SOUTH SEA BUBBLE.——There existed at that time *long* annuities to the amount of 666,821*l.* 8*s.* and *short* annuities, for 32 years from 1710, to the amount of 127,260*l.* 6*s.* The proprietors of these annuities were allowed to subscribe them into the *South Sea* trading stock; and the Company, for every 100*l.* of the *long* annuity which should be subscribed, were to receive from government an addition to their capital of 2000*l.* bearing 5 *per cent.* interest till 1727, and afterwards 4 *per cent.* till redeemed: and for every 100*l.* of the *short* annuities, they were to receive an addition to their capital of 1400*l.* bearing the same interests.——They were besides to take in the redeemable debts to the amount of 16.546,482*l.* and to receive an addition to their capital of 100*l.* for every 100*l.* subscribed.——By the subscription of the *long* and *short* annuities which followed this agreement, a capital due from government to the Company was created, which was greater by 3.034,769*l.* than the original sum advanced for the annuities subscribed. And as much of these annuities and of the redeemable debts were subscribed, as increased the *South Sea* trading capital to 37.802,203*l.*——In 1722, four millions of this capital was purchased by the BANK, (See Note 3.) which reduced it to 33.802,203*l.*——By 9 Geo. I. 1723, this remaining capital was divided into two equal parts, one of which alone (or 16.901,101*l.*) was ordered to be the trading capital of the Company, and the other part was directed to be called *South Sea Annuities.*——In 1733, the *South Sea* trading capital had been reduced by payments at different times to 14.691,137*l.* 12*s.* By an Act of Parliament in that year, this remaining stock received a farther division; and only a fourth part, or 3.662,784*l.* was allowed to be the Company's stock; and the other three parts, or 10.988,353*l.* were directed to be called NEW South Sea Annuities, in order to distinguish them from the former annuities, which have ever since gone under the name of OLD South Sea annuities.——From 1733, to the present time, SOUTH SEA STOCK has continued the same; but the capital of the OLD South Sea annuities has been reduced, by redemptions, to 11.907.470*l.* and of the NEW South Sea annuities, to 8.494,830*l.* And of the whole *South Sea* debt, which in 1722 was 33.802,203*l.* there has, since that year, been paid off in all 9.737,119*l.* This should have reduced it to 24.065,081*l.* but it is in reality 25.984,685*l.* The reason of this is, that the diminution just mentioned of the *South Sea* debt was made in part with money borrowed in 1751, to pay off such proprietors of South Sea annuities as had refused to consent to the reduction of interest proposed to them in 1749. The sum borrowed for this purpose was 2.100,000*l.* bearing 3 *per cent.* with 1181*l.* 5*s.* for management. This debt is now reduced by redemptions to the sum specified in the preceding account; or to 1.919,600*l.*

NOTE (11).——EAST-INDIA STOCK. See page 123.——In 1698, a company of merchants, in consideration of two millions lent to government at 8 *per cent.* were incorporated, and entitled to the sole privilege of trading to the *East-Indies.*——These two millions formed the first capital of the present *East-India* Company.——In 1702, an old company of traders to the *East-Indies* was united to this company; and in

1708, these united companies lent to government 1.200,000*l.* without additional interest, which made their capital 3.200,000*l.* bearing 5 *per cent.*——In 1730, this interest was reduced to 4 *per cent.* and by the 23d Geo. II. 1749, to 3 *per cent.*——The salt duties, and some additional stamp duties, were at first charged with the annuity due on this capital; but at present the duties constituting the aggregate fund are charged with it.

NOTE (12).—EAST-INDIA ANNUITY. See page 123.—The capital of this annuity was advanced to government in 1744, at 3 *per cent.* and, in consideration of this loan, the exclusive charter of the Company was continued to Lady-day 1783, at which time it is to cease, provided three years notice has been given, and the debt due from government discharged.

An observation here forces itself upon me, which I have often had occasion to make.——Part of this loan was a compensation from the *East-India* Company for prolonging the term of its charter; and, therefore, ought not to have been included in the loan. The Company would have lent 750,000*l.* on the interest common at the time, or 4 *per cent.* and the remainder would have been advanced as a gratuity.—It is a pity those who managed these contracts for the public, did not attend to the absurdity and extravagance of making a *debt* of purchase money, and *borrowing* in the very act of *selling*.

NOTE (13).——EXCHEQUER LONG ANNUITIES. See page 123.——These are the *long* annuities which, in 1720, remained unsubscribed to the South Sea Company. See Note 10.——They consist first of annuities to the amount of 54,900*l.* 14*s.* 6*d.* purchased by the 4th, 5th, and 6th of *William* and *Mary*, for 96 years, from January 1695, with the addition of 1350*l.* *per ann.* for salaries to exchequer officers. These annuities were originally 14 *per. cent.* life-annuities. By the 6th and 7th of *William* and *Mary*, in order to raise more money, these annuitants, or any other persons

persons for them, were offered a reversionary interest in the annuities after the failure of the lives, till the end of 96 years from January 1695, on paying 4½ years purchase, (that is 63*l.*) for every annuity of 14*l.*——The predecessors of the present company of the MILLION BANK (so called from the MILLION lottery 1694, in which they were some of the principal adventurers) purchased 30,669*l.* 4*s.* of these reversionary annuities. The life annuitants being now reduced to a very small number, almost the whole of this annuity is lapsed to the *company*; and though they have divided for several years 5 *per cent.* on a capital of half a million, yet their growing savings, from the falling in of lives, have been such, that, when their annuity ceases in 1791, they will, I am informed, have accumulated a fund considerably larger, than the capital on which they have made their dividends. But to return.

These EXCHEQUER Annuities consist farther of

| £. | s. | d. | |
|---|---|---|---|
| 30,400 | 6 | 8 | purchased for 99 years from *Christmas* 1705, by 2d and 3d of *Anne*, with 1450*l.* for management. |
| 23,234 | 16 | 6 | purchased for 99 years from *Lady-day*, 1706, by 4 *Anne*, with 1470*l. per ann.* for management. |
| 7,776 | 10 | 0 | purchased for 99 years from *Lady-day*, 1707, by 5 *Anne*, with 375*l.* 12*s. per ann.* for management. |
| 4,710 | 0 | 0 | purchased for 99 years from *Lady-day*, 1708, by 6th of *Anne*, with 208*l.* 2*s. per ann.* for management. |
| 10,181 | 0 | 0 | purchased for 99 years from *Lady-day*, 1707, by a 2d Act of 5th of *Anne*, with 416*l. per ann.* for management. |
| Add 54,900 | 14 | 6 | |
| 131,203 | 7 | 8 | Total. |

 The

The original ſum contributed for theſe annuities was 1.836,276*l.* They are even now worth more than this ſum. The public has already paid above TEN MILLIONS; and by the time they are all extinct, it will have paid above THIRTEEN MILLIONS, on their account. This is great extravagance; but it is nothing to the extravagance conſtantly practiſed of borrowing on perpetual annuities, without putting them into a fixed courſe of redemption.

NOTE (14).—TONTINE by an act of 6 Geo. III. See page 124.—The intention of this Act was to raiſe 300,000*l.* towards paying off navy bills, by offering to ſubſcribers for every 100*l.* advanced, an annuity of 3*l.* for their lives, with benefit of ſurvivorſhip. But the ſcheme did not ſucceed, and only 18000*l.* was ſubſcribed.

NOTE (15) ——LIFE ANNUITIES. See page 124.—— The annuities on *two* lives in 1694, were ſold at 12*l.* *per ann.* during *two* lives, of any ages, and the annuities on *three* lives, at 10*l.* *per ann.* during *three* lives, for every 100*l.* advanced.——This was very extravagant; for, ſuppoſing the annuitants in general, about the age of 20 or 30, it was the ſame, in the caſe of *two* lives, with giving above 10 *per cent.* for money, and in the caſe of three lives, 9 *per cent.*—— It is, likewiſe, extremely abſurd in theſe caſes to pay no regard to difference of ages. A *ſingle* life at the age of 60, ſuppoſing money improved at 4 *per cent.* is intitled to 11 *per cent.* but at the age of 10, ſcarcely to 6 *per cent.* *Two* lives at 60, are entitled, on the ſame ſuppoſition, to 8½ *per cent.* but at 10, not to 5 *per cent.*——The original amount of theſe annuities was 22,700*l.* nearly. In 1762, that is, in 68 years, they were reduced by deaths no lower than 9,215*l.*

The other life-annuities mentioned in the preceding account were *douceurs* granted for loans in 1745, 1746, and 1757. An account of the annuities granted in the laſt of theſe years may be ſeen in page 101.

The life-annuities in 1745, amounted to 22,500*l.* and were granted, together with the profits of a lottery, for a loan of two millions at 4 *per cent.*

The

The life-annuities in 1746, amounted to 45,000*l.* and were granted, with the profits of another lottery, for a loan of three millions, at the same interest.——The remarks made in the 3d section of the last part, and particularly in the note, p. 101, are applicable to these two loans. The value of the life-annuities, and the profits of the lotteries, were made a part of the public debt. And, supposing the life-annuities worth, one with another, only 14 years purchase, and the profits of the two lotteries worth 300,000*l.* it will follow, that the capital created by these loans, instead of being 5.000,000*l.* should have been only 3.755,000*l.*

But there is another remark, which it is proper to mention here. The life-annuities granted in 1757, amounting to 33,750*l.* were, in January 1775, that is in 18 years, reduced by deaths to 28,732*l.* or but a little more than a seventh part. But, supposing the annuitants all in the firmest stage of life, or between the age of 10 and 30, they ought, according to some of the best tables of observations, to have been reduced a *quarter*. These life-annuities have, therefore, fallen in much more slowly than could have been expected; and I have found the same to be true of all the other life-annuities.——The reason, undoubtedly, is, that the tables exhibit the rate of mortality among all sorts and orders of men taken together; whereas, the lives on which annuities are bought, are a selection of the better sort of lives from the general mass, and therefore must be of greater value.——Indeed I am not acquainted with any table of observations which gives the probabilities of the duration of life high enough to be a guide in this case; except that which was formed by Mr. *De Parcieux*, from the French *Tontines*.——A calculation, therefore, of the values of lives, agreeably to this table, would be of considerable use.

NOTE (16).——UNFUNDED DEBT. See page 124.—— I have given the navy debt, as it was in January, 1775.— The civil list debt in 1775, was probably more than the sum at which I have reckoned it. Lord STAIR, in his account of the national debt, income, and expenditure, reckons it at 800,000*l.*



Much

Much the greatest part of the foregoing debts, with the taxes for paying the interest, including the duties composing the *Aggregate*, *South-Sea*, and *General* Funds, have, by the 25th of *George* the Second, 1751, and several subsequent acts of Parliament, been thrown into one general account; and the *surplus* of the whole, after deducting the interest, 800,000 l. *per ann.* to the civil list, and a few other payments, forms the SINKING FUND.——The debts not brought to this account are about seven millions and a half in the *South-Sea* House; 11.186,800 l. of the *Bank* capital; the Civil List million; four millions and a half borrowed at 3 ½ *per cent.* in 1758; the capital of the East-India annuity; and the Exchequer long and life annuities, except those granted in 1758. But the *surplusses* of the duties which pay the interest of these debts, are either carried *immediately* into the *Sinking Fund* account; or brought *first* to the *Aggregate* Fund, and from thence carried into that account.——On the contrary. Deficiencies in these duties when they happen, are made good out of the Sinking Fund; and afterwards replaced from the supplies.

For example. Three old nine-penny excises on beer, with an additional three-pence per barrel, producing above half a million annually; also, 3,700 l. *per* week out of the hereditary excise on beer,

beer, together with ſome duties on paper, coals, &c. and ⅓ additional ſubſidy of tonnage and poundage, are appropriated to the payment of the Banker's Annuity; the Life Annuities granted in 1693 and 1694; the Exchequer Long Annuities; and annuities on various ſums ſubſcribed to the South-Sea Company in 1720. The ſurpluſſes make a part of the *Aggregate Fund*; and after contributing to ſatisfy the charge on that fund, are carried into the *Sinking Fund.*—— Again. Certain additional duties on ſoap, parchment, coals, &c. are appropriated to pay the intereſt of 1.250,000l. and of 1.750,000l. parts of the Bank capital.——The ſurpluſſes are carried *directly* to the *Sinking Fund.*——In like manner. The duties on houſes and windows impoſed by an act of the 20th of *George* the Second, 1747, (*a*) after deducting from them 91,485l. *per ann.* to ſatisfy certain charges on old houſe-duties in the *Aggregate Fund*; and, alſo, other duties on houſes and windows impoſed by the 2d and 6th of *George* the Third, amounting in all to about 205,000l. *per ann.* are carried into the Sinking Fund, together with the capitals, the in-

(*a*) Theſe duties were appropriated to the payment of the intereſt at 4 *per cent.* of a capital of 4.400,000l. created in 1747, for which four millions only had been advanced. It is now a part of the capital of the reduced 3 *per cent.* annuities.



tereſt

tereſt of which has been charged upon them. But the addition to theſe duties (with a tax on penſions) granted in 1758, and charged with the intereſt (at 3 ½ *per cent.*) of the loan in that year, having not been carried into the *Sinking Fund*, and proving deficient; the deficiency is conſtantly made good out of this fund, and afterwards replaced from the ſupplies.

*State and Amount of the* NATIONAL DEBT *at Chriſtmas* 1753; *with the Charges of Management.*

BANK OF ENGLAND.

| | Principal. £. | Intereſt. £. |
|---|---|---|
| BANK capital — | 11.686,800 | 393,038 |
| Of this capital 3.200,000l. bore at this time 3 *per cent.* intereſt; and the remainder bore 3 ½ *per cent.* till 1757, by 23d Geo. II. 1749.——See note (1) p. 125. | | |
| Management 5,898l. *per ann.* | | |
| Three *per cent.* BANK Annuities conſolidated by 25 Geo. II. 1751.—See note (6) p. 127. — | 9.137,821 | 274,135 |
| Management 4,450l. *per ann.* | | |
| Total | £20.824,621 | 667,173 |

BANK

| | Principal. | Interest. |
|---|---|---|
| | £. | £. |
| Brought over | 20.824,621 | 667,173 |
| BANK Annuities consolidated by 25 Geo. II. 2.713,618l. carrying 3 ½ *per cent.* interest till 1755; and 14.857,956l. carrying the same interest till 1757. See note (7) p. 128. — | 17,7401,32 | 619,546 |
| Management 9,884l. *per ann.* | | |
| Civil List million, 1726 | 1.000,000 | 30,000 |
| Management 360l. *per ann.* | | |
| Whole charge of Management at the Bank in 1753—20,592l. *per ann.* | | |
| SOUTH-SEA COMPANY. | | |
| SOUTH-SEA Stock carrying 4 *per cent.* till 1757 — | 3.662,784 | 146,511 |
| Old and New SOUTH-SEA Annuities carrying 3 ½ *per cent.* till 1757 — | 21.362,525 | 747,688 |
| Three *per cent.* 1751— See note (10) p. 131. | 2.100,000 | 63,000 |
| Whole charge of management at the *South-Sea-House* on stock and annuities, 15,748 l. *per ann.* | | |
| EAST-INDIA HOUSE. | | |
| EAST-INDIA STOCK, reduced to 3 ½ till 1757 | 3.200,000 | 112,000 |
| | £.69.851,254 | 2.385,918 |

EAST

| | Principal. | Interest. |
|---|---|---|
| | £. | £. |
| Brought over | 69.851,254 | 2.385.918 |
| EAST-INDIA annuity 1744 | 1.000,000 | 30,000 |
| Management 1,687l. 10s. *per ann.* | | |
| Total (*a*) | £.70,851,254 | 2.415,918 |

(*a*) The whole of this sum, (except 16.437,821 l. consisting of the old Bank capital, the consolidated 3 *per cents*, the South-Sea 3 *per cent.* annuities 1751, the Civil List million, and the East-India annuity) that is, 54.413,433l. was reduced by 23 Geo. II. 1749, from an interest of 4 *per cent.* to 3 ½ till 1757, and afterwards to 3 *per cent.*——The proprietors of a capital of 3.290,042l. refused to consent to this reduction, which, therefore, was paid off; 1.190,042l. with *Exchequer* Bills (afterwards cancelled); and 2.100,000l. with money borrowed at 3 *per cent.* and added to the capital of the *South-Sea* annuities. The whole sum, therefore, reduced and paid off, was 57.703,475l. which produced a saving to the public, and an addition to the Sinking Fund after 1757, of 612,735l. *per ann.*

The SALT DUTIES in 1753, had been for some time mortgaged to pay the principal and interest of a million borrowed in 1745. In 1757, after clearing the mortgage, they became free, and were carried into the Sinking Fund, of which they have ever since formed a part. This produced a farther addition to the *Sinking Fund*, after 1757, of about 220,000 l. *per ann.*

I have not included the million now mentioned in the account given above of the public debts in 1753, because it was in a fixed course of redemption; nor have I included 499,600l. in Exchequer Bills charged on the duty on sweets, because these Exchequer Bills were paid off in 1754.

EXCHEQUER

| | Principal. | Interest. |
|---|---|---|
| | £. | £. |
| Brought over | £70.851,254 | 2.415,918 |
| EXCHEQUER. | | |
| ANNUITIES for 96 and 99 years from various dates in King *William*'s and Queen *Anne*'s times being the original sum contributed. See note (13) page 132. — | 1.836,276 | 131,203 |
| Management 5,230l. *per ann.* inclusive of management for the two next articles. | | |
| ANNUITIES for lives with benefit of survivorship, being the original sum contributed — | 108,100 | 7,567 |
| ANNUITIES for two and three lives, being the remainder after deducting the annuities fallen in by deaths, and reckoned worth 10 years purchase — — | 106,650 | 10,665 |
| ANNUITIES for single lives 1745, being the remainder after deducting the annuities fallen in by deaths; and reckoned worth 14 years purchase — — | 296,142 | 21,153 |
| | £.73.198,422 | 2.586,506 |

| | Principal. | Intereſt. |
|---|---|---|
| | £. | £. |
| Brought over | 73.198,422 | 2.586,506 |
| ANNUITIES for ſingle lives 1746, being the remainder after the lives fallen in — | 582,274 | 41,591 |
| Navy debt in 1754—Intereſt reckoned at 2 *per cent.* — | 1.296,568 | 25,931 |
| Total of the principal and intereſt of the public debts in 1753 — | £.75.077,264 | 2.654,028 |

STATE *and* AMOUNT *of the* NATIONAL DEBT *in* 1739.

BANK OF ENGLAND.

| | Principal. | Intereſt. |
|---|---|---|
| | £. | £. |
| BANK CAPITAL, conſiſting of 1.600,000l. old capital carrying 6 *per cent*; and 7.500,000l. carrying 4 *per cent.* See note 1, p. 123. — — | 9.100,000 | 396,000 |
| BANK ANNUITIES at 3 *per cent.* for the lottery in 1731. — — | 800,000 | 24,000 |
| | £.9.900,000 | 420,000 |

SOUTH-

| | Principal. £. | Interest. £. |
|---|---|---|
| Brought over | 623,312 | 2.321,215 |
| SOUTH-SEA COMPANY. Stock and annuities bearing 4 *per cent.* — — | 27.302,203 | 1.092,088 |
| EAST-INDIA COMPANY. EAST-INDIA ſtock carrying 4 *per cent.* — | 3.200,000 | 128,000 |
| EXCHEQUER ANNUITIES. Annuities at 3 ½ by 4 Geo. II. paid off in 1752 | 400,000 | 14,000 |
| ANNUITIES at 4 *per cent.* charged on the duty on wrought plate by 6 Geo. I. 1720 — — | 312,000 | 12,480 |
| 182,250l. of this capital was paid off in 1750. The remainder is now included in the capital of the reduced 3 *per cent.* annuities. | | |
| ANNUITIES at 3 *per cent.* charged on the Sinking Fund by 9 and 10 Geo. II. Now included in the conſolidated 3 *per cent.* annuities — | 900,000 | 27,000 |
| ANNUITIES on *Nevis* and St. *Chriſtopher* Debentures at 3 *per cent.* Now included in the conſolidated 3 *per cents.* — | 37,821 | 1,135 |
| | £.42.052,024 | 1.694,703 |

EXCHEQUER

| | Principal. | Intereſt. |
|---|---|---|
| | £. | £. |
| Brought over | 42,052,024 | 1.694,703 |
| EXCHEQUER BILLS charged on a duty upon victuallers by 12 Geo. I. 1726—Carrying 3 *per cent.* — — | 480,000 | 14,400 |
| EXCHEQUER BILLS charged on a duty on ſweets by 10 of Geo. II. 1737—Carrying 3 *per cent.* and paid off in 1754—See the note p. 140. — | 499,600 | 14,988 |
| ANNUITIES for long terms from various dates — | 1.836,276 | 131,203 |
| ANNUITIES for lives with *benefit* of *Survivorſhip* granted in 1693 — | 108,100 | 7,567 |
| ANNUITIES for two and three lives, 1694 — | 106,650 | 15,000 |
| *Navy* debt (*a*) — | 1.300,000 | 26,000 |
| Total of the *Principal* and *Intereſt* of the National Debt in 1739 (*b*) | £.46.382,650 | 1.903,861 |

(*a*) Having met with no account of the Navy Debt at this time, I have choſen, rather than omit it, to ſuppoſe it nearly the ſame that it was at the commencement of the laſt war; which, probably, is reckoning it too high.

(*b*) In this account I have omitted a million borrowed in 1734, becauſe the redemption of it was near being completed by the Salt Duties. I have alſo omitted *Short Annuities* amounting to 24,334l. being the remainder of 9 *per cent.* annuities for 32 years created in 1710, becauſe the term for which they were created was near expiring.

From

From the account in the POSTSCRIPT, at the end of this tract, it will appear, that 10.639,793l. of the public debt was discharged between the years 1763 and 1775; and also that the *funded* debt was, in 1775, 1,400,000l. greater than it was at the end of the last war. From hence, and from the amount of the public debt in 1775, as stated in page 124, it follows, that the funded debt at the end of the war was 130.943,051 l. and the whole debt 146.582,844l. and, consequently, that the war left upon the nation an *unfunded debt* amounting to (*a*) 15.639,793l. This unfunded debt consisted of the following particulars—Of 3,500,000l. borrowed after the peace in 1763, and applied towards bearing such expences of the war as could not immediately cease with its operations.——Of near *eight millions* in navy, victualling, ordnance, and transport debts.——Of 1.800,000l.

(*a*) The author of the *Considerations on the Trade and Finances of this Kingdom* makes this debt 1.318,000 l. more than the sum at which I have here stated it. See page 22; and *State of the Nation* by the same auther, page 15, quarto editions.——The reason of this difference is, that this writer has included in the unfunded debt left by the war the deficiencies of grants and funds in 1763 and 1764, and the *whole* army debt not provided for in those years; whereas I have excluded the former entirely; and admitted only as much of the latter as exceeded the army debts common in subsequent years. See the Postscript.

*Exchequer bills*; and the remainder, of ſubſidies to foreign princes, extraordinaries of the army, and German demands.

In the interval of peace between 1748 and 1755 the following debts were paid off.

| | £. |
|---|---|
| *Bank Annuities* bearing 4 *per cent.* — | 1.013,148 |
| SOUTH-SEA Annuities bearing 4 *per cent.* —— — | 176,893 |
| *Annuities* bearing 3 ½ *per cent.* charged by 4 Geo. II. on additional Stamp-duties — — — | 400,000 |
| EXCHEQUER Bills bearing 3 *per cent.* charged by 10 Geo. II. 1737 on the duties on ſweets — | 499,600 |
| Borrowed in 1745 at 3 ½ *per cent.* on the credit of the Salt duties — See note, page 140. | 1.000,000 |
| (*a*) Total | £.3.089,641 |

(*b*) In 1751 there was applied to the payment of Navy debts 200,000l. and in 1752, the ſum of 900,000l. But I have not reckoned theſe ſums, becauſe they did little more than make up the conſtant deficiency in the *Peace Eſtabliſhment* for the Navy.

From

From the whole, the following account of the progreſs of the National Debt, from 1739 to 1775, may be deduced.

| | Principal £. | Intereſt. £. |
|---|---|---|
| *Amount* of the *principal* and *intereſt* of the national debt before the war which begun in 1740 — — | 46.382,650 | 1.903,861 |
| Amount in 1749 immediately after the war | 78.166,906 | 2.765,608 |
| Increaſed by the war — | 31.784,256 | 861,747 |
| Diminiſhed by the Peace from 1748 to 1755 | 3.089,641 | 111,590 |
| Amount at the commencement of the laſt war — — | 75.077,264 | 2.654,018 |
| Amount at the end of the war in 1763 — | 146.582,844 | 4.840,821 |
| Increaſed by the laſt war | 71.505,580 | 2.186,803 |
| Diminiſhed by the Peace, in twelve years from 1763 to 1775 — | 10.639,793 | (*a*) 400,000 |
| Amount at *Midſummer*, 1775 — — | 135.943,051 | 4.440,821 |

We are now involved in another war, and the public debts are increaſing again faſt. *Exchequer* Bills have been increaſed from 1.250,000l. to 1.500,000l. A new capital of 2.150,000l. has been added to the 3 *per cent*. Conſolidated Annuities.

(*a*) See the Poſtſcript.

nuities. And a vote of credit was given in the laſt ſeſſion of Parliament for a million. The laſt year, therefore, has added 3.400,000l. to our debts, beſides a vaſt ſum not yet provided for, conſiſting of navy, ordnance, victualling, tranſport and army debts.——The preſent year (1777) muſt make another great addition to them; and what they will be at the end of theſe troubles, no one can tell.——The union of a *foreign* war to the preſent *civil* war might perhaps raiſe them to TWO HUNDRED MILLIONS; but, more probably, it would ſink them to——NOTHING.

## SECT. III.

### *Of the* DEBTS *and* RESOURCES *of France.*

MINISTERS have of late ſought to remove the public apprehenſions by general accounts of the weakneſs of powers, which, from the circumſtances of former wars as well as national prejudices, have been felt by the people as jealous rivals or formidable enemies.——I wiſh it was poſſible for me to confirm theſe accounts; and by contraſting the preceding ſtate of our own debts with a ſimilar one of thoſe of FRANCE, to ſhew, that from this power in particular we have nothing to fear. The following particulars, on the

the correctness of which I can rely, may give some assistance in judging of this subject.

The whole expence of the last war to FRANCE was 1.118.307,047 livres; that is, 49.702,000 l. sterling. of which 23.152,000 l. (520.926,000 livres) consisted of money procured by the sale of taxes, by free-gifts, and extra-impositions during the war, which left behind them no debts: And 26.550,000 l. (597.380,100 livres) consisted of LOANS, or money raised on perpetual annuities, life-annuities, and lotteries.—At the beginning of 1769 the whole amount of the debts of *France*, including all arrears and capitals advanced on annuities and lotteries, was 128.622,000 l. sterling, or 2.894.053,616 livres. The annual charge derived from this debt was 6.707,500 l. sterling (150.919,284 livres)——All the appropriations amounted to 8.218,500 l. sterling (184.919,284 livres).——The expences of the army, navy, king's houshold, prince's houshold, foreign affairs, &c. amounted to 8.947,000 l. or 201.307,312 livres. So that the whole annual expence was 17.165,000 l. (386.226,596 livres).--The whole revenue had amounted, before 1769, to 13.484,500 l. sterling (303.401,696 livres).——The public expence, therefore, had exceeded the revenue 3.681,000 l. (82.800,000 livres) *per ann.*



From

From the year 1769 to the prefent King's Acceffion, by forced reductions of intereft, and by new taxes, the public revenue was carried to 16.289,000l. fterling (366.508,000 livres) and the public expence was reduced fo as not to exceed the revenue above 766,800l. *per annum* (17.253,000 livres).——The anticipations alfo of the revenue, which before 1769 had extended to *feventeen* months, were reduced to *five* months.— Such was the progrefs of reformation; namely, an increafe of revenue amounting to little lefs than THREE MILLIONS fterling *per ann.* in a few years, under an unpopular minifter, in the latter days of a reign never characterized by an attention to oeconomy, or a regard to the public intereft; and at this time particularly ftamped by unprecedented profufion and a general relaxation.

A new reign produced a new minifter of finance whofe name will be refpected by pofterity for a fet of meafures as new to the *political* world, as any late difcoveries in the fyftem of nature have been to the *philofophical* world.—Doubtful in their operation, as all unproved meafures muft be, but diftinguifhed by their tendency to lay a folid foundation for endlefs peace, induftry, and a general enjoyment of the gifts of nature, arts, and commerce.——The edicts iffued during his adminiftration exhibit indeed a phænomenon of the moft extraordinary kind. An abfolute king ren-

dering

dering a voluntary account to his ſubjects, and inciting his people to *think*; a right which it has been the buſineſs of all abſolute princes and their miniſters to extinguiſh in the minds of men.—— In theſe edicts the king declared in the moſt diſtinct terms againſt a bankruptcy, an augmentation of taxes, and new loans; while the miniſter applied himſelf to increaſe every public reſource by principles more liberal than *France*, or any part of *Europe*, ever had in ſerious contemplation.——It is much to be regretted, that the oppoſition he met with, and the intrigues of a court, ſhould have deprived the world of thoſe lights which muſt have reſulted from the example of ſuch an adminiſtration.

After a ſhort interval, a nomination, in ſome reſpects ſtill more extraordinary, has taken place in the court of FRANCE. A court which a few years ſince was diſtinguiſhed by its bigotry and intolerance, has raiſed a *Proteſtant*, the ſubject of a ſmall but virtuous republic, to a deciſive lead in the regulation of its finances. It is to be preſumed, that ſo ſingular a preference will produce an equally ſingular exertion of integrity and talents. Though differing from Monſieur TURGOT in ſeveral principles, which regard the larger lines of government, he appears by his firſt ſteps, and, particularly, the preamble to a late edict

 for

for raiſing 24 millions of livres by a lottery, to put his foot on the ſame great baſis of general juſtice, and a ſtrict conſervation of the faith of the king; and points more particularly at the ſureſt of all reſources in any modern ſtates, a ſimplification of taxes and a reformation in the collection of them. This adminiſtration, making improvements in the Revenue its immediate object, is more capable of preſent exertion; and, as ſuch, is more formidable.

From theſe facts and obſervations it is impoſſible not to conclude, that if we truſt our ſafety to the difficulties of FRANCE, we may find ourſelves fatally deceived. I will add, that though (like the 3 s. land-tax and lotteries among ourſelves) ſome of the extraordinary impoſitions of the laſt war have been continued in *France*, there are ſome which ceaſed with the war, and which they can renew. It is, particularly, an advantage of unſpeakable importance to them, that they can carry on a war, as they did the laſt, at *half* our expence; and that, having no dependence on the flattering deluſion of paper, they can, as they did in 1759, bear even a bankruptcy in the middle of a war, and yet carry it on vigorouſly.—Their debts time itſelf is ſinking faſt. Of 3.111,000 l. (ſeventy millions of livres) in annuities on the *Hotel de Ville* at *Paris*, 1.777,000 l. (forty millions of livres) conſiſted

in

in 1774 of Life Annuities, which were falling by deaths at the rate of 71,000l. (1.600,000 livres) every year.——Even their loſs of credit, whatever preſent embarraſſment attends it, favours them upon the whole. To this they owe the advantages juſt mentioned. The facility with which our high credit has enabled us to run in debt enſnares us; and, if a change of meaſures does not take place, *(a)* muſt *ruin* us. Experience has given them a juſt horror at borrowing on permanent funds; and were they inclined to do it, they are not able to do it to any great amount; and, conſequently, they cannot go on mortgaging one reſource after another till none is left.—While we loſe ſight of the capital in the intereſt, they carry their views chiefly to the reimburſement of the capital; and after receiving high intereſt, for ſome years, can be ſatisfied with receiving back a part of their capital.——Their debts, being confined in a great meaſure to the *Farmers General* and others at PARIS, are not circulated and diffuſed among the body of the people in the manner ours are: And it is well known, that they can make uſe of methods to diſcharge them which our government muſt never think of. The acts of arbitrary power and unjuſt expedients to which, on many occa-

(*a*) "Either the nation (Mr. Hume ſays) muſt deſtroy "public credit, or public credit will deſtroy the nation." Political Eſſays, page 135.

ſions,

ſions, they have had recourſe for this purpoſe without producing any tumults, are ſuch as appear to us almoſt incredible; and ſhould the time ever come, when it will be neceſſary in this country to make uſe of any violence of the ſame kind, all government will probably be at an end.

In point of territory and number of inhabitants, the two countries will bear no compariſon *(a)*. We have hitherto oppoſed *France* by our free ſpirit, and our colonies; and to them chiefly we owe our proſperity and victories. Our colonies once ſeparated from us, the iſlands will ſoon follow. But ſhould they remain ours, our comparative advantages will beſt appear from the following authentic account of the imports into *France* from their iſlands.

In 1774.

| | Weight in Pounds. |
|---|---|
| Sugar imported into *France* — | 147.986,959 |
| Indigo — — — | 1.734,206 |
| Rocou — — — | 210,187 |
| Coffee — — — | 58.247,133 |
| | 208.178,485 |

*(a)* The number of inhabitants in *France* is 26 millions. In *Britain* it cannot exceed ſix or ſeven millions. See p. 66. And *Obſervations on Reverſionary Payments*, page 185, third edition.

In

In 1775.

| | Weight in Pounds. |
|---|---|
| Sugar imported into *France.* — | 171.932,972 |
| Indigo ——— ——— | 2.134,247 |
| Rocou — — — — | 169,831 |
| Coffee — —— — | 58.545,000 |
| | (*a*) 232.782,050 |

Value of the above commodities re-exported from *France*, taken upon the average price.

| | Livres. | | Sterling. |
|---|---|---|---|
| In 1774 — | 75.901,373 | — | 3.373,000 |
| In 1775 — | 74.961,318 | — | 3.331,000 |

The whole importation from the *West Indies* into *Britain* is about three millions *per ann.*

But I have gone much beyond the views with which I begun this ſection. The facts which have been ſtated, and the reflections which they have occaſioned, are intended principally to ſhew that we ought not to ſuffer ourſelves to be drawn into ſecurity by any aſſurances of the weakneſs of *France.* — May ſhe, however, find herſelf the weakeſt of kingdoms whenever, from motives of

(*a*) Near one half of all this importation is made into *Bourdeaux* only; and the reſt into *Rochelle, Marſeilles, Nantz, Havre,* and *Honfleur.*

intereſt or ambition, ſhe ſhall attempt to injure any of her neighbours.——May *Britain*, hitherto the moſt favoured ſpot under heaven, always preſerve her diſtinguiſhed happineſs, and eſcape the danger which now threatens her. And may the time ſoon come, when all mankind, ſenſible of the value of the bleſſings of peace and equal liberty, ſhall ſuffer one another to enjoy them, and learn war no more.

## SECT. IV.

*Containing an Account of the National Income and Expenditure; the Surplus of the Revenue; and the Money drawn from the Public by the Taxes; with Remarks on Lord* STAIR's *Account.*

APPROPRIATED REVENUE *at Midsummer*, 1775.

| | £. |
|---|---|
| Intereſt of the national debt — | 4.440,821 |
| Civil liſt revenue. See the note in page 163 —— | 800,000 |
| Expences of management attending the national debt; of which 71,432 l. is the expence of management at the Bank, South-Sea Houſe, and *India* Houſe; and 5.900 l. ſalaries to *Exchequer Officers.* See Page 119, &c. — | 77,332 |
| Annuities payable out of the Aggregate Fund to the DUKE OF GLOUCESTER, 8000 l.—DUKE OF CUMBERLAND, 8000 l.—the Repreſentatives of ARTHUR ONSLOW, Eſq; 3000 l.—And the Sheriffs of ENGLAND and WALES, 4000 l.—In all | 23,000 |

Clerk

Clerk of the Hanaper in Chancery—Coinage (*a*) expence——Tenths and firſt-fruits of the Clergy appropriated to the augmentation of ſmall livings—Extra revenues of the crown, conſiſting of *American* quit-rents; duty of 4½ *per cent.* in the Leeward Iſlands; revenues of Gibraltar and dutchy of *Cornwall*, &c.—Fees for warrants and orders, for auditing and engroſſing accounts of dividend warrants, and other charges at the EXCHEQUER and TREASURY (*b*) —— 100,000

Total of the Appropriated Revenue £. 5.441,153

(*a*) In order to defray the expence of coinage, a duty of 10 s. *per* ton has been laid on wines imported; and, as far as this duty happens to fall ſhort of 15,000 l. the deficiency is made good out of the ſupplies.

(*b*) I am not able to give the exact amount of this part of the appropriated revenue. I have, therefore, reckoned it at ſuch a round ſum, as, I think, cannot much exceed or fall ſhort of it.

## *State of the* Surplus *of the* Revenue *for* 11 *years ended at* 1775.

### Unappropriated Revenue.

| | £. |
|---|---|
| Neat Produce of the Sinking Fund, for five years, including casual surplusses, reckoning to *Christmas* in every year; being the annual medium, after deducting from it about 45,000 l. always carried to it from the supplies, in order to replace so much taken from it every year to make good a deficiency in a Fund established in 1758. — — | 2.610,759 |
| Neat annual produce of Land Tax at 3s. militia deducted; and of the Malt Tax *(a)* — — | 1.800,000 |
| (N. B. These two taxes in 1773, brought in only 1.665,475 l.) | |
| There are some casual Receipts, not included in the Sinking Fund, such as Savings in Pay-Office, duties on Gum Senega, American Revenue, &c. But they are so uncertain and inconsiderable, that it is scarcely proper to give them as a part of the permanent Revenue. Add however on this account — | 50,000 |
| Total of unappropriated Revenue | £. 4.460,759 |

(*a*) The Land-tax at 3 s. is given by Parliament for 1.500,000 l.; and the Malt-tax for 750,000 l. but they are always greatly deficient.—Both these taxes (and also sometimes the income of the Sinking Fund) are borrowed of the *Bank*, and spent long before they come into the Exchequer; and therefore, are debts constantly due to the Bank, for which interest is paid.

*Produce*

*Produce of the* SINKING FUND, *reckoned to* Chriſtmas *in every Year.*

| | | |
|---|---|---|
| 1770 | —— | £.2.486,836 |
| 1771 | —— | 2.553,505 |
| 1772 | —— | 2.683,831 |
| 1773 | —— | 2.823,150 |
| 1774 | —— | 2.731,476 |

The average of theſe five years is 2.655,759 l. or, deducting 45,000 l. (as directed in the laſt page), 2.610,759 l.

In 1775, the Sinking Fund was taken for 2.900,000 l. including an extraordinary charge of 100,000 l. on the *Aggregate* Fund; but it produced 2.917,869 l. The average of ſix years, including 1775, was 2.654,443 l. The average of five years before 1770, was 2.234,780 l.

ANNUAL EXPENDITURE.

| | £. |
|---|---|
| Peace Eſtabliſhment, for the Navy and Army, including all miſcellaneous and incidental expences | 3.700,000 |
| Annual increaſe of the Navy and Civil Liſt debts — — | 350,000 |
| Intereſt at 2 *per cent.* of 3.600,000 l. unfunded debt, which muſt be paid out of the unappropriated Revenue — — — | 72,000 |
| Total | 4.122,000 |
| ANNUAL SURPLUS of the Revenue | 338,759 |
| Annual income £. | 4.460,759 |

The

The eſtimate for the peace eſtabliſhment, including miſcellaneous expences, amounted, in 1775, to 3.703,476 l.—But the extraordinary expences, occaſioned by the war with America, made it fall very ſhort.—In 1774 it amounted to 3.784,452 l. excluſive of 250,000l. raiſed by Exchequer Bills, towards defraying the expence of calling in the gold coin. And the medium for eleven years, from 1765, has been nearly 3.700,000 l. —According to the accounts which I have collected, the expence of the peace eſtabliſhment (including miſcellaneous expences) was, in 1765, 1766, and 1767, 3.540,000 l. *per ann.*—In 1768, 1769, and 1770, it was 3.354,000 l. *per ann.*—— In 1771, 1772, 1773, 1774, and 1775, the average has been nearly four millions *per ann.* excluſive of the expence of calling in the coin.

The parliament votes for the ſea ſervice 4 l. *per* month *per* man, including wages, wear and tear, victuals and ordnance. This allowance is inſufficient, and falls ſhort every year more or leſs, in proportion to the number of men voted. From hence, in a great meaſure, ariſes that annual increaſe of the navy debt mentioned in the ſecond article of the *National Expenditure.* This increaſe in 1772 and 1773 was 691,350 l. or 345,675l. *per ann.* The number of men voted in thoſe two years, was 20,000. I have ſuppoſed them reduced to 16,000, and the annual increaſe of the Navy

M Debt

Debt to be only 250,000 l.——Add 100,000 l. for the annual increaſe of the Civil Liſt Debt, and the total will be 350,000 l.

Soon after the publication of the preceding account in *February* 1776, the EARL OF STAIR obliged the public with another account of the ſame kind, which brings out a concluſion much more unfavourable. According to this account, were lotteries aboliſhed, and the land-tax at 3 s. in the pound only, there would be a *deficiency* in the revenue, inſtead of ſuch a *ſurplus* as I have ſtated. The following remarks will ſhew the reaſon of this difference.

The EARL OF STAIR has taken the annual produce of the *Sinking* Fund at 2.506,400 l. being the average produce of EIGHT years ended at *Lady-day* 1775.——I have taken it at 2.610,759 l. being the average of FIVE years ended at *Chriſtmas* 1775.——The neat produce of the land and malt taxes has been alſo taken near 50,000 l. higher in my account; and I have beſides admitted 50,000 l. *per ann.* for caſual ſupplies, which his Lordſhip has not charged.

The annual increaſe in the Navy Debt, LORD STAIR ſtates at 300,000 l. and of the Civil Liſt at 200,000 l. I have ſtated the former at 250,000 l. and the latter at 100,000 l.—In order alſo to avoid, as much as poſſible, all exaggeration, I have thrown out the expence of the new coinage. LORD STAIR has admitted it, and given an yearly

expence

expence derived from hence of 100,000 l.—— He has alſo taken the Peace Eſtabliſhment for 1774, as a fair medium for common years of peace, becauſe it was lower in that year than in the three years preceding 1775. I have taken the average of *eleven* years of peace, which is 75,000 l. leſs.

In conſequence of theſe differences, the PEACE expenditure in *Lord Stair's* account comes out 325,000 l. *per ann. higher* than in mine; and the national income comes out 204,359 l. *lower*; from whence it follows, that without lotteries, and the land being at 3 s. in the pound, the kingdom muſt, according to his Lordſhip's calculation, run out at the rate of about 200,000 l. every year.

In ſome of the particulars I have mentioned, this account may be neareſt to the truth; but, I hope, it will be conſidered, that I have ſtudied to give moderate accounts, and aimed at erring always rather on the favourable than the unfavourable ſide. (*a*)

## *Second Method of deducing the* SURPLUS *of the* REVENUE.

From the year 1763 to the year 1775, or during a period of 12 years, 10.739,793 l. of the public debt was paid off.—The money employed for

(*a*) It ſhould be remembered, that all theſe accounts were publiſhed before the application to the *Houſe of Commons* in April, 1777, for the payment of the debts of the Civil liſt.

 this

this purpose must have been derived from the surplus of the *ordinary* revenue, added to the *extraordinary* receipts. These receipts have con-

On that occasion it appeared that these debts amounted then to 618,340 l. At the same time that this sum was granted, the income of the Civil List was advanced from 800,000 l. to 900,000 l. *per ann.* I have therefore been right in giving the *increase* of the Civil List income at 100,000 l.; and nearly so in giving the Civil List debts in 1775 at half a million. See Pag. 124; and Note 16, Pag. 135.

By an Act of the first of George IId. the Civil List was to be made up to 800,000, whenever in any year the duties and revenues appropriated to it fell short of that sum. The clear produce of these duties for 33 years, or from Midsummer 1727 to Midsummer 1760, was 26.182,981 l. 17 s. 6 d. or 793,424 l. *per ann.* They fell short, therefore, taking one year with another, more than they exceeded.—In 1747 they had been deficient for seven years together; and the whole deficiency amounted to 456,733 l. 16 s. which, in conformity to the Act I have mentioned, was made good to his Majesty out of the supplies for that year.—In 1729 also, 115,000 l. was granted out of the supplies for the like reason——This is all the money received by his late Majesty from Parliament towards supporting his houshold and the dignity of his civil government; or 810,749 l. *per ann.*—— At the accession of his present Majesty, the clear sum of 800,000 l. *per ann.* was settled upon him for his life, in lieu of all the Civil List duties and revenues. But this income proving insufficient, 513,511 l. was granted by Parliament in 1769 towards paying debts which had been incurred; and in 1777 (as I have just mentioned) 618,340 l. more, besides raising the King's income to 900,000 *per ann.* as a step, it is expected, towards raising it to a million *per ann.*

sisted

fifted of the following articles.——1ft. The land-tax at 4 s. in the pound in 1764, 1765, 1766, and 1771; or 1 s. in the pound extraordinary for four years, making 1.750,000 l.——2. The profits of ten lotteries (*a*) making (at 150,000 l. each lottery) 1.500,000 l.——3. A contribution of 400,000 l. *per ann.* for five years from the EAST INDIA Company, making 2,000,000 l.—4. Savings by debts difcharged at a difcount, (*b*) making at leaft 400,000 l.——5. Paid by the Bank in 1764 for the renewal of their charter, 110,000 l.—6. Savings on high grants during the war; produce of *French* prizes taken before the declaration of war; fale of lands in the ceded iflands; and compofition for maintaining *French* prifoners (*c*) making

(*a*) Four of thefe lotteries have been annexed to annuities; but it would be a great miftake to think that they have not been equally profitable with the other lotteries. For inftance; in 1767, a million and a half was borrowed on an annuity of 45,000 l. with a lottery of 60,000 tickets annexed. In the fame year, 2.616,777 l. was paid off; but, had it not been for the lottery, only 1.350,000 l. could have been raifed on the annuity; and 150,000 l. lefs muft have been paid off.

(*b*) The difcounts on a million and a half paid off in 1772, and two millions paid off in 1774 and 1775, amounted nearly to this fum.

(*c*) The particular fums may be found in a pamphlet, entitled, *The Prefent State of the Nation*, p. 28, quarto edition. But I have not included all the fums there enumerated; nor have I admitted the Army favings in 1772, and fome other fmaller fums.

 2.620,000 l.

2.620,000 l.——All these sums amount to 8.380,000l. There remains to make up 10.739,793l. (the whole debt discharged) 2.359,793 l. and this, therefore, is the amount of the whole surplus of the *ordinary* revenue for twelve years; or 196,000l. *per ann.* (*b*)

The Earl of STAIR has also, in this method, calculated the *surplus* of the Revenue; and makes the total, for eleven years, to be no more than 2.557,378 l. even with the assistance of lotteries, and the land-tax at 4s. in the pound for five years; from whence it follows, that *without* these assistances, there would have been a deficiency of near 60,000 l. *per ann.*—The reason is, that his Lordship has taken the whole debt paid since 1763, at no more than 7.053,855 l. or three millions and

(*b*) This surplus, being the medium for the whole 12 years of peace, is less than that in p. 160, which is the medium at the end of this period, when the Sinking-Fund produced above a quarter more than it did at the beginning of it.——He who chuses to make the enquiry will, I believe, find the following account to be nearly accurate.——For the first five years after 1763, the Sinking-Fund, after making good the deficiencies of all the other Funds, produced nearly two millions *per ann.* Add 1.800,000l. by pag. 159, and the whole disposable Revenue during this period, exclusive of extraordinary receipts, will appear to be 3.800,000 l.——The current expence (including 38,000 l. for the interest of 1.800,000 l. Exchequer Bills and 350,000 l. for the annual increase of the Civil List and Navy Debts) was 3.779,000 l. The surplus, therefore, was no more than 30,000 l. *per ann.*

a half

a half leſs than I have made it; and he has taken it ſo much leſs, chiefly in conſequence of including in the amount of the public debt in 1775, the exceſs of the expences of that year above the common peace expences. This exceſs is to be charged to the preſent war; and, in determining the ordinary peace *ſurplus*, which is my object, it was proper to exclude it, and to terminate the account at the commencement of the war.— I will only add, that Lord STAIR has alſo included more in the extraordinary receipts than I have; and, particularly, 700,000 l. which he ſuppoſes the public gained by the TEA INDEMNITY.—— But this was only a compenſation made by the *Eaſt-India* Company for the loſs which the public ſuſtained by taking off, in 1766, a part (or 1s. *per* pound) of the duty on tea. In 1772 it was reſtored; and the exciſe upon tea has ſince produced as much as ever. *Before* 1766, it produced annually 474,091 l. Immediately (*a*) after 1766, it produced 341,284 l.—But in 1775, it produced 490,292 l. and in 1776, 463,013.

(*a*) I have here taken the average of two years before and after 1766.

*Sketch of an Account of the Money drawn from the Public by the Taxes, before the Year* 1776.

| | £. |
|---|---|
| CUSTOMS in ENGLAND, being the medium of the payments into the Exchequer, for 3 years ending in 1773. (*b*) | 2.528.275 |

Amount

(*b*) The annual medium of the payments into the Exchequer from the CUSTOMS in ENGLAND, for the laft five years, has been 2.521,769 l.—In 1774 the payment into the Exchequer was 2.547,717 l.—In 1775, it was 2.476,302 l.—The produce of the CUSTOMS, therefore, has been given rather too high.

The produce of the EXCISES in England has been higher, in 1772 and 1775, than in any two years before 1776; but the average of any three fucceffive years, or of all the five years fince 1770, will not differ much from the fum I have given.—In 1754, or the year before the laft war, the CUSTOMS produced only 1,558,254 l. ——The Excifes, exclufive of the Malt-tax, produced 2.819,702 l.——And the whole revenue, exclufive of the Malt-tax and Land-tax at 2 s. was 5.097,617 l. —In 1753 the whole revenue was 5.189,745 l. And the appropriation or annual charge upon it, (confifting of the Civil Lift, 834.443 l. intereft of the national debt, exclufive of navy debt, 2.628,087 l. expences of management, 43,691 l. 4½ *per cent.* from the Leeward iflands, 27,378 l. annuity to the late Duke of Cumberland 25,000 l. firft fruits and tenths of the Clergy 13,597 l. &c. &c.) was 3,733,713 l. The Sinking Fund, therefore, produced 1.456,000 l.; which, added to 1.500,000 l. (the neat produce, at that time, of Land at 2 s. and

| | £. |
|---|---|
| Amount of the EXCISES in ENGLAND, including the malt tax, being the medium of 3 years ending in 1773 — — | 4.649,892 |
| Land Tax at 3 s. — — | 1.300,000 |
| Land Tax at 1 s. in the pound. — | 450,000 |
| SALT DUTIES, being the medium of the years 1765 and 1766. — | 218,739 |
| Duties on Stamps, Cards, Dice, Advertiſements, Bonds, Leaſes, Indentures, News-papers, Almanacks, &c. — — | 280,788 |
| Duties on houſes and windows, being the medium of 3 years ending in 1771 — — | 385,369 |
| Poſt Office, Seizures, Wine Licences, Hackney Coaches, Tenths of the Clergy, &c. — — | 250,000 |
| EXCISES in SCOTLAND, being the medium of 3 years ending in 1773 | 95,229 |

and Malt-tax) made the unappropriated revenue 2.956,032 l. The expence of the peace eſtabliſhment, conſiſting of 10,000 ſeamen, and 18,857 landmen, was, in 1753 and 1754, (including an allowance for the increaſe of the Navy-debt) 2.400.000 l. nearly; which left an annual ſurplus in the national income of 556,000 l. *without* lotteries, and land at 2 s. This ſurplus (with land at 3 s.) has of late ſcarcely exceeded 300,000 l.; and, therefore, has not been a THIRD of what it was in the laſt peace, and before the reduction of intereſt to 3 *per cent.* was compleated.

CUSTOMS

| | £. |
|---|---|
| CUSTOMS in SCOTLAND, being the medium of 3 years ending in 1773 — — — | 68,369 |
| Annual profit from Lotteries — | 150,000 |
| Inland taxes in SCOTLAND, coinage duties, casual revenues, such as the duties on Gum-Senega, American revenue, &c. — — | 150,000 |
| EXPENCE of collecting the EXCISES in ENGLAND, being the average of the years 1767 and 1768, when their produce was 4.531,075 l. *per ann.* | |
| 6 *per cent.* of the gross produce — | 297,887 |
| EXPENCE of collecting the Excises in SCOTLAND, being the medium of the years 1772 and 1773, and the difference between the gross and nett produce——31 *per cent.* of the gross produce — | 43,254 |
| EXPENCE of collecting the CUSTOMS in ENGLAND, being the average of 1771 and 1772, bounties included, and 15 *per cent.* of the gross produce, exclusive of drawbacks and over-entries — — | 468,703 |

N. B. The bounties for 1771 were 202,840 l.—for 1772, 172,468 l.

The charges of management for 1771, were 276,434 l.

For

| | |
|---|---|
| For 1772, 285,764 l. or 10 *per cent.* nearly. | |
| Intereſt of loans on the land tax at 4 s. expences of collection, militia, &c. — — | £. 250,000 |
| PERQUISITES, &c. to Cuſtom-houſe officers, &c. ſuppoſed — — | 250,000 |
| EXPENCE of collecting the Salt-duties in ENGLAND, $10\frac{1}{2}$ *per cent.* — | 27,000 |
| Bounties on fiſh exported — — | 18,000 |
| EXPENCE of collecting the duties on Stamps, Cards, Advertiſements, &c. $5\frac{1}{4}$ *per cent.* — — | 18,000 |
| Total £. | 11.9000,505 |

The *Earl of Stair* has in his papers made this total to be above 400,000 l. more, by including in his eſtimate ſeveral articles which I have omitted; particularly, the intereſt and management on the equivalent to *Scotland*, the Scotch crown Revenues, Dutchy of *Cornwall* and *Lancaſter* Fines, &c. He has alſo given an eſtimate of the fees and perquiſites of office of every kind, and reckoned them at half a million; whereas, I have only reckoned the perquiſites of office at the *Cuſtom-houſe*.

I cannot quit the notice which I have made ſo free as to take of *Lord Stair*'s papers, without mentioning

mentioning the particular gratititude due to him for publishing them; and for stepping forth at this time to draw the attention of the public, by the weight of his name and character, to calculations, which, as he justly says, "it be-"comes every man of property among us to "understand; to awaken the nation from the "lethargy into which the mockery of paper "wealth has plunged it; and to bear his testimony "against the present unnatural war."

It must be seen, that the foregoing account is imperfect and defective. It may, however, be sufficient to prove, that the whole money raised DIRECTLY by the taxes before 1776 could not have been much less than TWELVE MILLIONS. An addition of above 300,000 l. *per ann.* was made to it in 1776 and 1777. And in this year a yet greater addition must be made.——It should be farther considered, that as the increased price of one commodity has a tendency to raise the price of other commodities; and as also dealers generally add more than the value of a tax to the price of a commodity, besides charging interest for the money they advance on the taxes; for these reasons, it seems certain, that the taxes have an INDIRECT effect of great consequence; and that a larger sum is drawn by them from the public, than their *gross* produce. It is also to be considered confidered, that many of the perfons who are now fupported by collecting the taxes, would have fupported themfelves by commerce or agriculture; and, therefore, inftead of taking away from the public ftock, would have been employed in increafing it.——Some have reckoned, that on all thefe accounts the expence of the taxes is *doubled*; but this muft be extravagant. Let us fuppofe a *fourth* only added: and it will follow, that the money drawn from the public by the taxes (exclufive of tithes, county rates, and the taxes which maintain the poor) is near 15 millions *per ann.*; a fum not far lefs than the whole fpecie of the kingdom; which, therefore, had we no paper currency, would be totally inadequate to the wants of the kingdom.

Without all doubt fuch a ftate of things, in a great commercial nation, is dangerous and frightful; but it admits of no remedy, while the public debt continues what it is.—With a view, therefore, to the quick reduction of this debt, I will juft mention the following propofals.——It has appeared, that, fuppofing the taxes not to become lefs productive, and the current national expence to continue the fame that it has been for ten years before 1775, a furplus may be expected in the revenue of about 300,000 l *per ann.*—With a furplus fo trifling, nothing can be done; but it might be increafed, firft of all, By keeping the

LAND

LAND TAX for the future at 4 s. in the pound. As rents have been almoſt doubled, this will not be much more to the preſent proprietors of land, than 2s. in the pound was formerly. 'Tis, therefore, equitable; and will add to the national income near 450,000 l.

*Secondly*, All the money now ſpent in maintaining troops in America might be ſaved.—— The Colonies are able to defend themſelves. They wiſh to be allowed to do it. Should they ever want the aid of our troops, they will certainly pay us for them. Indeed, I am of opinion, they will never be willing to make peace with us, without ſtipulating that we ſhall withdraw our troops from them. Were there any external power that claimed and exerciſed a right of ſtationing troops in this country, without our conſent, we ſhould certainly think ourſelves entirely undone.——I will eſtimate this ſaving at no more than 200,000 l. *per ann.*

*Thirdly*, I do not ſee why the peace eſtabliſhment might not be reduced to what it was, at an average, in 1768, 1769, and 1770. This would produce a ſaving of 350,000 l. *per ann.*—I might here propoſe reducing the peace-eſtabliſhment for the *Navy* to what it always was before the laſt war, or from 16,000 to 10,000 men. But it would be infinitely better to reduce the ARMY; and this might produce a farther ſaving of great confequence.——But waving this, I fhall only mention,

*Fourthly*, That contributions might be obtained from *North America* and other parts (*a*) of the British Empire, on the principles ftated, from the EARL of SHELBURN's authority, in the firft Tract, p. 106. ——I will eftimate thefe at no more than 400,000 l. *per ann.*———Add the *Surplus* now in our poffeffion; and the total will be 1.700,000.——In the *Introduction* to the third edition of the Treatife on *Reverfionary Payments*, I have explained a method of paying off, with a finking fund of a million *per ann.* (*b*) a hundred millions of the national debt in forty years. What then might not be done with fuch a fund as this?

In

(*a*) We drew, fome years ago, this contribution from ASIA only; and it cannot be unreafonable to expect, that the greateft part of it may be again drawn from thence after the expiration, in 1780, of the charter of the EAST-INDIA company. At that period alfo, it is much to be wifhed that fome effectual meafures may be eftablifhed for making amends to the inhabitants of BENGAL for the fhocking injuries they have fuffered, and for fkreening them from all farther injuries; and likewife for withdrawing from the crown that patronage of the Eaft-India Company, which it has lately acquired, and which has given one of the deepeft wounds to the conftitution.

(*b*) At the time of writing the introduction here referred to, four years ago, I *thought* the furplus of the revenue might be taken at 900,000 l. *per ann.* But it muft be confidered, that the nation was then in poffeffion of a Contribution

In four years 13.986,300 l. will fall from an interest of 4 *per cent.* to 3 *per cent.*——Also, 4.500,000 3½ *per cent.* 1758, will fall, in five years, to an interest of 3 *per cent.*——The Long Annuities granted in King William's time, will, in 14 years, become extinct; and in 29 years those granted in Queen Anne's time will become extinct, as will also the greatest part of the Life-Annuities specified in p. 124.—All these savings will not amount to much less than 400,000 l. *per ann.* And were they to be added to the fund as they fall in, its operations would be so much accelerated, that in a few years we should see this country above all its difficulties.——Still more might be done by striking off unnecessary places and pensions; by giving up all the means of corruption; by reducing the pay of the great officers of state; and simplifying the taxes. A minister who appeared determined to carry into execution such a system, would soon gain the confidence of the public; endear himself to all honest men; and in time come to be blessed as the Saviour of his country.

tribution of 400,000 l. *per ann.* from the India Company, which has been since lost.—See the Additional Preface to the 2d Edition *of the Appeal to the Public on the Subject of the National Debt.*

POST-

# POSTSCRIPT.

THE following POSTSCRIPT was published only in a few of the last Editions of the *Observations on Civil Liberty*. It has been often referred to in the preceding work; and therefore, it is necessary to give it a place here.

ACCOUNT *of Public Debts discharged, Money borrowed, and Annual Interest saved from* 1763 *to* 1775.

| Debts paid off since 1763. | | Annuity decreased. | |
|---|---|---|---|
| | £. | £. | s. |
| 1765— | 876,888 funded, bearing interest at 4 *per cent.* | 34,835 | 10 |
| | 1.500,000 unfunded, 4 *per cent.* | 60,000 | 00 |
| 1766— | 0.870,888 funded, 4 *per cent.* | 34,835 | 10 |
| | 1.200,000 unfunded, 4 — | 48,000 | 00 |
| 1767— | 2.616,777 funded, 4 — | 104,671 | 0 |
| 1768— | 2.625,000 funded, 4 — | 105,000 | 0 |
| 1771— | 1.500,000 funded, 3½ *per cent.* | 52,500 | 0 |
| 1772— | 1.500,000 funded, 3 *per cent.* | 45,000 | 0 |
| 1773— | 800,000 unfunded, 3 — | 24,000 | 0 |
| 1774— | 1.000,000 funded, 3 — | 30,000 | 0 |
| 1775— | 1.000,000 funded, 3 — | 30,000 | 0 |
| Total | 15.483,553 | Total 568,842 | 0 |

In 1764, there was paid off 650,000 l. navy-debt; but this I have not charged, becauſe ſcarcely equal to that annual increaſe of the navy-debt for 1764, 1765, and 1766, which forms a part of the ordinary peace eſtabliſhment. The ſame is true of 300,000 l. navy debt, paid in 1767; of 400,000l. paid in 1769; of 100,200 l. paid in 1770; 200,000l. in 1771; 215,883l. in 1772; and 200,000l. in 1774.

## *Account of money borrowed and debts contracted ſince* 1763.

| | | £ | Annual intereſt increaſed. |
|---|---|---|---|
| Borrowed and funded, at 3 *per cent.* - in | 1765— | 1.500,000— | 45,000 |
| in | 1766— | 1.500,000— | 45,000 |
| in | 1767— | 1.500,000— | 45,000 |
| in | 1768— | 1.900,000— | 57,000 |
| Unfunded in | 1774— | 250,000— | 7,500 |
| Civil liſt debt in | 1775 (*a*) | 500,000 | |
| | Total | 7.150,000— | 199,500 |

(*a*) This article was omitted in the firſt editions of this *Poſtſcript.*——It might have been proper to add, the exceſs of Navy debts *contracted* above the Navy debts *diſcharged*, from 1763 to 1775; and had this been done, the ſurplus in p. 166, would have been reduced to 150,000l. *per ann.*

5 From

From 15.483,553l. the total of debts discharged, substract 7.150,000l. the total of debts contracted; and the remainder, or 8.333,553l. will be the diminution of the public debts since 1763. Also, from 568,842l. the total of the decrease of the annual interest, subtract 199,500l. (the total of its increase), and the remainder, or 369,342l. will be the interest or annuity saved since 1763.—To this must be added 12,537l. *per ann.* saved by changing a capital of 1.253,700l. (part of 20.240,000l.) from an interest of 4 to 3 *per cent.* pursuant to an act of the 10th of George III.; also the life-annuities that have fallen in; which will make a saving in the whole of near 400,000l. *per annum:* And it is to this saving, together with the increase of luxury, that the increase of the *Sinking Fund* for the last ten years has been owing.

To the debts discharged the following additions must be made.

In 1764 there was paid towards discharging the extraordinary expences of the army, 987.434l. In 1765, these expences amounted to 404,496l. In 1766, to 479,088l.—Total 1.871,018l.——This sum is 1.100,000l. higher than the extraordinary expences of the army for three years in a time of peace. This excess, being derived from the preceding war, must be reckoned a debt left by the war. And the same is true of 1.106,000l. applied, in 1764, 1765, and 1766, towards satisfying

fying *German* demands.——There are likewife fome fmaller fums of the fame kind; fuch as fubfidies to *Heffe-Caffel*, *Brunfwick*, &c. And they may be taken at 200,000l.——The total of all thefe fums is 2.406,240 l. which, added to 8.333,553l. makes the whole diminution of the public debts, or the whole faving of the kingdom, fince 1763, to be 10.739,793l.

Soon after the peace in 1763, an unfunded debt, amounting to 6.983,553l. was funded on the *Sinking Fund*, and on new duties on wine and cyder, at 4 *per cent.* There has been fince borrowed and funded on coals exported, window-lights, &c. 6.400,000l. The funded debt, therefore, has increafed fince the war 13.383,553l. It has decreafed (as may appear from page 177) 11.983,553l. and, confequently, there has been on the whole an addition to it of 1.400,000l.——During feven years, from 1768 to 1774, 1.115,883l. navy-debt was paid off. See page 178. But, as this is a debt arifing from conftant deficiencies in the peace eftimates for the navy, it is a part of the current peace expences.——On the 31ft of December, 1767, this debt was 1.213,072l.—On the 31ft of December, 1774, it was 1.850,000l. and confequently, though 1.115,883l. was paid off, an addition was made to it, in feven years, of 673,028l. It increafed, therefore, at the rate of 255,558l. *per ann.*

SUPPLE-

# SUPPLEMENT
## TO
## SECTION III. PART II.

*Containing additional Obſervations on Schemes for raiſing Money by Public Loans.*

IT is impoſſible, that any attentive perſon can reflect without concern, on that monſtrous accumulation of artificial debt for which no value has been received; which has been pointed out in different parts of the preceding Tract; and, particularly in the third Section of the ſecond Part. This being a ſubject which, in the preſent ſtate of our finances, is highly intereſting; I have been induced to return to it in this place; and to offer ſome further obſervations and propoſals which have occurred to me in re-conſidering it, and which I think neceſſary to explain and confirm thoſe which have been already offered.

There are two methods in which money is capable of being borrowed for public ſervices. The firſt is, by offering ſuch *high* intereſt as may of itſelf be ſufficient to induce lenders to advance the ſums that are wanted: And the ſecond is, by offering a *low* intereſt, with a *gratuity* or *doceur* to produce the acceptance of it.—The laſt has been the method in which our government has moſt commonly borrowed money; and the gratuity offered has been either a right to a greater capital than the ſum advanced, or a *long* or *ſhort* or *life* annuity, or the profits of a lottery, or ſome advantages of trade.——The firſt without doubt, is the moſt rational method of borrowing; and the latter is ſo abſurd and extravagant as to be incapable of being adopted in the common tranſactions of life. —In order to give a juſt and full idea of this, I ſhall inſtance in the laſt loan; ſpecifying the manner in which it *would* have been made if the uſual method of borrowing had been followed; and comparing this with the manner in which it *was* made; and the manner in which, I think, it *might* have been made to the greateſt advantage.

Five millions, it is well known, were borrowed laſt year; and, had the old plan of borrowing been adopted, this ſum would have been borrowed by ſome ſuch ſcheme as one of the *two* following.

Firſt. Intereſt in the public funds being then near 4 *per cent. per ann.* an intereſt of only 3 *per cent.* would have been offered; or, in other words, for every 100l. in *money*, 100l. *ſtock* carrying 3 *per cent.* (worth then 78l.) would have been given; but at the ſame time, as a *premium* or *compenſation* for accepting ſuch low intereſt, a life-annuity, or

 a ſhort

a ſhort annuity would have been offered worth ſomewhat more than the difference between 100l. and 78l. or about 24l. The whole premium, therefore, in raiſing *five millions*, would have been equal in value to about 1,200,000l. and, ſuppoſing it to have been either a life-annuity, or a ſhort annuity for 17 years of 2l. worth 12 years purchaſe, annexed to every 100l. ſtock, the whole annual charge incurred by the loan would have been 250,000l. for a term of years, and 150,000l. for ever till the capital is redeemed.

It is manifeſt that the capital including in it according to this account almoſt the whole *premium*, the public makes itſelf, by this mode of borrowing, a *debtor* for the very thing it *gives*; and, beſides paying the annuity, obliges itſelf to advance at redemption the whole value of it.—It is proper to add, that this is done *unneceſſarily*, becauſe 1.200,000 might have been procured by ſelling the annuity, and the remaining 3.800,000l. neceſſary to make up five millions, might have been procured, as will be ſhewn preſently, without any *doceur* by giving higher intereſt.

But there is another method of borrowing which has been practiſed by government on former occaſions, and which might have been adopted in the laſt loan.

For every 100l. advanced a new capital in the 3 *per cent.* funds worth that ſum would have been ſold, including a funded 10l. lottery ticket. This new capital would have been nearly 127l. three *per cent. ſtock* for every 100l. in *money*, or 6.343,954l. ſtock for FIVE MILLIONS in money; of which ſtock 5.718,954l. would have been ſold, to encourage ſubſcriptions, at 2 *per cent.* below the market price, that is, at 76l. ½; and the remaining ſtock, having a lottery annexed, would have been ſold at *par*. A fictitious or artificial capital, therefore, would have been created, or a debt incurred more than the value received, of 1,343,954l. beſides relinquiſhing about 150,000l. which might have been obtained by the profits of the lottery.

I have been ſeldom more ſurprized than at the preference of this ſcheme, which, at the time of ſettling the laſt loan, was expreſſed by ſome very reſpectable members of the Houſe of Commons; nor can this preference be eaſily accounted for on any other ſuppoſition than that they conſider the public debts as incumbrances, never to be removed, and, therefore, think it of no conſequence with what difficulties the redemption of them is loaded by an increaſe of capitals bearing low intereſt. It muſt be acknowledged indeed that this method of borrowing would have been attended with a ſmall preſent advantage; for the intereſt of 6.343.954l. at 3 *per cent.* is 190,318l. and this, together with the intereſt of 150,000l.

or 6000l. *per ann.* loſt by giving up the profits of a lottery, would have been the whole preſent annual charge it would have brought on the public. But if this be a ſufficient reaſon for preferring ſuch a ſcheme, it would perhaps be beſt to create capitals bearing 2 *per cent.* or even 1 *per cent.* intereſt; for probably ſuch capitals would bear a better price, in proportion to the rates of intereſt, than any 3 *per cent.* capitals, and conſequently, a greater preſent ſaving might be made by ſelling them. No other objection can be made to this than that by lowering intereſt, and laying the public under an obligation to return *double* or *triple* every ſum it receives; the redemption of the public debts might be rendered ſo expenſive and difficult as to be entirely impracticable. But this would be of no conſequence if indeed their redemption is already become impracticable; and if, therefore, every new charge they bring on the public is to be conſidered as laid on for eternity.

With theſe ſchemes let us now compare the ſcheme actually adopted for the laſt loan.

Inſtead of a 3 *per cent.* capital, a new capital bearing 4 *per cent.* intereſt, irredeemable for ten years, was offered at 95l. for every 100l. *ſtock*, with two *douceurs* to raiſe the value of the ſtock above 100l. in money; namely, a ſhort annuity of a HALF *per cent.* for ten years, (reckoned worth 4l. 2s.) and the profit (reckoned at 3l.) of one ticket in a money lottery consisting of 50,000 tickets.

The chief difference between this scheme and the first I have described is, that the new stock created is a FOUR *per cent.* instead of a THREE *per cent.* stock. But this is a difference of particular importance, and brings it near to such plans of borrowing as appear to me the best.——In the *first* scheme, the artificial capital is 1.200,000l. In the *second*, 1.343,954l. In this *third* scheme it is only 250,000l. This scheme, therefore, has evidently great merit; and perhaps, in the present state of the public debts, it does not admit of any great improvement. There is, however, an easy alteration which, I think, would have been an improvement, and which I shall take the liberty to mention.

According to a preceding observation, the two *douceurs* being included in the capital, are granted, and must be paid twice over. This is so absurd and extravagant that it ought to be avoided as far as possible; and it might have been avoided, in a great measure, by offering for every 100l. advanced 95l. stock, carrying 4 *and a quarter* interest irredeemable for ten years, with the same

short

ſhort annuity and a lottery ticket annexed.(*a*) In this caſe, the new capital would have been 4.750,000l. carrying (at $4\frac{1}{4}$ *per cent.*) 201,875l. *per ann.* intereſt. There would, therefore, have been a ſaving of 250,000l. in the capital; and the annual charge would have been nearly the ſame.

It muſt be obſerved that this ſcheme ſuppoſes that a ſtock bearing $4\frac{1}{4}$ *per cent.* intereſt would have been valued nearly at *par*; and, according to the principles on which the ſcheme was calculated, it could not have been valued at much leſs; or, ſuppoſing it valued at 1 or 2 *per cent.* leſs, the difference might have been made up by only adding two or three years to the duration of the ſhort annuity and the term of irredeemableneſs.—Had a *ſtock* been offered bearing $4\frac{1}{2}$ *per cent.* intereſt irredeemable for ten years, one *half* at leaſt of the ſhort annuity might have been ſaved. The annual charge for ten years would have been ſomewhat leſs; (*b*) and the exceſs afterwards would have been

(*a*) Or, for every 105l. contributed, 100l. STOCK irredeemable for 10 years might have been given, carrying $4\frac{1}{4}$ *per cent.* intereſt, with the ſame ſhort annuity and a lottery ticket annexed; and then the new capital would have been 4.762,000l. carrying (at $4\frac{1}{4}$ *per cent.*) 202,385l. *per ann.* intereſt. The amount of the ſhort annuity would have been 23,810l. and the number of lottery tickets 47,620.

(*b*) 211,375l. the intereſt at $4\frac{1}{2}$ of 4.750,000l. and 12,500l. a ſhort annuity of a QUARTER *per cent.* annexed to every 100l.

 contributed,

been much more than compenſated by the advantages at redemption attending a higher intereſt and a ſmaller capital.

But, perhaps, ſuch a ſcheme as the following would have been preferable to any of thoſe now propoſed.

For every 100l. in *money* 75l. ſtock irredeemable for 10 years and carrying $4\frac{1}{4}$ *per cent.* intereſt, might have been offered, together with an annuity for 27 years of $1\frac{1}{2}$ *per cent.* (valued cheap at 16 years purchaſe, or 24l.) and the advantage of a lottery ticket. This ſcheme would have been as likely to be attended with a profit as that which was adopted. The new capital would have been only 3.750,000l. bearing 159,375l. intereſt. The ſhort annuity would have been 75,000l. and the whole annual charge (ſuppoſing no redemptions of the capital to take place after ten years) 234,375l. for 27 years, and afterwards 159,375l. It appears, therefore, that 1.250,000l. or a *quarter* of the capital that was actually created, would have been ſaved; and alſo a rent charge on the public after 27 years of 40,750l. *per ann.* for ever.—The additional expence to balance theſe advantages would have been 9.650l. *per ann.* for ten years, and 34,375l. *per ann.* for 17 years. In other

contributed, make 223,875l. This laſt ſum, therefore, would have been the annual charge for 10 years; and the firſt ſum the annual charge after ten years till redemption.

words;

words; the public would have abſolutely ſecured the redemption of a *quarter* of the loan, (or of 1.250,000l.) beſides an eaſier redemption of the remainder, at the expence of 680,875l. in the whole, (*a*) to be paid annually in ſmall ſums during the courſe of 27 years.

All that has been now ſaid has gone on the ſuppoſition that, agreeably to the calculations on which the laſt loan was formed, 100l. *ſtock* irredeemable for ten years and bearing 4 *per cent.* intereſt, would ſell at 17l. more than 100l. ſtock bearing 3 *per cent.* intereſt; (or at 95l. when the latter ſtock is at 78l.) and alſo, that a ſhort annuity for ten years would ſell at $8\frac{1}{10}$ years purchaſe.—— But events have ſhewn that theſe valuations were too high. The new ſubſcription (including 100l. four *per cent.* ſtock, a half *per cent.* ſhort annuity, and the profit of a lottery ticket) ſhould have ſold, according to theſe valuations, at about $102\frac{1}{2}$. But it never bore ſo high a price; and in a little time it fell to *par*, and at laſt to 3 *per cent.* diſcount.— Various reaſons have been aſſigned for this; but the true reaſons were the following.

Firſt. A general fall of near 2 *per cent.* which took place in the ſtocks ſoon after the loan was ſettled.

(*a*) Ten payments of 9,650l. and ſeventeen payments of 34,375l. make 680,875l.

Secondly,

Secondly. A lower valuation of the new 4 *per cent.* ſtock and the ſhort annuity which took place in the ALLEY.—This was the principal reaſon; and it will be proper particularly to explain it. In doing this, it will be neceſſary to look back a little to the hiſtory of the public funds.

In 1717 the public debts were reduced from an intereſt of 6 *per cent.* to 5 *per cent.* and in 1727, from 5 *per cent* to 4 *per cent.* In 1737 a bill was brought into the HOUSE of COMMONS by Sir *John Barnard*, for a farther reduction from 4. to 3 *per cent.* At this time the 3 *per cents.* were above *par*; and even, during the three firſt years of the war which began in 1740, they continued ſo high that government was able to raiſe the neceſſary ſupplies by borrowing at 3 *per cent.*——In ſuch circumſtances, it was impoſſible the public creditors ſhould avoid expecting a *third* reduction; and this expectation would neceſſarily ſink the value of the FOUR PER CENTS. by leading the public to conſider them as no more than a THREE *per cent.* ſtock having a ſhort annuity of ONE *per cent.* annexed. Accordingly; *before* the war the difference of price between the THREE and the FOUR *per cent.* ſtocks was about 10 or 11 *per cent.* After the commencement of the war, a reduction becoming more doubtful and more diſtant, this difference became greater, and generally kept between

tween 14 and 17 *per cent.* At the approach of the PEACE in 1748, it ſunk to 11 *per cent.* and ſoon *after* the PEACE, the 3 *per cents.* having riſen conſiderably above *par*, (*a*) and an univerſal expectation of a ſpeedy reduction taking place, it ſunk to 6 *per cent.*——It is evident, therefore, that the price of the FOUR *per cents.* has been governed by the expectation of their reduction, (*b*) and that, had there been no ſuch expectation, their price, compared with the 3 *per cents.* would have been much higher. It will appear preſently to be moſt probable, that had it not been for this expectation, the prices of theſe ſtocks would not have differed much from the proportion of the rates of intereſt.

In taking this account, I have only compared the THREE *per cents.* with the SOUTH-SEA FOUR *per cent.*

(*a*) It may be worth obſerving, that during this whole war they never fell below 82, except for a few months during the rebellion in 1745; that after the PEACE in 1748 they roſe to 105, and in the ſucceeding war never fell ſo low as they are now, except in the two laſt years; that after the PEACE in 1763 it was expected they would again riſe above *par*; but that, inſtead of this, they have in general during the whole peace kept 12 or 13 *per cent.* below *par*, and 15 or 16 *per cent.* below the price they bore before the two laſt wars.——One of the reaſons of the great alteration which has taken place ſince the laſt war is, I think, pointed out in the 3d Section of the 3d Part of this Tract.

(*b*) Since the reduction in 1749 there has been no FOUR *per cent.* capital created except that of the laſt year.

*cent.* capitals before their reduction in 1749, at which time they amounted to above 27 millions, and were (as the consolidated three *per cent.* annuities are now) the grand staple stock of the kingdom. In 1746 and 1747, two new FOUR *per cent.* capitals were created redeemable at any time, and transferrable at the BANK. The price of these new capitals kept for some time after their creation, considerably below the price of the old SOUTH-SEA four *per cents.* the reasons of which were, I suppose, the general reasons which make new funds bear a lower price than old ones; and, particularly, their having less traffic in them, and being small and detached parcels likely to be first selected for the operations of finance.

Were the cause now assigned, or the expectation of a reduction of interest, the only cause that governed the comparative prices of 3 *per cent.* and 4 *per cent.* capitals, the excess of one above the other would never be more than the supposed value of a short annuity of 1l. till *reduction.* ——— But there is another cause which may operate in this instance, and which ought not to be overlooked; I mean, the expectation of a greater payment at *redemption.* The effect of the former is to *diminish*, and of the latter to *increase* the value of FOUR *per cent.* capitals.——In order to understand this it must be remembered, that when the 3 *per cents.* are at any considerable

considerable discount, it becomes practicable to redeem them under *par*, while debts bearing 4 *per cent.* interest must be redeemed at *par*. This will make a difference in favour of the latter, which will be greater or less in proportion to the greater or less discount at which the *three per cents.* are sold, the greater or less quantity of stock bearing 4 *per cent.* interest, and the greater or less probability that the whole or a considerable part of it will be soon redeemed (*a*)——Let us suppose, for instance, that all the public debts bearing 4 *per cent.*

(*a*) What is here said has been verified, in the particular instance of a *million and a half* borrowed in 1756, which was to carry 3½ *per cent.* interest till 1771, and then to become redeemable.——During the last war, and for about three years after the commencement of peace, there was a general expectation that the THREE *per cents.* would rise above *par* as they had done in the former peace; and while this expectation continued, this stock was reckoned no better than a THREE *per cent.* stock with a short annuity of a *half per cent.* annexed; and for this reason it bore, during that period, a lower price than another stock of 4 millions and a half which was to bear the same interest till 1782, and then to become redeemable, and to sink to an interest of 3 *per cent.*——In the latter end of 1767 and beginning of 1768 the price of the former stock rose above that of the latter, and continued not far from *par* from that time to the time of its redemption in 1771. The reason must have been, that being a small stock bearing a higher interest than the other stocks, it was expected, that it would be paid off at *par*, and therefore with a considerable profit, as soon as it became redeemable; which accordingly happened. See Postscript, page 177.

interest

interest, consist of a single capital of FIVE MILLIONS redeemable at any time; and that all the rest of the public debts are THREE *per cent.* capitals sold at a discount of 12 *per cent.* or at 88l. for every 100l. stock. In these circumstances, there would be a certainty that the small stock bearing 4 *per cent.* interest would be selected for redemption as soon as possible; and, as a stock carrying such high interest could not be expected, when the 3 *per cents.* are at 88, to be redeemed under *par*, its real value would on this account exceed that of the THREE *per cents.* more or less in proportion as its redemption was more or less distant. And its *whole* excess of value in these circumstances is to be computed in the following manner.—It would consist of a 3 *per cent.* capital, for every 100l. of which 100l. in money is to be received; and of an additional annuity of 1 *per cent.* till redemption. Its excess of value, therefore, if the whole capital was to be redeemed immediately, would be the same with the discount of the 3 *per cents.* or 12 *per cent.* If the capital was not to be redeemed till the end of 7 years, its excess of value would consist of 12 *per cent.* payable seven years hence, and the present worth of an annuity of 1 *per cent.* for the intermediate term of seven years. 12l. payable at the end of 7 years is worth in present money (allowing compound interest at 4 *per cent.*) 9l. 2s. 6d. An annuity of 1l. for seven years is worth

worth (reckoning the ſame intereſt) 6l. The whole exceſs of value, therefore, will be 15l. 2s. 6d. for every 100l. ſtock. If the redemption of the capital is to be delayed 15 years, the exceſs of value computed in the ſame manner will be 17l. 15s. 6d. —if 20 years, 19l. 1s.—if 30 years, 21l.

If the 3 *per cents.* had been ſuppoſed at a greater diſcount, it is evident that theſe ſeveral values would have been likewiſe greater; and had the quantity of 4 *per cent.* ſtock been ſuppoſed *double* or *triple*, the effect would have been the ſame with a delay of redemption; and had it been ſuppoſed thirty or forty millions, the effect (in conſequence of our ſlow progreſs in redeeming our debts) would not have fallen very ſhort of an eternal delay of redemption.

Before 1749, the amount of the public debts carrying 4 *per cent.* intereſt was near 58 millions. The expectation, therefore, of the advantage now explained could not *then* have any effect; and the only cauſe which could have influenced, in any conſiderable degree, the comparative prices of theſe ſtocks muſt have been the firſt I have aſſigned, or the expectation of their *reduction*; that is, in other words, the expectation of a *ſudden redemption* of them, as ſoon as the 3 *per cents.* got above *par*, by borrowing money at that intereſt. Had not this been foreſeen, or had there been an act of parliament rendering it impractica-

ble,

ble, there is no reaſon to doubt but the price of the FOUR *per cents.* compared with the THREE *per cents.* would have approached nearly to the proportion of the rates of intereſt, agreeably to what is ſaid in page 191.

The ſtate of the public funds has been much changed ſince the two laſt wars; but it is an alteration that has increaſed the comparative value of 4 *per cent.* capitals.

I have already obſerved, that during the laſt war there was reaſon to expect, that, as ſoon as peace came, the THREE *per cents.* would riſe above *par.* No one can now entertain any ſuch expectation. On the contrary; it is moſt probable, that they will never again riſe to that which has been their average price during the laſt peace from 1763 to 1775, and which, I think, may be ſtated at 87 or 88.——My reaſon for this aſſertion is,

Firſt, that after the preſent war, ſhould we be ſo happy as to eſcape the ruin with which it threatens us, our taxes and expences will be ſo much increaſed, and at the ſame time our reſources ſo much diminiſhed, as neceſſarily to leave the credit and value of our public ſecurities lower than ever.

Secondly. Though our credit and reſources ſhould continue undiminiſhed, yet the great addition which the preſent war will make to the public debts, is alone likely to ſink their value; becauſe

because every increase of a saleable commodity has always a tendency to lower its price.——It follows from hence, that the purchasers of FOUR *per cent.* capitals have now a prospect of an advantage of 12 or 14 *per cent.* at redemption, which they could not have had before the last peace.

In connexion with this it must be considered, that it is now highly probable, that it will never be again practicable to reduce the interest of any 4 *per cent.* capitals. In order to such a reduction, government must be able to offer to the proprietors of these capitals their *principal*, should they not chuse to take lower interest, and consequently to borrow at an interest of 3½ or 3¾ *per cent.* But no sums will be lent on such lower interest, unless it can be depended upon that capitals bearing that interest, when brought to market, will bear a premium of 1 or 2 *per cent.*; and this, when the *three per cents.* are not higher than 87 or 88, would require the excess of value of such capitals to be estimated at 14 or 15 *per cent.* whereas it has been lately found, that even FOUR *per cent.* capitals irredeemable for ten years, will not bear such an excess of value.—A *reduction*, therefore, of the interest of FOUR *per cent.* capitals, or a *redemption* of them by borrowed money, cannot now be reckoned upon; and the only cause that can REASONABLY sink their value compared with the THREE *per cents.* below the ratio of the rates of interest, is the probability of a redemption of them by the ſurplus of the national revenue. I need not ſay how little is to be expected from hence. Suppoſing, however, that much may be expected, I have ſhewn what effect it ought to have; and from the obſervations I have made, and particularly the computation in page 194, &c. it appears, I think, that the price of the capital of five millions four *per cent.* annuities lately created ought to have been near 18 *per cent.* more than the price of the THREE *per cents.* This appears to be true on the ſuppoſition that this capital will be redeemed in fifteen years; (that is, in five years after the expiration of the term for which it is made irredeemable) that the 3 *per cents.* will riſe to as high a price as they bore during the laſt peace; and that purchaſers are allowed to make FOUR *per cent.* compound intereſt of their money.——Were we to ſuppoſe this capital diſcharged even in two years after it becomes redeemable, the value, made out in the ſame way, would be nearly 17l.

He who will conſider all this, and alſo recollect the general price of the 4 *per cents.* before their reduction in 1749, (ſee page 190) muſt be convinced that the TREASURY, at the time the laſt loan was ſettled, had good reaſon for taking the price of the new *four per cent.* capitals 17 *per cent.* higher than the price of the three *per cents.*——It has, however, been found that this was too high a valuation. Inſtead of being ſold at 17l. more for every 100l. ſtock than the 3 *per cents.* they have been ſold at only 13l. or 14l. more; and this has been the chief reaſon of the diſcount to which the laſt ſubſcription fell.——It is hard to ſay, by what principles the money'd men who traffic in the funds have governed themſelves in this inſtance; but certain it is, that they have not been guided by any of the rules of juſt calculation: And the ſame muſt be ſaid of the value at which they have reckoned the ſhort annuity of a half *per cent.* for ten years annexed to the new 4 *per cents.* In forming the ſcheme for the laſt loan this annuity was, I have ſaid, eſtimated at $8\frac{1}{10}$ years purchaſe, agreeably to its real value, ſuppoſing the payments yearly, the firſt payment to be made at the diſtance of a year, and money improved at 4 *per cent.* compound intereſt. But it has in general been ſold at about $7\frac{1}{2}$ years purchaſe; which is *leſs* than its value, ſuppoſing money improved at $5\frac{1}{2}$ *per cent.* compound intereſt. (*a*)

(*a*) Nothing has been more undervalued in the ALLEY than *Annuities on lives.* They have been always granted, very unreaſonably, without any limitation of age; and their value has been taken at no more than 12 or 13 years purchaſe; tho' really worth one with another 16 or 17 years purchaſe. This is a ſtrong reaſon for preferring ſhort annuities to them in all ſchemes for raiſing money. Short annuities for 21 years will be taken for as much as life-annuities; and yet experience has proved that in this time not a *quarter* of the life-annuities will drop; and the whole expence brought by them on the public will not be removed in leſs than 70 or 80 years. See Note 15, Page 134.

From this account it appears, that could the caprice of the public have been foreseen, the price of the new four *per cents.* should not have been reckoned at more than 91l.; (the 3 *per cents.* being at 78l.) and that, consequently, to make up a value which would have produced 102l. for every 100l. advanced, either the term of irredeemableness and of the short annuity should have been lengthened; or, supposing this term the same, the short annuity should have been more than doubled. An artificial capital, indeed, of near half a million would in this case have been created. But this disadvantage might have been avoided, without bringing any additional expence on the public, by such alterations as I have before proposed; and by increasing in the corrected schemes, page 186, &c. either the term of irredeemableness, or the short annuity, or the rate of interest, or all of them together.

The preceding account will, I fancy, help to shew what is practicable, *taking things as they are*, in borrowing money for public uses. It proves, that the nation loses greatly by the low price of all capitals bearing a higher interest than 3 *per cent.* and that could their value be raised, it would be greatly benefited.——For example. Could the new FOUR *per cents.* have been taken at 99l. for every 100l. stock, instead of 95l. the whole expence

pence of the ſhort annuity in the ſcheme of the laſt loan, and of a *quarter per cent.* perpetual intereſt, in the corrected ſchemes, page 186, &c. might have been ſaved. But had the value of the 4 *per cents.* been raiſed in proportion to the rate of intereſt, or *nearly* in that proportion, a farther ſaving might have been made, in all the ſchemes, of the profits of the lottery, and, conſequently, of 6000l. *per annum* in the annual charge.——My next enquiry, therefore, ſhall be, in what manner and by what regulations this may be done. I have written in the ſection on loans, on the ſuppoſition that ſuch regulations are practicable; and I have propoſed one of them; but I will here be more explicit.

It has been ſhewn, that before 1749 the cauſe which depreſſed the value of the 4 *per cents.* was the expectation of their being reduced; and that *now* this cauſe is the expectation of their being ſoon *redeemed.* Remove, therefore, theſe cauſes in any degree, and their value muſt riſe in the ſame degree.——With reſpect to the firſt, it is in my opinion certain that it would be doing great ſervice to the public to exclude it entirely. Our reductions of intereſt have proceeded from a policy too narrow; and the nation is likely to ſuffer by them much more than it has gained. (a) The ſavings they produce, being expended on current ſervices, tempt to extravagance; give a fallacious appearance of opulence; and, by making our debts ſit lighter, render us leſs anxious about redeeming them, and leſs apprehenſive of danger from the increaſe of them. At the ſame time they render their redemption a work of more difficulty, and oblige government, when under a neceſſity of contracting new debts, either to give extravagant intereſt, or to offer extravagant premiums. That accumulation of artificial debts which I have pointed out has been owing principally to this cauſe; and had it not been, in particular, for the reduction in 1749, the public debts would now have been near 14 millions leſs; and a debt of above a hundred millions, inſtead of conſiſting of capitals bearing intereſt at 3 *per cent.* would have conſiſted of capitals bearing ſome of them 3½, ſome 4, and ſome 4½ and 5 *per cent.* intereſt, which (ſuppoſing them all at a medium to bear 4 *per cent.*) a million *per ann.* would have redeemed in ſix years leſs

(*a*) I would except here the firſt reduction in 1717. This was then neceſſary to gain a fund for ſinking the public debts; and had the fund thus gained been applied, as the laws required, invariably to this purpoſe, and all farther reductions been avoided, we ſhould now have been burthened with no debts.

time,

time, and at twenty-one millions lefs expence.— In fhort; reducing of intereft is one of thofe unhappy TEMPORARY EXPEDIENTS to which ftatefmen are apt to betake themfelves; and by which *prefent* relief is gained at the expence of *future* fafety, and diftrefs poftponed by rendering it in the end more unavoidable and dreadful.——There cannot, therefore, be any fufficient reafon againft making the intereft of the new capitals which may be created by any future loans, IRREDUCIBLE. (*a*) Should this raife the price of capitals bearing high intereft in proportion to the increafe of intereft, government would be enabled to borrow to equal advantage whatever intereft it offered; the new loans would not bring any greater annual charge on the nation than would have been neceffary had the fame fums been obtained by felling 3 *per cent.* capitals; and, at the fame time, all the immenfe expence of *douceurs* and *fictitious capitals* would be faved, and all the advantages in redeeming the public debts obtained, arifing from fmaller capitals bearing higher intereft.

Such a regulation as that now propofed would be alone fufficient for thefe purpofes, when the amount of the debts bearing high intereft and declared irreducible, is confiderable, as appears

(*a*) That is; never capable of being redeemed by fubftituting one debt for another; or of being faved from redemption by accepting lower intereft.

 from

from what is ſaid in page 195. But when a debt happens to bear a higher intereſt than any other, and is at the ſame time ſmall, the probability of a *quick redemption* will operate in the ſame manner on its price with the expectation of a *reduction*; and in this caſe, therefore, it will become neceſſary, in order to avoid the inconveniences I have deſcribed, to POSTPONE REDEMPTION; and one of the beſt methods of doing this will be, by ordering, that ſuch a debt ſhall be redeemed *after* ſome other given part of the funded public debts.—So ſlow has been our progreſs in redeeming debts, that this (ſuppoſing the part to be firſt redeemed conſiderable) would be reckoned, in the preſent circumſtances of the funds, the ſame with making the debt to be laſt redeemed, irredeemable for ever. And ſhould ſuch an apprehenſion prove right, the public would loſe nothing, becauſe the debt whoſe redemption was poſtponed, would bring no greater annual charge on the public, than if the ſame ſum had been obtained by ſelling a capital bearing any lower intereſt. But ſhould it prove falſe, or ſhould our debts be ever put into a fixed courſe of redemption, the public would gain greatly by being able, after diſcharging one part of its debts, to diſcharge the remainder more expeditiouſly and eaſily.

I ſhall beg leave to illuſtrate what has been now ſaid by having recourſe again to the laſt loan of

FIVE MILLIONS.——During the laſt 60 years, or from the firſt eſtabliſhment of the ſinking fund to the year 1777, no more than about FIFTEEN MILLIONS of the public funded debts have been paid. An order, therefore, that the capital of five millions bearing 4 *per cent.* created by the laſt loan, ſhould not be diſcharged unleſs a capital of twenty-five or thirty millions in the three *per cents.* ſhall have been *firſt* diſcharged, would have carried its redemption to ſo diſtant a period, as might probably have raiſed it to the ſame comparative value with any 3 *per cent.* capitals.

Let it, however, be ſuppoſed to advance its price only to 102l. when the 3 *per cents.* are at 78; that is, when the ratio of the rates of intereſt required the price to be at 104. In theſe circumſtances, 4.850,000l. of the five millions would have been advanced for an equal capital carrying 194,000l. intereſt at 4 *per cent.*; and the remaining 150,000l. would have been advanced for the lottery: And thus the whole expence of the ſhort annuity, and 150,000l. capital, would have been ſaved. —And had the ſame ſum been obtained by ſelling a 3 *per cent.* capital, the amount of intereſt, though the leaſt poſſible, would not have been much leſs;(*a*)

(*a*) Suppoſing the 3 *per cents.* ſold at 76½, the capital neceſſary to produce 4.850,000l. in money would be 6.339,869l. the intereſt of which at 3 *per cent.* is 190,195l.

but,

but, at redemption, there would have been a neceſſity of paying above a MILLION AND A QUARTER for which no value had been received.——When ſuch advantages, uncompenſated by any loſs, can be obtained by ſo eaſy and ſimple a regulation as only changing the ORDER of paying the public debts, (*a*) what poſſible reaſon can there be againſt adopting it?

There is another method by which the value of any ſtocks bearing high intereſt might be raiſed, which would probably be no leſs effectual; I mean, by ordering that no part of ſuch ſtocks ſhall be redeemed, without at the ſame time redeeming an *equal*, or any *larger* ſum, in other capitals. This is the regulation propoſed in the ſection on public loans, page 98; and it will not be amiſs here to give an illuſtration of it, by ſuppoſing, that EIGHT MILLIONS will be wanted for the neceſſary ſupplies of this year; and that this ſum will be procured by ſelling, as was done in the laſt loan, a capital equal to the ſum advanced, bearing 4 *per cent.* intereſt. Were the

(*a*) When the amount of intereſt, payable for a ſum obtained by ſelling a 4 *per cent.* capital, is the ſame with the amount of intereſt, payable for an equal ſum obtained by ſelling a 3 *per cent.* capital, which is nearly the preſent caſe, poſtponing, in the manner I have propoſed, the redemption of the former, becomes as indifferent as it would be to poſtpone in the ſame manner the redemption of any 3 *per cents.*

intereſt in this caſe made irreducible, and the capital incapable of being redeemed without at the ſame time redeeming four times as much of the 3 *per ct.* or ſome other ſtocks, an increaſe of value would be communicated to it which would render all Douceurs unneceſſary. For it would be a capital, the redemption of which could not be completed without diſcharging in all FORTY (*a*) MILLIONS of the public debts.——I cannot doubt but that, in theſe circumſtances (ſuppoſing the price of the 3 *per cents.* to continue near 78) a 100 l. in money would be given for 100 l. in ſuch a ſtock, and the whole extravagant expence of ſhort annuities, lotteries, and artificial capitals would be ſaved.

(*a*) In this caſe only a FIFTH of the *ſurplus* to be at any time employed in redeeming debts could be applied to the redemption of this *particular* loan. The reſt after nine years might be employed in redeeming the 4 *per cent.* ſtock created laſt year; or jointly with it, ſuch parts of future loans bearing high intereſt, as, in borrowing on the ſame plan, might be left redeemable. And thus no obligation would ariſe from this mode of borrowing to prefer the redemption of 3 *per cents.* to the redemption of capitals bearing higher intereſt. In particular; had this been the plan of borrowing through the laſt war, all ſurplus monies might have been ever ſince employed intirely in paying off 4, 4½ and 5 *per cent.* capitals preferably to any others; and at the ſame time, no *douceurs* would have been granted in order to procure the loans, no artificial debt contracted, or extraordinary charge incurred.

In

In ſhort. With the aid of ſuch regulations as thoſe now propoſed, EIGHT MILLIONS might this year be borrowed (ſuppoſing the 3 *per cents.* not lower than 78 or 77) *probably* at an intereſt of 4 *per cent.*, but *certainly* at an intereſt an EIGHTH or a QUARTER higher, without offering any *premiums.* Whereas, if no ſuch regulations are eſtabliſhed, either an artificial debt of near (*a*) *two millions and a half* muſt be created; or 5 *per cent.* for 15 or 20 years certain, together with the profits of a lottery, muſt be given; and a new tax laid which will produce 400,000 l. *per ann.*

It may deſerve to be added, that an unproſperous ſtate of public affairs, and apprehenſions of public danger, would have a tendency, by placing the redemption of our debts at a greater diſtance, to promote, rather than obſtruct the ſucceſs of ſchemes attended with ſuch regulations.

There remains one propoſal more on this ſubject which I wiſh may be attended to.

(*a*) Should this be diſregarded, and a long annuity offered, as a *douceur*, of $1\frac{1}{2}$ *per cent.* for 90 or 100 years, *eight millions* might perhaps be borrowed at an intereſt, including the long annuity, of $4\frac{1}{2}$ *per cent.* even though the 3 *per cents.* ſhould fall as low as 73.—And this, probably, would be the very ſcheme a miniſter would prefer, who, minding chiefly preſent eaſe, did not care how much he burdened the nation hereafter.

I have

I have obſerved, that our reductions of intereſt have been the effect of too narrow a policy. It ſeems to me, that one of the beſt meaſures that could now be adopted, would be to undo what we have done in this inſtance, by reſtoring the 3 *per cent.* capitals to a higher intereſt, and making this reſtoration, one of the means of raiſing the neceſſary ſupplies. That this is practicable, and that it would be advantageous, will appear from the following ſcheme, and obſervations.

For 20 l. in money, let 110 l. ſtock bearing 3½ *per cent.* intereſt, be offered, in exchange for every 100 l. of the 3 *per cent.* ſtocks; and let the new 3½ *per cent.* ſtock be capable of being redeemed at any time, but never under *par*, unleſs when the price of the 3 *per cents.* happens to be below 85 l.—By this ſcheme the public would procure 20 l. from the converſion of every 100 l. 3 *per cent.* ſtock into 110 l. ſtock carrying 3½ *per cent.*; or FIVE MILLIONS from the converſion of TWENTY-FIVE MILLIONS. The new *additional* capital would be only TWO MILLIONS AND A HALF, (or 10 *per cent.* of the old capital); and the *additional* intereſt would be 17 s. (that is, a half *per cent.* added to 7 s. the intereſt of 10 l. at 3½ *per cent.*) for every 20 l. advanced; or 4¼ *per cent.* for the whole loan.

That ſuch a ſcheme would afford ample encouragement to ſubſcriptions, ſuppoſing the 3 *per*

*cents.*

*cents.* at or near 78, will appear from confidering, that the intereft offered is above a *quarter per cent.* more than could be made by purchafing any perpetual annuities, and at the fame time, in confequence of forming a part of the intereft of a THREE AND A HALF *per cent.* capital, is incapable of reduction, and therefore nearly on an equal footing with the intereft of any 3 *per cent.* capital.——But to be a little more explicit.

The new capital of 110 l. bearing 3½ *per cent.* intereft would be better than the 100 l. THREE *per cent.* capitals for which it would be fubftituted, in the following refpects.——1ft. It would carry 17 s. *per ann.* more intereft; and fuch an intereft, when the price of an annuity of 3 l. is 78 l., ought to be worth 22 l. 2 s. The additional intereft, therefore, would be difpofed of at 2 l. 2 s. for every fum of 22 l. 2 s. (or at 9½ *per cent.*) lefs than its true value, compared with the price of the 3 *per cent.* annuities.

Secondly. The 3 *per cents.* when *peace* comes, will probably be capable of being redeemed at 88 l. (*a*) But this ftock, in the fame circumftances, muft be redeemed at *par.* It will, therefore, produce 12 l. more in every 100 l. at redemption. Add the 10 l. additional ftock; and the whole additional fum to be received at redemption

(*a*) In 1774, a million of the 3 *per cents.* was redeemed at this price; and in 1772, a million and a half at 90.

will

will be 22 l.——There will, therefore, be a profit at redemption of 10l. *per cent.* of the money advanced; and this profit deserves the more notice, because the stock to which it is annexed, being redeemable at any time, and bearing a higher interest than the 3 *per cents.*, will be selected for redemption before them; and therefore its price will be so much the more likely always to keep near *par.*—Setting aside, however, this advantage, and supposing only the 20l. advanced likely to be received at redemption, it may be found by calculating in the manner explained in p. 194, &c. that the substitution of 110l. stock carrying THREE AND A HALF *per cent.* for 100 l. carrying THREE *per cent.*, or, in other words, that 20 l. to be received some time hereafter, besides an annuity of 17s. for the intermediate time, is worth in present money more than 20 l., reckoning compound interest at 4 *per cent.*

Such a scheme, therefore, in whatever way its value was rightly calculated, would appear to offer an advantageous bargain. Should there, however, be reason to fear that the public might judge otherwise; or should the 3 *per cents.* be at 74 or 75, the value might be easily increased near nine *per cent.* by making the substituted stock 112 l. instead of 110 l. in which case, the interest for the 20 l. advanced would become

18 s.

18 s. 5d. *per ann.*, or a little more than four and a half *per cent.* inftead of *four and a quarter.*

The advantages to the public which would arife from fuch a fcheme are——1ft. That it would be one of the beft preparations for meafures that muft fome time or other be entered into for putting the public debts into a *fixed* courfe of redemption. (*a*)——In confequence of being raifed to a higher intereft, a confiderable part of them would be made capable of being redeemed with more eafe and expedition; and for this reafon, it is certain that, if there remains a poffibility of our efcaping

(*a*) I mean fuch a courfe of redemption as fhould not be liable to interruption by a WAR; or, as would be the effect of the eftablifhment of fuch an unalienable *finking* fund as has been defcribed in the *Appeal to the Public on the Subject of the National Debt*, and the *Obfervations on reverfionary Payments.*——Nothing can fave us from bankruptcy but fuch a fund; and were it eftablifhed, the 3 *per cents.*, when they came to be redeemed, would foon rife to *par*; and, confequently, the obligation implied in this fcheme to pay a part of them at *par* would occafion no additional expence. It is, however, fo little to be expected, that fuch a fund will be ever eftablifhed, that it would have been folly to have made the calculation given above, on any fuppofition lefs favourable, than that the 3 *per cents.* will bear the fame price after the prefent war, that they bore after the laft; and that we fhall go on as we have hitherto done, paying off a *million*, or a *million and a half*, now and then in a time of peace.

ing a public bankruptcy, the time muſt come when we ſhall wiſh all our debts bore a high intereſt. (*b*)

Secondly. A capital of TWO MILLIONS AND A HALF would be ſaved in raiſing FIVE MILLIONS. That is; the nation in procuring *five millions* would incur a debt of only *half* that ſum; and inſtead of having a QUARTER OR A THIRD *more* to pay at redemption than had been received, it would have ONE HALF *leſs* to pay.

Thirdly. Such a ſcheme would keep up public credit; and, by its neceſſary operation, contribute to carry *itſelf* into execution. For the advantages attending it being grounded entirely upon the old 3 *per cent.* ſtocks, few at ſuch a time would chuſe to ſell them, but many would be induced to buy; and, conſequently, their price would be advanced, contrary to the common effect of public loans.——Theſe ſeem to me advantages ſo un-

(*b*) The converſion of a 3 *per cent.* ſtock into a 3½ *per cent.* ſtock gives the ſame advantage in redeeming it, that the power of redeeming it at 85¾ for every 100 l. would give.——A million *per ann.* ſurplus would redeem 114 millions and a quarter of the latter ſtock in the ſame time, and therefore at the ſame expence, that it would redeem 100 millions of the former. I ſuppoſe here the 3 *per cents.* paid at *par*; and this I have before obſerved will be found to be neceſſary ſhould a time (ſcarcely the object of hope) ever come when government will ſet itſelf in earneſt and with any effect to pay the public debts.

ſpeakably important, that I cannot but think it would be right to go to ſome extraordinary expence, in making at leaſt one experiment of this kind. If, in conſequence of offering high terms in *one* trial for a ſmall ſum, ſuch an experiment ſhould ſucceed, it might be renewed on lower terms; and the way might be diſcovered of managing, in the beſt manner, larger loans on the ſame plan.——I cannot help thinking indeed, that it would be found that in this way great ſums might be raiſed without creating *any* new capitals, or making any addition to the public debts. I fancy, for inſtance, that few, when the 3 *per cents.* are about 78, would ſcruple to pay 25l. for the converſion of 100l. THREE *per cent.* ſtock into a 100l. FOUR *per cent.* ſtock, provided this laſt ſtock was not to become redeemable till THIRTY OR FORTY MILLIONS of our preſent debts have been diſcharged: And ſuppoſing this true, money for public ſervices would be raiſed at 4 *per cent.* or at an intereſt nearly as low as poſſible; and, at the ſame time, a ſum equal to the whole money advanced would be ſaved. But were it neceſſary to take for ſuch a ſubſtitution 24l. or even 23l. (that is, to pay about 4¼ *per cent.* for money) the gain, if our debts are ever to be redeemed, would abundantly overbalance the increaſed expence of intereſt.

CORRECTIONS

## CORRECTIONS and ADDITIONS.

IN THE SECOND TRACT, page 120, after the words *Lent at 4 per cent. in 1746, charged on licences for retailing spirituous liquors, and reduced to 3 per cent. by 23d of George II.* 1749, add, *and consisting of old Exchequer Bills then cancelled and converted into a debt from Government to the Bank, for which the Bank was allowed to add to its capital an equal sum by 19th George II. Ch. 6.*

In page 128, instead of the words, *In* 1751, *certain Exchequer tallies and orders, amounting to* 129,750*l.* read, *In* 1751, *the remainder of certain Exchequer tallies and orders charged on the duties on wrought plate, and amounting to* 129,750*l.*

Page 136, line 17, instead of 1758 read 1757.

Page 137, line 2d from the bottom, for 205,000l. read 215,000l.

Page 139, for 17.7401,32l. read 17.701,324l.

Page 144, after *Exchequer Bills charged on a duty upon victuallers by 12th Geo. I.* 1726, add, *and afterwards by 16th Geo. II.* 1743, *charged on the duties on licences for retailing spirituous liquors. Now included in the Bank Capital by 19th Geo. II. Ch. 6.*

4 Page

Page 144, Note (*b*) after the words, *In this account I have omitted a million borrowed in* 1734, add, *and half a million borrowed in* 1736; *becauſe theſe debts had for ſome time been in a fixed courſe of redemption by the ſalt-duties.*

In page 145, line 2d, for 10.639,793l. read 10.739,793l.—Ibid. line 10th, for 146.582,844l. read 146.682,844l.—Ib. line 12th, for 15.639,793l. read 15.739,793l.——Ibid. note, line 2d, for 1.118,000l. read 1.218,000l.

P. 147. For 146.582,844l. read 146.682,844l. —For 71.505,580l. read 71.605,580l.—And for 10.639,793l. read 10.739,793.

F I N I S.